Cybersecurity with AWS

Fortifying Digital Frontiers

Syed Rehan

Apress®

Cybersecurity with AWS: Fortifying Digital Frontiers

Syed Rehan
London, UK

ISBN-13 (pbk): 979-8-8688-1553-9   ISBN-13 (electronic): 979-8-8688-1554-6
https://doi.org/10.1007/979-8-8688-1554-6

Managing Director, Apress Media LLC: Welmoed Spahr
Acquisitions Editor: Spandana Chatterjee
Editorial Assistant: Gryffin Winkler

Cover designed by eStudioCalamar

Cover image designed by Freepik (www.freepik.com)

Distributed to the book trade worldwide by Springer Science+Business Media New York, 1 New York Plaza, New York, NY 10004. Phone 1-800-SPRINGER, fax (201) 348-4505, e-mail orders-ny@springer-sbm.com, or visit www.springeronline.com. Apress Media, LLC is a Delaware LLC and the sole member (owner) is Springer Science + Business Media Finance Inc (SSBM Finance Inc). SSBM Finance Inc is a **Delaware** corporation.

For information on translations, please e-mail booktranslations@springernature.com; for reprint, paperback, or audio rights, please e-mail bookpermissions@springernature.com.

Apress titles may be purchased in bulk for academic, corporate, or promotional use. eBook versions and licenses are also available for most titles. For more information, reference our Print and eBook Bulk Sales web page at http://www.apress.com/bulk-sales.

Any source code or other supplementary material referenced by the author in this book is available to readers on GitHub. For more detailed information, please visit https://www.apress.com/gp/services/source-code.

If disposing of this product, please recycle the paper

First and foremost, I thank God, the source of all knowledge and grace; verily my success is only by the Almighty.

To my mother and my father – your steadfast love, your wisdom, and your silent sacrifices built the foundation upon which this work now stands.
To my wife, my unwavering partner and daily source of inspiration – thank you for your patience through late-night drafts and for believing in this project whenever my own resolve faltered.
And to my daughters, whose boundless curiosity about the digital world reminds me why its protection matters so deeply – may you grow fearless, kind, and endlessly inquisitive.
This book is for you, offered with my deepest faith, love, and gratitude.

Table of Contents

About the Author

Syed Rehan is a seasoned technology leader with over two decades of experience in cybersecurity, cloud computing, IoT, AI, and machine learning. He began his career as a C developer working on embedded systems, where he discovered his passion for security by identifying and mitigating vulnerabilities in firmware and operating systems.

Syed has held senior engineering and security leadership roles across multiple industries, from telecommunications and IoT to cloud infrastructure and AI.

Since joining Amazon Web Services (AWS) in 2017, Syed has shaped the security posture of AWS offerings through both strategic leadership and hands-on technical implementation. He has supported the development of key security services, including AWS Security Hub, AWS IoT security solutions, AWS GenAI security solutions, AWS Verified Access, AWS KMS, AWS Private Certificate Authority (CA), and AWS IAM features, all focused on military-grade security implementations. Before joining AWS, Syed served at Nokia, where he laid much of the groundwork for modern mobile security standards, engineering hardened software stacks, introducing robust cryptographic controls, and stress-testing critical systems against the emerging threats that now shape today's smartphone defenses.

An active contributor to the open source community, Syed works on Linux loadable kernel modules (LKMs) for security and other projects that strengthen system defenses. His expertise spans hands-on system diagnostics (e.g., *lsof, lsmod, lscpu*), service management with systemd, and low-level architecture hardening including GPU instruction set security.

A recognized thought leader, Syed speaks regularly at major industry conferences, including AWS re:Invent, AWS Summits, and Black Hat, where he shares insights on cloud infrastructure security, IoT protection frameworks, and emerging AI security challenges. Syed's blogs, whitepapers, and training materials help demystify complex security concepts for the global tech community.

Beyond his professional achievements, Syed is deeply committed to technology education accessibility. He volunteers with organizations providing STEM training to underserved youth in London, Toronto, and New York and through virtual initiatives worldwide, focusing on cloud computing, cybersecurity fundamentals, and responsible technology use.

Syed pairs deep technical authority with collaborative leadership, channeling a lifelong dedication into advancing security practices, driving innovation, and mentoring the next generation of security professionals. He's always open to idea sharing, collaboration, and mentoring anyone eager to grow their cybersecurity skills. You can connect with him on LinkedIn: https://www.linkedin.com/in/iamsyed.

About the Technical Reviewer

Rodrigo Merino is Generative AI and IoT Solutions Architect Manager at AWS with over a decade of experience deploying emerging technologies, ranging from generative AI to IoT. Throughout his career, Rodrigo has successfully implemented numerous enterprise-grade deployments focusing on security, reliability, performance, and resilience. His deployment expertise encompasses hardening AI systems against vulnerabilities, implementing automated fallback mechanisms, and designing architectures that maintain performance integrity under varying loads. Rodrigo guides customers across various industries to accelerate their AI/ML and generative AI journeys by developing robust deployment strategies that ensure business continuity while meeting stringent security and compliance requirements. Rodrigo's expertise lies in bridging the gap between cutting-edge technology and practical business applications, enabling companies to harness the full potential of AI through resilient infrastructure designs that scale securely.

Acknowledgments

First and foremost, I offer my deepest gratitude to God, whose grace and guidance have illuminated every chapter of my life and this book.

To my father and mother – your steadfast love, sacrifices, and unwavering faith in me laid the foundation for every endeavor. Every page is a testament to the values you instilled.

To my wife, the heart of our home, and to our wonderful daughters, whose laughter and encouragement remind me daily why knowledge and curiosity matter – your patience during countless late-night writing sessions means more than words can convey.

I am indebted to the teachers who opened the doors to new ideas and challenged me to think deeper and to the mentors who sharpened my skills and guided my career, especially Yasser Al Saied, Bob Pitts, and Nigel Page. Through your example, I have learned that true leadership is rooted in generosity and integrity.

A special thanks to Rodrigo, the technical reviewer, whose keen eye and insightful feedback strengthened the accuracy and clarity of these pages.

Finally, "thank you," the reader. By choosing this book, you have invested your time and trust in these words. Your curiosity fuels authors everywhere, and it is my sincere hope that what you find here sparks new insights, **knowledge**, conversations, and possibilities.

With gratitude,
Syed Rehan

Introduction

Cloud adoption is surging, and so are the tactics adversaries use to target cloud workloads. *Cybersecurity with AWS: Fortifying Digital Frontiers* narrows that gap by blending battle-tested Zero-Trust (ZT) design patterns, step-by-step labs, and lessons drawn from real incidents into one practical playbook you can start using the moment you sign in to the AWS Console.

What This Book Offers

You will find equal parts strategy and execution. Early chapters ground you in the foundational concepts of Zero Trust, the shared responsibility model, and modern cryptography, while latter chapters walk you through step-by-step labs for IAM (identity and access management) hardening, VPC (virtual private cloud) micro-segmentation, SIEM (Security Information and Event Management) rule-writing, automated incident response (IR), and even post-quantum preparedness. Every control is mapped to its business driver and compliance requirement, so you always know *why* as well as *how*. Sidebars flag cost considerations, operational gotchas, and shortcuts for multi-account environments, letting you adapt advice to startups and large enterprises alike.

How to Use the Book

If you are new to cloud security, read sequentially: each chapter builds on the last, culminating in a full defense-in-depth architecture. If you are a seasoned practitioner, feel free to jump straight to the domain you are tackling, data-centric Zero Trust in Chapter 6 or generative artificial intelligence (GenAI) security in Chapter 10, and then circle back for context. Hands-on sections assume only a free-tier AWS account; they are sandbox-safe so you can follow along in real time. Each chapter ends with an operational checklist that can be copied into your runbooks or GRC (Governance, Risk, and Compliance) tooling.

Who Should Read This Book?

- **Cloud and Security Architects**: Designing multi-account landing zones or re-architecting legacy estates for Zero Trust in AWS

- **DevOps/Platform Engineers**: Embedding "shift-left" security, Infrastructure as Code (IaC) guardrails, and automated remediation into continuous integration/continuous deployment (CI/CD) pipelines

- **SOC (Security Operations Center) and Incident Response Teams**: Modernizing detections, playbooks, and forensics for container, serverless, and multi-region workloads

- **Compliance, Risk, and Audit Professionals**: Mapping AWS controls to NIST (National Institute of Standards and Technology), ISO (International Organization for Standardization) 27001, PCI DSS (Payment Card Industry Data Security Standard), HIPAA (Health Insurance Portability and Accountability Act), GDPR (General Data Protection Regulation), and emerging AI/PQC (post-quantum cryptography) regulations

- **CTOs, CISOs, and Technology Leaders**: Balancing protection, agility, and cost while crafting a cloud-first security strategy

- **Application and Cloud Security Engineers**: Hardening APIs, serverless functions, and microservices against real-world TTPs (tactics, techniques, and procedures)

- **Data Protection and Privacy Officers**: Enforcing encryption, data sovereignty, and classification requirements at scale

- **AI/ML (Machine Learning) and DevSecOps Practitioners**: Securing generative AI pipelines and integrating threat-aware ML into security operations

- **Network and Systems Administrators**: Migrating on-prem architectures to AWS and implementing least-privilege networking

- **Consultants, Trainers, and Students**: Preparing for AWS Security Specialty or CISSP-Cloud or simply seeking hands-on reference material

Why Cybersecurity Matters

Regulators, customers, and boards now treat security as a first-order feature rather than an afterthought. A single breach can erode brand trust overnight, derail digital transformation roadmaps, and trigger fines that dwarf cloud migration savings. Robust security, by contrast, unlocks competitive advantage: faster product releases, smoother audits, lower insurance premiums, and the freedom to collaborate across regions and business units without fear of compromise. In short, sound cyber-hygiene is no longer optional; it is a prerequisite for innovation.

How to Use This Book for Maximum Impact

Treat the guidance as iterative, not static. Spin up a lab environment, implement a control, validate it with the supplied hands-on steps, and then fold the hardened pattern into production. Revisit the maturity checklists quarterly; cloud services evolve rapidly, and so should your defenses. Pair the technical chapters with the business-focused notes in Chapter 11 so that every engineering improvement feeds directly into board-level risk metrics and future-state planning.

Armed with this approach and the detailed chapters that follow, you will be able to turn AWS's vast security and non-security services into a coherent, continually improving defense program that keeps pace with both innovation and threat.

CHAPTER 1

Building Secure Cloud Infrastructures: A Cybersecurity Overview

Welcome to the fascinating world of cybersecurity. In this opening chapter, we invite you to explore a realm where digital fortifications protect against unseen threats and the battlefields of modern warfare are defined by lines of code. Together, we will delve into a dynamic and critical field where the defenders of our digital future relentlessly strive to outsmart those who seek to exploit our interconnected world. Prepare to discover the intricacies of this captivating domain, where technology and human intellect intertwine in a constant dance of protection and innovation.

In today's digital age, cybersecurity has become an essential requirement for safeguarding digital assets. The rapid growth of online services and the increasing complexity of cyber threats have made securing our digital resources a paramount concern. This book aims to be a comprehensive guide to mastering and implementing robust cybersecurity measures within the Amazon Web Services (AWS) environment. As organizations increasingly migrate their infrastructure to the cloud, AWS has emerged as a leading Cloud platform, providing a myriad of tools and services designed to protect data, applications, and networks. In this introductory chapter, we will examine the fundamental principles of cybersecurity, the unique security challenges posed by cloud computing, and how AWS Services can effectively tackle these challenges. Whether you are an experienced IT professional or a newcomer to cloud security, this book will equip you with the vital knowledge and skills to protect your AWS infrastructure from the ever-evolving cyber threats.

© Syed Rehan 2025
S. Rehan, *Cybersecurity with AWS*, https://doi.org/10.1007/979-8-8688-1554-6_1

What Is Cybersecurity

Cybersecurity involves protecting computers, networks, software applications, AI applications, critical systems, and data from digital threats. Organizations must secure data, applications, and solutions to maintain customer trust and meet regulatory requirements. They utilize various cybersecurity measures and tools to safeguard sensitive information and prevent business disruptions caused by unauthorized network activities. Implementing cybersecurity requires a coordinated effort among people, processes, and technologies.

The Importance of Cybersecurity

In today's digital landscape, organizations across every sector – from healthcare to finance, education to government, and beyond – have become deeply reliant on sophisticated digital systems and high-speed connectivity. These technological advancements drive operational efficiency and elevate customer service to unprecedented levels.

However, this digital transformation brings with it a crucial imperative: the need for robust cybersecurity. Just as businesses safeguard their physical assets with locks, alarms, and security personnel, they must now extend equally stringent protection to their digital realm. This includes not only data but also the very systems and networks that form the backbone of modern Interconnected world.

The threat landscape is ever-present and evolving. Cyber-attacks deliberate and often highly sophisticated attempts to infiltrate digital defenses pose a constant risk. These malicious efforts aim to breach systems and networks, potentially resulting in a range of devastating consequences: from the exposure of sensitive information to outright data theft, deletion, unauthorized alteration, blackmail, or sabotage.

In this context, the implementation of effective cybersecurity measures is not merely advisable; it's essential. A robust cybersecurity strategy offers a multitude of benefits, safeguarding not just an organization's digital assets, but also its reputation, financial stability, and the trust of its stakeholders. As we navigate this interconnected digital ecosystem, cybersecurity must evolve to support continued growth and innovation ensuring that progress remains sustainable and secure in the long run.

Effective cybersecurity measures provide numerous benefits:
Robust cybersecurity isn't just about protection; it's a strategic investment that delivers tangible advantages across compliance, resilience, and risk mitigation.

1. **Preventing or Reducing Breach Costs**: Implementing cybersecurity strategies minimizes the negative impacts of cyber-attacks on business reputation, financial health, operations, and customer trust. For example, disaster recovery plans help contain intrusions and maintain business continuity.

2. **Ensuring Regulatory Compliance**: Certain industries and regions mandate compliance with data protection regulations, such as the General Data Protection Regulation (GDPR) in Europe, which requires appropriate cybersecurity measures to ensure data privacy.

3. **Mitigating Evolving Threats**: As technology evolves, so do cyber threats. Organizations must continually update their cybersecurity measures to counter new and sophisticated attack methods.

Types of Cyber-Attacks: The Ever-Evolving Threat Landscape

Cybersecurity is an ever-evolving field, with professionals facing a diverse and continuously changing array of threats. Understanding these various attack vectors is crucial for developing robust defense strategies. Here's an extensive overview of the types of cyber-attacks that organizations must guard against:

- **Malware**: This broad category encompasses malicious software designed to infiltrate and damage systems, including Trojans, spyware, and viruses.

- **Ransomware**: A particularly insidious form of attack where cybercriminals encrypt data and demand payment for its release.

- **Man-in-the-Middle Attacks**: These involve intercepting communications between two parties, often to steal sensitive information.

- **Phishing**: Social engineering tactics used to trick individuals into revealing personal information or installing malware.

- **DDoS (Distributed Denial of Service) Attacks**: Overwhelming servers with a flood of traffic to render them inaccessible.

- **Insider Threats**: Security risks posed by individuals within an organization who have authorized access.

- **SQL Injection Attacks**: Exploiting vulnerabilities in databases to gain unauthorized access to sensitive data.

- **Cross-Site Scripting (XSS) Attacks**: Injecting malicious scripts into trusted websites to compromise user data or impersonate legitimate users.

- **Password Attacks**: Attempts to crack or guess passwords to gain unauthorized system access.

- **Zero-Day Attacks**: Exploiting previously unknown vulnerabilities before patches are available.

- **Advanced Persistent Threats (APTs)**: Sophisticated, long-term attacks targeting high-value information or infrastructure.

- **Supply Chain Attacks**: Compromising a supplier or partner to indirectly access the target organization.

- **Crypto Jacking**: Unauthorized use of computing resources for cryptocurrency mining.

- **Fileless Attacks**: Malware that operates in memory without leaving traces on the hard drive.

- **Social Engineering Attacks**: Manipulating individuals to divulge sensitive information or perform actions that compromise security.

- **Watering Hole Attacks**: Compromising websites frequently visited by the target audience to spread malware.

- **Botnets**: Networks of infected computers used for large-scale attacks.

- **Credential Stuffing**: Using stolen credentials across multiple platforms to gain unauthorized access.

- **Drive-By Downloads**: Malicious code that infects a device simply by visiting a compromised website.

- **Form Jacking**: Injecting malicious code into online forms to steal sensitive data.

- **IoT (Internet of Things) Attacks**: Exploiting vulnerabilities in Internet of Things devices.

- **Brute-Force Attacks**: Systematically attempting all possible password combinations to gain access.

- **Spear Phishing**: Targeted phishing attacks that focus on specific individuals (celebrity or famous individual) or organizations.

- **Whaling**: Phishing attacks aimed at high-level executives, such as CEOs or CFOs.

- **Business Email Compromise (BEC)**: Attacks that involve impersonating a legitimate business or employee to trick victims into transferring funds or disclosing sensitive information.

- **Rogue Software**: Deceptive software that claims to be legitimate but is actually malware.

- **Clickjacking**: Tricking users into clicking hidden or obscured elements to initiate unintended actions or download malware.

- **Eavesdropping**: Intercepting and listening to private communications without the knowledge or consent of the parties involved.

- **Spoofing**: Impersonating a trusted entity, such as a website, email sender, or IP address, to gain unauthorized access or steal sensitive information.

- **Keylogger Attacks**: Using hardware or software tools to record keystrokes, often to capture login credentials or other sensitive information.

- **Rootkits**: Malware designed to provide attackers with persistent, undetected access to a system by modifying the operating system (OS) or other software.

- **Wiper Malware**: Malicious software designed to erase data from infected systems, often used in destructive attacks against organizations.

- **DNS (Domain Name System) Tunnelling**: Exploiting the Domain Name System (DNS) protocol to exfiltrate data or communicate with remote servers, often bypassing traditional security measures.

- **Session Hijacking**: Taking over a user session by obtaining the session ID, allowing attackers to impersonate the user.

- **AI-Powered and AI-Targeted Attacks**:

  - **Prompt Injection**: Manipulating AI models by feeding malicious or misleading prompts to produce unintended or harmful outputs

  - **AI Impersonation Attacks**: Using AI-generated voices, images, or text to convincingly mimic real individuals or systems in phishing, fraud, or misinformation campaigns

  - **Data Poisoning Attacks**: Corrupting the training data used by AI models to introduce vulnerabilities or bias or degrade model performance

  - **Model Inversion Attacks**: Exploiting an AI model to reconstruct sensitive information about the data it was trained on, potentially exposing private or confidential data

  - **Adversarial Example Attacks**: Crafting inputs that are intentionally designed to mislead AI models into making incorrect or harmful decisions

  - **Model Theft (Model Extraction) Attacks**: Stealing proprietary AI models by querying them extensively to recreate their functionality or duplicate their intellectual property

  - **Evasion Attacks**: Modifying malicious content so that it bypasses AI-based detection systems, such as spam filters or malware detectors

As the cybersecurity landscape continues to expand, these threats underscore the growing complexity organizations face in protecting digital assets. While it's impossible to list every form of attack, this collection highlights the critical need for layered, adaptive, and forward-looking security strategies. In a world where both attackers and defenders increasingly rely on AI, staying vigilant, informed, and resilient has never been more essential.

How Cybersecurity Works

Organizations implement cybersecurity strategies through

- **Risk Assessment**: Cybersecurity specialists evaluate existing systems, networks, and data storage to identify vulnerabilities.

- **Comprehensive Frameworks**: Developing and implementing protective measures tailored to the organization's needs.

- **Employee Education**: Training staff on security best practices to reduce the risk of accidental breaches.

- **Automated Defense Technologies**: Utilizing tools to detect and respond to threats across all data access points.

- **Continuous Risk Assessment and Improvement**: Regularly reassessing security measures, mitigating emerging risks, and applying lessons learned from incidents to strengthen future defenses.

Types of Cybersecurity

A robust cybersecurity strategy addresses various areas:

- **Critical Infrastructure Security**: Protecting essential systems like energy, communication, and transportation from disruptions

- **Network Security**: Safeguarding connected devices and managing user permissions with technologies like firewalls

- **Cloud Security**: Ensuring the protection of data and applications in the cloud through shared responsibility models, where the cloud provider secures the infrastructure, while the customer is responsible for securing their data, applications, and access controls

- **IoT Security**: Securing Internet of Things devices that pose additional risks due to constant connectivity and being out in the field (outside of organization security perimeter)

- **Data Security**: Using encryption and backups to protect data in transit and at rest

- **Application Security**: Implementing secure coding practices to prevent vulnerabilities in software

- **Endpoint Security**: Protecting remote access points from threats

- **Disaster Recovery and Business Continuity**: Preparing for prompt responses to incidents while maintaining operations

- **End User Education**: Training employees to recognize and respond to potential threats

Components of a Cybersecurity Strategy

Effective cybersecurity requires a coordinated approach involving

- **People**: Educating employees on the latest threats and best practices to prevent oversight

- **Processes**: Developing a security framework for continuous monitoring and rapid response to vulnerabilities

- **Technology**: Utilizing tools like firewalls, antivirus software, and Zero-Trust security models to protect systems

Modern Cybersecurity Technologies

Organizations employ advanced technologies to enhance their cybersecurity:

- **Zero Trust**: Assumes no user or application is trusted by default, requiring strict authentication and continuous monitoring.

- **Behavioral Analytics**: Monitors data patterns to detect suspicious activities and anomalies in the pattern and telemetry.

- **Intrusion Detection Systems (IDSs)**: Identify and respond to cyber-attacks using machine learning and data analytics.

- **Cloud Encryption**: Scrambles data in cloud storage to prevent unauthorized access.

Balancing Cybersecurity and Business Needs

Effective cybersecurity should seamlessly integrate with business operations, providing protection without hindering usability. It should enable the business to operate efficiently while safeguarding against potential threats. By finding the right balance, organizations can achieve robust protection and meet their business objectives.

In summary, cybersecurity is a critical practice for protecting digital assets and ensuring the smooth operation of businesses. By employing comprehensive strategies and modern technologies, organizations can defend against evolving threats and maintain the trust of their customers.

Introduction to Zero-Trust Principles and Their Importance in Modern Cybersecurity

Zero Trust is a cybersecurity model based on a simple principle: trust nothing, verify everything. Unlike traditional security models that assume everything inside an organization's network is trustworthy, Zero Trust requires strict verification for any entity attempting to access resources.

Key elements of Zero Trust include

- **Least-Privilege Access**: Granting only the permissions necessary for an entity to perform its required tasks

- **Continuous Monitoring**: Constantly assessing the security posture and behavior of entities to detect anomalies

- **Micro-segmentation**: Dividing networks into small, isolated segments to limit the spread of breaches

- **Strong Authentication**: Using multi-factor authentication (MFA) and robust identity verification processes

AWS Security Best Practices

Implementing security best practices in AWS ensures a robust defense against potential threats. Here are key practices to follow.

1. Least-Privilege Principle

- **Definition**: Granting users the minimum levels of access – or permissions – needed to perform their job functions.

- **Implementation**: Use IAM (identity and access management) roles and policies to define and enforce the principle of least privilege (PoLP). Regularly review and update permissions to ensure they are appropriate.

2. Multi-factor Authentication (MFA)

- **Definition**: An authentication method that requires two or more verification factors to gain access to a resource.

- **Implementation**: Enable MFA for all users, especially those with privileged access. AWS IAM supports MFA through hardware devices and virtual MFA apps.

3. Encryption at Rest and in Transit

- **Definition**: Protecting data by encrypting it when it is stored (at rest) and during transmission (in transit).

- **Implementation**:
  - **At Rest**: By default use TLS AWS KMS (Key Management Service) to manage encryption keys and encrypt data stored in services like Amazon S3 (Simple Storage Service), Amazon RDS (Relational Database Service), and Amazon EBS (Elastic Block Store).
  - **In Transit**: By default use TLS (Transport Layer Security) to encrypt data being transmitted across networks. AWS services such as CloudFront and Elastic Load Balancing (ELB) support TLS.

4. Network Segmentation and Security Groups

- **Definition**: Dividing a network into smaller segments and using security groups (SGs) to control traffic between them.

- **Implementation**:

  - Use VPC (virtual private cloud) to create isolated sections of AWS Cloud.

  - Configure security groups to allow only necessary traffic to and from instances. Utilize network access control lists (NACLs) for additional layer of security.

5. Secure Configuration Management

- **Definition**: Ensuring that systems and services are configured securely from the start.

- **Implementation**:

  - Use AWS Config to track changes to resource configurations and compliance status.

  - Implement AWS Systems Manager for automated configuration management and patching.

6. Incident Response and Forensics

- **Definition**: Preparing for, detecting, responding to, and recovering from security incidents.

- **Implementation**:

  - Develop and test incident response plans (IRPs) regularly.

  - Use AWS CloudTrail and AWS Config to log and track changes for forensic analysis.

  - Utilize Amazon GuardDuty for real-time threat detection.

7. Compliance and Governance

- **Definition**: Adhering to regulatory requirements and managing the overall governance of security practices.

- **Implementation**:

  - Use AWS Artifact to access compliance reports and select AWS services compliant with standards such as GDPR, HIPAA, and ISO.

  - Implement governance frameworks and tools like AWS Organizations to manage multiple AWS accounts.

By integrating these AWS services and security best practices, organizations can significantly enhance their cybersecurity posture, ensuring robust protection for their digital assets.

What You Have Learned

This chapter introduced the essential principles of cybersecurity and its role in safeguarding digital assets such as data, applications, and infrastructure in today's interconnected world. You learned that as threats evolve in complexity and scale, cybersecurity becomes increasingly critical for maintaining trust, ensuring compliance, and protecting operations.

The chapter explored how AWS supports cybersecurity with scalable, secure, and flexible tools and services. These offerings help organizations defend against a wide array of threats including malware, ransomware, phishing, insider risks, and DDoS attacks.

You also discovered key cybersecurity domains, including network, cloud, IoT, endpoint, and data security along with foundational practices like risk assessment, employee education, and automated threat detection. Additionally, modern concepts such as Zero Trust, behavioral analytics, and cloud encryption were introduced to illustrate how organizations can strengthen their security posture in a dynamic threat landscape.

This foundation prepares you for more advanced topics and practical implementation as you continue your journey into cybersecurity with AWS.

Summary

Cybersecurity plays a vital role in protecting digital systems from a constantly evolving range of threats. This chapter highlighted the strategic, technical, and operational components required to build effective cybersecurity programs, with a focus on the capabilities offered by AWS. You've laid the groundwork to understand, implement, and manage security in the cloud, preparing you for more advanced topics in the chapters ahead.

CHAPTER 2

Cloud Security Responsibilities and the AWS Security Ecosystem

In the chapter, we will dive deep into something called the shared responsibility model and how important it is with regard to how you will use the cloud – be it AWS, Azure, or Google Cloud Platform (GCP). The shared responsibility model is the key concept that is used to describe and clearly delineate what the cloud provider is responsible for and what the customer is responsible for with regard to security and compliance to make sure the application/solution in the cloud is secure.

We'll make a rundown of AWS services that relate to cybersecurity and, when needed, explain how those services can fortify your AWS cloud environment. Understanding and implementing these in-place mechanisms and best practices will drive your AWS environment to a whole new level of security and let you safely operate the cloud services your business is dependent on.

This chapter will help you understand how to gain knowledge and skills on the use of AWS cloud deployments for stronger security.

The Shared Responsibility Model

The shared responsibility model is one of the most critical concepts in cloud security because it defines the clear boundary between the cloud service provider's (CSP) responsibility and the customer's. Understanding this model is rather like renting an office building.

© Syed Rehan 2025
S. Rehan, *Cybersecurity with AWS*, https://doi.org/10.1007/979-8-8688-1554-6_2

Put differently, this analogy shows that AWS plays the role of the cloud provider that secures the outside and structure of the building, thus the physical security of the data centers, network infrastructure, and core services they provide. This means that AWS ensures the structure is strong and the building is guarded against external attacks.

However, what you do inside the building – how you set up your office, the security of your processes, and who you allow inside your office – is all up to you. Likewise, when you are using AWS services, it is your responsibility to secure your applications, your data, and any configurations that you create in the AWS environment. That would include controlling who has access, encrypting data that you collect, and making your applications resilient to common attacks.

Security roles are shared between AWS, the cloud provider, and you the consumer of the services. Thus, following the set best practices and security guidelines is important. In this way, your applications dependent on AWS services are not exposed to the possible threats resulting from malicious individuals. But who are the malicious individuals?

Threat Landscape

Within the threat landscape, we have "bad actors" at the center. These refer to individuals or groups with malicious intent who seek to exploit vulnerabilities in your cloud environment.

They can be categorized as follows:

1. **Hackers**: These are individuals or groups who attempt to gain unauthorized access to your systems for various purposes, such as stealing data, defacing websites, or disrupting services. They often exploit weaknesses in security configurations or software vulnerabilities.

2. **Cybercriminals**: These are financially motivated cybercrimes. Activities may range from ransomware attack, where they lock up your data and ask for money in return for unlocking it, to stealing sensitive information like credit card details to be used in fraudulent activities. Among cybercriminals, we also have some sponsored by governments; these threat actors conduct sophisticated cyber-espionage and cyber-attacks to gather intelligence, disrupt critical infrastructure, or steal intellectual property.

3. **Insider Threats**: Threats are internal, meaning inside the organization. Disgruntled employees or contractors with access to critical information may leverage that access to harm an organization, through data theft or system sabotage, among other methods.

4. **Script Kiddies**: These are inexperienced individuals who use pre-written scripts or tools to launch attacks without a deep understanding of how they work. They often seek to gain notoriety or simply cause disruption for fun.

5. **Hacktivists**: These are individuals or groups motivated by political or social causes. They use hacking as a form of protest to draw attention to their cause, often targeting organizations or governments they perceive as adversaries.

These are all various forms of threats that are ever-changing in nature; thus, detailed security and watchfulness should be performed. AWS does provide a secure base; that does not mean you should not build securely on top.

We'll dive deeper into best practices to see the ways in which additional hardening can be performed to make your AWS environment even more secure. The more completely you understand the shared responsibility model, the more secure and resilient your cloud infrastructure will be for your applications.

Overview of AWS Services Relevant to Cybersecurity

Amazon Web Services provides a host of security tools and functionalities to safeguard your cloud resources: data, applications, and infrastructure. Each of these services interfaces with others to establish a robust security model in your AWS environment.

Understanding the capabilities of these AWS services is critical for cybersecurity professionals committed to designing resilient and secure cloud architectures.

While not all services are strictly security-focused, each contributes significantly by enabling, enhancing, or supporting broader cybersecurity and compliance objectives across AWS environments.

AWS Services of Strategic Relevance to Cybersecurity Professionals Aiming to Strengthen AWS Security Posture

Identity and Access Management

Manage who can access what in your AWS environment and how they authenticate.

- **AWS Identity and Access Management (IAM)**: Fine-grained access control across AWS resources:

  - **AWS IAM Identity Center**: Centralized access for AWS accounts and applications (SSO (Single Sign-On))

- **Amazon Cognito**: Authentication for web and mobile apps with user sign-up/sign-in

Networking and Infrastructure Security

Protect your network boundaries, manage traffic, and enforce segmentation using AWS-native tools.

- **AWS Virtual Private Cloud (VPC)**: Isolated cloud network for AWS resources:

  - **AWS PrivateLink**: Private, secure connectivity to AWS services without public internet

- **AWS Network Firewall**: Managed, stateful firewall for VPC traffic inspection

- **AWS Firewall Manager**: Centralized management of firewall rules and policies

- **Amazon Route 53 Resolver DNS Firewall**: DNS-level threat protection for VPCs

- **AWS Verified Access**: Secure application access without VPNs (ZTA (Zero-Trust architecture))

- **AWS Web Application Firewall (WAF):** Protects web apps against common exploits (e.g., SQL injection)

- **AWS Shield:** DDoS protection for websites and applications

Threat Detection and Monitoring

Continuously monitor for malicious activity and vulnerabilities across your AWS workloads.

- **AWS GuardDuty:** Intelligent threat detection and continuous monitoring

- **Amazon Detective:** Investigation tool for analyzing GuardDuty and VPC Flow Logs

- **Amazon Inspector:** Automated vulnerability management for EC2 and containers

- **AWS Security Hub:** Centralized view of security posture and compliance checks

- **AWS IoT Device Defender:** Security audit and monitoring for IoT devices

Logging, Audit, and Governance

Ensure visibility, accountability, and regulatory compliance through logging and automated audit tools.

- **AWS CloudTrail:** Records account activity and API calls for governance and auditing

- **AWS Config:** Tracks resource configurations and compliance over time

- **Amazon CloudWatch:** Monitoring and observability of AWS resources and applications

- **AWS Audit Manager:** Automates evidence collection for audit and compliance reporting

Data Protection and Cryptography

Secure your data at rest and in transit using encryption, key management, and secure storage services.

- **AWS Key Management Service (KMS)**: Managed service for creating and controlling encryption keys.

- **AWS Secrets Manager**: Securely stores, rotates, and retrieves credentials and secrets.

- **Amazon Macie**: Machine learning–based service to discover and protect sensitive data (like PII (personally identifiable information)) in S3.

- **AWS CloudHSM**: Dedicated hardware security module (HSM) for secure key storage.

- **AWS Certificate Manager (ACM)**: Provision and manage SSL/TLS certificates for AWS workloads.

- **AWS Payment Cryptography**: Cryptographic operations for payment systems and PCI DSS compliance.

- **AWS Private Certificate Authority**: Private CA service to create and manage certificates.

Identity and Access Management

Let's see how we can control who can access what, when, and how across our systems and data within our AWS environment using AWS IAM.

AWS Identity and Access Management (IAM)

AWS Identity and Access Management (IAM) offers precise, granular control over who can do what. IAM allows you to manage users and use permissions to allow or deny their access to AWS resources. IAM is integrated with all AWS services and enables you to secure your AWS resources in a reliable way.

Key IAM Features:

IAM comes with a powerful set of features designed to help you manage access to AWS resources securely and efficiently.

- **Authentication and Authorization**: IAM, by default, denies access unless policies explicitly allow it. This feature greatly enhances security.

- **Principle of Least Privilege**: Assign just the needed permissions to reduce risk to an adequate level.

- **Roles vs. Users**: IAM roles give temporary, secure credentials for AWS services or federated identities. Prefer roles over IAM users, which have long-term credentials; if users are necessary, ensure they rotate credentials regularly.

IAM Policies:

Policies express permissions in JSON documents that specify the actions, resources, and conditions that are allowed.

IAM policies come in different forms to suit varying access control needs, from broad AWS-managed options to fine-tuned, custom policies. **Types include**

- **AWS-Managed Policies**: These are created by AWS and used for typical scenarios.

- **Customer-Managed Policies**: Custom-made policies that fit specific requirements.

- **Inline Policies**: Put directly into roles, when a one-to-one relationship is required.

- **Resource-Based Policies**: This type of policy is directly attached to resources, such as S3 buckets, and allows for access across different accounts.

Access Control Models:

Different models help define how access is granted within AWS, enabling you to tailor permissions to your organization's structure and needs.

- **Role-Based Access Control (RBAC)**: Simplifying management by assigning permissions to job roles

- **Attribute-Based Access Control (ABAC)**: Employs tags to permit access based on attributes, allowing for an easily scalable and flexibly manageable permissions system

Restricting Access:

In addition to granting permissions, IAM provides mechanisms to explicitly limit or block access, helping enforce security boundaries and governance policies.

- **Deny Statements**: Clearly control actions and override "allow" statements.

- **Service Control Policies (SCPs)**: Enforce account access restrictions on all AWS Organizations accounts without having to grant permissions in those accounts. This is primarily a governance and compliance feature.

Achieving Least Privilege:

Granting only the permissions needed and nothing more is key to reducing risk. By using AWS IAM, you can regularly review and tighten access controls.

- Periodically sharpen your permissions with IAM Access Analyzer, AWS CloudTrail, and last accessed information.

- Remove permissions and users that are not in use. Use IAM Access Analyzer custom checks and the policy simulator to validate your policies.

Utilizing IAM ensures your AWS environment remains secure, compliant, and effective, making sure access is only given to authorized users.

AWS IAM Identity Center

AWS IAM Identity Center makes it easy to manage user access across multiple AWS accounts and cloud applications. It works in tandem with IAM to provide even better streamlined identity federation and portal-based, centralized user management. Whereas IAM alone is like a Swiss Army knife with many useful tools that aren't always easy to use together, IAM Identity Center is like an even better Segway for rolling down the path toward good identity access management.

Advantages:
Here's what makes AWS Identity Center a strong choice for centralized identity management.

- Managing several AWS accounts and applications in the cloud (e.g., Salesforce, Microsoft 365) from a single control point

- A portal with a single, customizable login that supports either existing corporate credentials or credentials managed by the Identity Center

- Heightened clarity regarding user accessibility and actions through the use of AWS CloudTrail integrations

Problems Solved:
AWS Identity Center addresses several common identity and access management challenges.

- Makes identity and permissions management uncomplicated throughout many AWS accounts and cloud applications

- Allows concentrated oversight and direction of user access, tackling the labyrinth IAM cannot navigate alone

Usage:
Here's how AWS Identity Center is typically used in real-world environments.

- AWS Identity Center (successor to AWS Single Sign-On) provides user identity and permissions management for AWS services and applications. The service works with existing identity sources (like Microsoft Active Directory (AD)) and provides consistent access to not just AWS services but also to a variety of cloud applications.

Capabilities:
These are some of the key things AWS Identity Center enables you to do.

- Rapidly grant access rights to Amazon Web Services accounts and a range of cloud/SAML applications.

- User activities can be easily monitored and tracked using CloudTrail.

Who Should Use It?

Designed for administrators who handle many AWS accounts as well as business applications and who need efficient, centralized identity and access management that is beyond the capability of traditional IAM.

How to Enable and Set Up IAM Identity Center:

Getting started with IAM Identity Center involves a few straightforward steps to configure user access across AWS accounts and cloud applications.

1. **Sign In:** Start with the AWS Management Console of the master account, and go to the IAM Identity Center console.

2. **Select Directory:** IAM Identity Center comes with a default user directory. You can use it or connect to a Microsoft AD (managed or via AD Connector) that you've set up.

3. **Grant Access to AWS Accounts:** All users in IAM Identity Center can access AWS accounts with SSO. To allow specific users or groups to access certain AWS accounts, you must select those accounts, choose the users or groups, and assign them permissions.

4. **Select Access to Business Applications:** You can give access to applications that are either integrated with IAM Identity Center or that you've provisioned in some other way. All users in IAM Identity Center can access every application that you've provisioned for them.

5. **IAM Identity Sign-In Web Page:** You can provide users now with this sign-in web URL that they can use to access their accounts and business applications provisioned for them.

Using IAM Identity Center, you can streamline and secure access management for your whole organization, allowing for enhanced productivity and security.

Amazon Cognito

An affordable, developer-friendly CIAM (customer identity and access management) solution, Amazon Cognito is designed to securely manage millions of user identities. It supports a myriad of authentication types, including

- Social

- Enterprise (SAML/OIDC)

- Custom authentication methods

Cognito is built on open standards such as OAuth 2.0, SAML 2.0, and OpenID Connect. It integrates very nicely with popular development frameworks and SDKs.

Key Features:

Amazon Cognito offers powerful tools to manage user identities, secure authentication, and control access with flexibility and ease.

- **Identity Store (User Pools)**: Securely manages user profiles with up to 50-plus customized attributes per user

- **Multitenancy**: Enables efficient reuse of authentication mechanisms and ensures tenant isolation

- **MFA**: Adding security with SMS and TOTP (time-based one-time password)-based MFA, customizable per user pool

- **Federation**: Enables logins through social (Facebook, Google, Apple) and enterprise providers using SAML/OIDC

- **Custom Authentication**: Lets you set up tailored sign-in flows and password-free methods using AWS Lambda

- **Lambda Triggers**: Personalizes user workflows such as sign-up, sign-in, and messaging with third-party integrations

- **Access Control**: Securely integrates with ALB (Application Load Balancer) and API Gateway and enforces policies through the use of tokens and scopes

- **AWS Resource Access**: Provides least-privilege access to AWS services (e.g., DynamoDB, S3) using identity pools

- **M2M (Machine-to-Machine) Authentication**: Enables M2M authentication, ensuring that the machines talk to each other securely, via the OAuth Client Credentials flow

- **Token Customization**: Allows for the creation of enriched access tokens that can be used for controlling at a more granular level who gets to access which resources and for maintaining a more personalized experience across Power BI

Advanced Security:

Amazon Cognito incorporates multiple layers of security features to protect your applications and users from evolving threats.

- Protection from web vulnerabilities through an integration with AWS WAF (Web Application Firewall).

- Immediate identification and thwarting of the reuse of compromised login information.

- Risky authentication attempts are met with additional verification. Otherwise, it's business as usual.

Auditing and Compliance:

To help meet regulatory requirements and maintain transparency, Amazon Cognito integrates robust auditing and monitoring capabilities.

- Amazon Web Services (AWS) CloudTrail, CloudWatch metrics, and Logs Insights enable a strong logging and monitoring foundation.

- Meets compliance standards like HIPAA, PCI DSS, SOC, and ISO (27001, 27017, 27018, 9001).

Amazon Cognito merges robust security, adherence to compliance mandates, and compelling usability to boost both developer experience and customer satisfaction.

Networking and Infrastructure Security

Building a strong security foundation starts with a well-designed network. AWS offers flexible tools to help you create secure, scalable, and isolated environments that protect your resources and data.

AWS Virtual Private Cloud (VPC)

Amazon VPC allows for the establishment of a logical, isolated, and virtual network within AWS while providing complete control over the IP address assignment, subnets, route tables, and gateways that make up the virtual network. VPC integrates securely with an on-premises network through the use of a VPN connection and can be configured to route either public or private traffic to the virtual network. The routing of all traffic to the virtual network can be controlled in such a way that backend systems are protected from direct exposure to the internet.

Key VPC Components:

These components form the building blocks of your virtual network, enabling you to design an architecture that balances accessibility, performance, and security according to your needs.

- **VPC**: Your customizable virtual network. It has IP ranges that you define.

- **Subnet**: An IP range inside a VPC that allows specific resources to not be accessible from the public internet.

- **Internet Gateway**: Allows interaction between VPC and the general internet.

- **Network Address Translation (NAT) Gateway**: Offers secure internet connectivity for private subnetworks.

- **Virtual Private Gateway**: VPC endpoint for VPN access to on-premises networks.

- **VPC Peering**: Jointly connects two VPCs in a private manner.

- **VPC Endpoint**: Allows for private connection to AWS services with no exposure to the internet.

- **Egress-Only Internet Gateway**: Enables IPv6 internet access without being directly exposed to inbound internet traffic.

Cybersecurity Benefits:

Implementing VPC architecture strengthens your security posture by isolating resources, controlling traffic flow, and minimizing exposure to external threats, all while enabling private and secure connections to AWS services and your own infrastructure.

- Allows for the creation of secure, separate network environments.

- Security groups, network ACLs (access control lists), route tables, and subnet isolation are secure and trustworthy. They provide layered security for networks.

- Lowers vulnerability by leveraging AWS PrivateLink to make direct, secure service connections.

VPC Endpoint Types:

Different endpoint options allow secure, private communication with AWS services without sending traffic over the public internet, helping to reduce attack surfaces and improve data privacy.

- **Gateway Endpoints**: Connect securely to AWS services such as S3 and DynamoDB and do so entirely via private routes.

- **Interface Endpoints**: Use AWS PrivateLink to connect in a private manner to the wider array of AWS and partner services.

Security Controls:

Robust controls like security groups and network ACLs enable precise traffic filtering at multiple levels, providing layered defense mechanisms that safeguard your cloud workloads.

- **Security Groups**: Stateful virtual firewalls that control inbound/ outbound traffic at the EC2 instance level.

- **Network ACLs**: Optional, stateless subnet-level firewall rules that add another layer of security. They complement security groups.

Cross-Region and Service Communication:

AWS offers flexible, secure options to connect resources across different regions and services, ensuring smooth, private data flow that respects your compliance and latency requirements.

- Regional traffic can be secured using VPC peering or AWS Direct Connect.

- Communicate securely with S3 using VPC endpoints.

Network Monitoring:

Comprehensive monitoring tools give you visibility into your network traffic and potential threats, empowering you to detect anomalies, troubleshoot issues, and maintain compliance through detailed logging and real-time analysis.

- **VPC Flow Logs**: Capture and check detailed IP traffic for auditing, troubleshooting, and security.

- **VPC Traffic Mirroring**: Duplicate network traffic from EC2 instances to external analysis tools for threat monitoring and diagnostics.

Amazon VPC provides a secure, adaptable network in AWS. It enables robust isolation and access controls, and it supports a solid suite of security best practices. VPC also provides convenient monitoring capabilities.

AWS PrivateLink

AWS PrivateLink provides secure, private, and direct connectivity from your VPCs to AWS-hosted services without using public IP addresses or traversing the internet. It ensures network traffic stays within AWS's secure network, enhancing security by reducing exposure to external threats.

Utilizing AWS PrivateLink:

AWS PrivateLink enables private connectivity between your VPC and supported AWS services or third-party applications without exposing traffic to the public internet. This approach ensures secure and efficient communication by keeping data within the AWS network boundaries.

- **End Users**: Set up interface endpoints (private network interfaces with private IP addresses) in your VPC to securely and privately access AWS services.

- **Service Providers**: Position a network load balancer (NLB) in front of your service, and then configure a PrivateLink service as a secure target group behind the NLB. Your customers access your service privately through PrivateLink.

Supported Services:

PrivateLink securely connects users to AWS services (e.g., EC2, ELB, Kinesis, SNS, Systems Manager, DataSync), third-party SaaS (Software as a Service) offerings from AWS Marketplace, and resources via AWS Direct Connect.

Cybersecurity Benefits:

By keeping all traffic within AWS's private network and enabling fine-grained access controls, AWS PrivateLink minimizes exposure to external threats. It helps you enforce strict security policies, reduce attack surfaces, and maintain compliance by ensuring data stays secure and private throughout its journey.

- Keeps all data traffic within AWS's secure network, eliminating public internet threats

- Provides detailed management and oversight of those utilizing your services, via IAM policy-based access

- Improves overall safety and security by ensuring that traffic remains private and access is carefully controlled

The security and privacy of your AWS workloads are significantly enhanced by AWS PrivateLink, allowing private, controlled, and safe service connectivity.

AWS Network Firewall

AWS Network Firewall is a managed, scalable firewall service that protects Amazon VPCs by filtering and monitoring network traffic. It provides flexible rules to detect threats, manage traffic flows, and ensure compliance across multiple accounts and VPCs.

Key Advantages:

AWS Network Firewall automates infrastructure management and scaling, enabling centralized, policy-driven security with flexible, customizable rule sets.

- **Managed by AWS**: No need to worry about setup or maintenance, AWS takes care of it all.

- **Centralized Policies**: Use Firewall Manager to apply consistent rules everywhere.

- **Flexible and Scalable**: Easily customize rules by IP, port, protocol, or domain, and the firewall scales as your traffic grows.

How It Secures VPCs:

It combines stateful inspection, intrusion prevention, and web filtering to protect VPC traffic at multiple layers.

- **Stateful Firewall**: A firewall that maintains the state of traffic flow. Tracks traffic flows to enforce precise, session-aware policies

- **Intrusion Prevention System (IPS)**: Actively finds and stops threats and exploits

- **Web Filtering**: Offers sophisticated traffic oversight and fine-grained control

Ideal Deployment Scenarios:

Perfect for monitoring inter-VPC traffic, ensuring compliance, and safeguarding sensitive applications.

- **Visibility and Control**: Ensuring the visibility and control of inter-VPC traffic, for instance, securing traffic between business applications and sensitive data.

- **Compliance and Security**: Outbound traffic is filtered by URL/IP/ domain to prevent data leaks.

- **Security of the connection**: Safeguards traffic routed through AWS Transit Gateway for Direct Connect and VPN.

- **Application Availability**: Screens incoming online traffic so that application-layer attacks are less likely to succeed.

Deployment Models:

Deploy firewalls within VPCs for local control or centrally via Transit Gateway for streamlined management.

- **Distributed**: Firewall placed directly within numerous VPCs for decentralized enforcement

- **Centralized**: Firewall connected to AWS Transit Gateway to filter centrally all traffic across linked VPCs

Activating AWS Network Firewall:

AWS Network Firewall looks at traffic that's coming into and going out of a VPC. It does this based on rules that are defined using AWS Firewall Manager. Those rules can enforce some pretty basic security, what security people would call "stateless" security, and also some really important security that requires the firewall to keep track of the state of a conversation between a client and a server.

- **Stateless Rules**: Basic allow/disallow rules based on IP, port, and protocol.

- **Stateful Rules**: Connect things and keep track of context so that the decisions you make can go deeper and be more session-aware.

Logging and Monitoring:

Capturing and storing detailed firewall logs is essential for visibility into network activity and for responding to security incidents effectively.

- Logs activity of the firewall to Amazon S3 or Kinesis Data Firehose for external analysis, threat detection, incident response, and forensic investigation

Integration and Traffic Control:

Seamless integration with AWS Transit Gateway and advanced traffic inspection features help you manage and secure network flows at scale.

- **AWS Transit Gateway**: Simplifies how you connect your VPCs and on-premises networks to a common network. With Transit Gateway, you can inspect network traffic in a scalable way

- **Outbound Traffic Control**: Provides URL filtering, protocol detection (DNS, HTTP/S), and ACL management

- **Encrypted Traffic Inspection**: Executes TLS decryption, analysis, and re-encryption (TLS 1.1, 1.2, 1.3 supported)

Cybersecurity Value:

AWS Network Firewall dramatically improves a cybersecurity posture. Such a thing is only possible because of what these firewalls allow users to do: define custom, even responsive, security policies; adapt protections to network behavior; and behave like something other than a dumb box that just says yes or no.

Amazon Firewall Manager

Amazon Firewall Manager simplifies the centralized management of firewall rules and security policies across multiple AWS accounts and resources within your AWS organization. It automatically enforces compliance with the policies you define, even as new accounts and resources are added. This service, really a set of tools for management and monitoring, is the simplest way to ensure that your security posture is consistently applied across your entire AWS environment.

Key Advantages:

Easily manage and enforce security policies centrally while staying quickly informed about potential threats.

- Control and administrate WAF policies and firewall rules in one location across all of AWS, using a single interface.

- **Automatic Enforcement**: New AWS accounts and their resources automatically have security policies applied.

- **Rule Grouping and Threat Alerts**: Organize WAF rules logically and get immediate notifications when a threat is detected.

Supported Resources:

- AWS WAF for Application Load Balancer and API Gateway

Prerequisites:

Make sure your AWS environment is properly organized and configured with the right permissions and monitoring tools in place.

- AWS Organizations containing management and member accounts that are clearly defined.

- Each managed account has AWS Config enabled.

- Necessary AWS resources and IAM permissions are set up correctly.

Policy Modes:

Start with manual setup to tailor policies exactly how you want, and then switch to automatic mode to keep everything consistently compliant without the hassle.

- **Manual Remediation**: At first, configure policies by hand for detailed command over policy configuration.

- **Automatic Remediation**: Firewall Manager automatically finds compliance drift and corrects it, ensuring that resources have consistent policy enforcement.

Cybersecurity Benefits:

Firewall Manager ensures a consistently secure AWS environment, enforcing uniform security standards across existing and future resources, significantly strengthening your cybersecurity posture.

Amazon Route 53 Resolver DNS Firewall

Amazon Route 53 Resolver DNS Firewall is a managed service providing control and filtering of DNS queries from AWS virtual private clouds (VPCs). It prevents queries to malicious domains, allows trusted domains, and supports customizable allowlists and blocklists.

Key Benefits:

Route 53 provides robust DNS traffic control with seamless AWS monitoring and regional management.

- **Fine Control**: Manages DNS query behaviors with pinpoint accuracy for even more secure internet communications

- **AWS Integration**: Integrates perfectly with AWS Resource Access Manager (RAM), CloudWatch, and Route 53 Resolver logs to monitor and log activities

- **Regional Control**: Manages outbound DNS traffic throughout various VPCs by means of rule groups that are prioritized

How It Works:

Blocks unauthorized queries while enabling precise filtering and real-time monitoring.

- **Protection**: Blocks unauthorized DNS requests, preventing DNS-based data exfiltration

- **Filtering**: Restricts resolution requests to private hosted zones, EC2 instance names, or other defined domains

- **Monitoring**: Uses CloudWatch and EventBridge for real-time visibility and logging of DNS traffic

Components and Settings:

Includes reusable rule groups, customizable domain lists, and detailed query handling options.

- **Rule Groups**: Sets of rules that apply to DNS queries. These can be reused across different virtual private clouds (VPCs).

- **Rules**: Separate filters that define domains and what actions to take (permit, obstruct, notify).

- **Domain Lists**: Lists that can be either custom or AWS-managed, specifying the domains that are permitted or prohibited.

- **Domain Redirection**: Choices to examine full DNS resolution pathways or just starting domains.

- **Types of Queries**: Specific types of records are sought in the DNS query.

Configuration Steps:

Set domain policies, create prioritized rules, and link them to your VPCs for enforcement.

- Define domain filtering strategy and lists.

- Create firewall rule groups per region.

- Add rules with priority settings for accurate order.

- Associate rule groups with targeted VPCs.

- Optionally configure VPC behavior if DNS Firewall response fails.

Cybersecurity Benefits:

Route 53 Resolver DNS Firewall strengthens your security posture by preventing malicious DNS queries, reducing risks of DNS-based attacks and data leaks. Comprehensive monitoring and logging enable rapid threat detection and incident response, while tight integration with AWS security services ensures a secure cloud environment.

AWS Verified Access

AWS Verified Access provides secure remote access to enterprise applications without VPNs, using Zero-Trust principles to evaluate and authorize each request in real time.

Key Features:

This service delivers real-time, Zero-Trust secure access with granular policy controls and broad integration.

- **Zero-Trust Security**: Authenticates each access attempt individually, preventing lateral threats.

- **VPN Alternative**: Removes VPN inconvenience, making remote access more user-friendly.

- **Real-Time Policy Evaluation**: Authenticates user identity, device security, and location in real time.

- **Fine-Grained Access Policies**: Allows granular and tailored access policies on a per-application or per-group basis.

- **Integration Capabilities**: AWS IAM Identity Center, third-party identity providers (IdPs) (Okta, JumpCloud, Ping Identity), and endpoint security (CrowdStrike, Jamf, Cisco Duo, VMware) are all supported.

- **Centralized Logging**: Logs detailed access logs for quick security incident analysis with standardized formats like OCSF (Open Cybersecurity Schema Framework).

- **Improved User Experience**: Provides seamless, secure application access without introducing extra authentication steps.

How It Works:

Verified Access evaluates access requests in real time against defined security conditions (identity, device posture, location). Admins centrally define and apply policies, simplifying security operations.

Security Enhancements:
Enhances protection through AWS WAF integration, device posture checks, and secure identity context passing.

- Integrates with AWS WAF for filtering common attacks (SQL injection, XSS)

- Allows for device posture checking via third-party device management

- Securely passes signed identity contexts to applications, minimizing reauthentication

Benefits from a Cybersecurity Perspective:
AWS Verified Access significantly improves cybersecurity by implementing principles of Zero Trust, reducing attack surfaces, and having centralized logging and integration with other security services, making security management easier and improving overall security stance in the end.

AWS Web Application Firewall (WAF)

AWS WAF is a managed service that helps protect web applications by filtering web requests based on rules you define, thereby blocking common attacks like SQL injection and cross-site scripting (XSS).

How AWS WAF Works:
AWS WAF examines incoming HTTP/S requests against defined security rules, allowing, blocking, or monitoring traffic based on conditions like IP addresses, headers, body content, or URI strings. It is natively integrated with Amazon CloudFront, Application Load Balancer (ALB), API Gateway, and AWS AppSync.

Protection Capabilities:
Provides robust filtering, blocks common web threats, controls bot traffic, and mitigates DDoS risks.

- **Malicious Request Blocking**: Prevents attacks like SQL injection and XSS

- **Bot Mitigation**: Differentiates between malicious and beneficial bots, providing visibility and control

- **Rate Limiting**: Limits request rates from specific IP addresses to avert DDoS attacks

Key Use Cases:

Some of the ideal use cases are

- Protecting web apps from common vulnerabilities

- Traffic direction by user agent, IP addresses, or headers

- Malicious bot traffic management and mitigation

Important Features:

Offers rate-based rules, IPv6 support, managed rule sets, and seamless logging integration.

- **Rate-Based Rules**: Controls request volumes to protect against DDoS

- **IPv6 Support**: Protects both IPv4 and IPv6 traffic

- **Managed Rules**: Preconfigured security rules from AWS and third parties

- **Logging and Monitoring**: Integrated with CloudTrail and CloudWatch for auditing and real-time visibility

Advanced Security:

Includes fraud prevention measures like account takeover and fake account creation blocking.

- **Account Takeover Prevention (ATP)**: Blocks unauthorized login attempts using stolen credentials

- **Account Creation Fraud Prevention (ACFP)**: Blocks fraudulent sign-ups and registrations to prevent fraud and phishing

Cybersecurity Benefits:

AWS WAF significantly enhances your cybersecurity with adaptive, scalable defense against web-based attacks. Its frictionless integration, robust real-time inspection, comprehensive logging, and bot mitigation capabilities ensure secure, compliant, and reliable application performance.

AWS Shield

AWS Shield is a managed DDoS protection service that protects applications in AWS Cloud. There are two levels of protection that AWS Shield offers: AWS Shield Standard, which is free, and AWS Shield Advanced, which is paid.

AWS Shield Standard:

Free, automatic protection against common DDoS attacks.

- Automatically safeguards against typical Layer 3 and Layer 4 attacks (e.g., SYN/UDP floods)

- Offered to all AWS customers at no additional charge

AWS Shield Advanced:

Enhanced, real-time defense with cost protection and expert support.

- Constant and assured monitoring and mitigation of advanced and large-scale Layer 3, 4, and 7 attacks (HTTP floods, DNS floods)

- Cost protection to cover usage that spikes because of an attack

- Real-time notification of attack types and also 24/7 access to the AWS Shield Response Team for fast incident management

Key Features:

Get full IPv4/IPv6 coverage and global reach, and become compliance-ready.

- **DDoS Cost Protection**: Protects you from the costs that can spike because of DDoS-triggered usage increases.

- **IPv6 Support**: Gives you total protection across all your traffic, whether it's IPv4 or IPv6.

- **Global Availability**: Standard protection can be used all over the world; if you're using the Advanced version, it also works with CloudFront, Route 53, and AWS Global Accelerator.

- **Compliance**: HIPAA-eligible, suitable for applications managing protected health information (PHI).

Visibility and Reporting:

Get real-time alerts, historical data, and global threat insights.

- Real-time notifications through CloudWatch metrics.

- Incidents that have occurred historically can be looked up for the past 13 months.

- The Global Threat Dashboard shows the recent global activity of DDoS attacks.

Cybersecurity Benefits:

The boost in cybersecurity posture by AWS Shield ensures robust defenses and, more significantly, reliable availability of applications that are threatened by various DDoS attacks. Furthermore, it integrates nicely across the AWS services and manages a wide comprehensive spectrum of attacks that one would find it hard to question its importance for the kind of applications that are crucial and also sensitive.

Threat Detection and Monitoring

AWS offers a range of threat detection and monitoring tools designed to keep your environment secure, continuously scanning for anomalies, suspicious activity, and potential risks so you can respond faster and smarter.

AWS GuardDuty

Amazon GuardDuty is a managed threat detection service that provides continuous security monitoring across AWS accounts, workloads, and data. Unlike many security services that provide low-level signals, GuardDuty identifies real threats and issues actionable security alerts. In fact, the service is fine-tuned to detect things like anomalous behavior and stolen credentials, two indicators of potential compromise that you might have difficulty finding with other services.

Key Benefits:

Constant, smart monitoring that fits seamlessly into your setup without slowing you down.

- **Continuous Monitoring**: Real-time threat detection that doesn't affect workload performance.

- **Threat Intelligence Integration**: Leverages AWS and external intelligence, along with machine learning, to spot new threats.

- **Total visibility**: Watches over CloudTrail, VPC Flow Logs, DNS queries, EKS audit log, and EC2/EBS activity, among other things.

- **Simple Integration**: Integrates without disruption with current event management, automation (EventBridge, Lambda), and remediation workflows.

- **Inexpensive**: You only pay for what you use, with no need to spend on extras like software or up-front costs.

- **Regional and Scalable**: Security findings remain specific to a given region but can be aggregated across regions; this service scales easily to accommodate workload demands.

Cybersecurity Advantages:
Early threat detection and fast, automated responses keep your systems safe and compliant with less hassle.

- Threats are detected before they can fully develop, enabling a prompt reaction.

- Reduced response times and less need for manual intervention are outcomes of automated remediation.

- Ensures that compliance is maintained (for instance, with PCI DSS) via in-depth and ongoing security oversight.

- Works without affecting the availability or performance of the system, making it fit for enterprise-level deployments.

AWS GuardDuty boosts your security posture through scalable, proactive threat detection. It gives you comprehensive visibility into what is happening in your AWS environment. And if it finds something that poses a threat, it has automated response capabilities to take care of the problem.

In short, it positions your AWS environment in a better and secure state.

Amazon Detective

Amazon Detective makes it easy to investigate security incidents. When AWS customers have a security event, they can look to Amazon Detective for help. Most AWS security tools rely on customers having some sort of base knowledge. At a minimum, customers need to understand the AWS logging infrastructure. Customers need to know how to configure and retrieve the right log files in order to make meaningful security assessments. And they need to be able to do this (to some degree) for the estimated time window of the security event.

Key Benefits:
Quickly investigate issues with centralized data, with no up-front costs.

- **Efficient Investigations**: Streamlined analyses of aggregated data, summaries, and contextual information make investigations more efficient.

- **Prolonged Data Storage**: Keeps and interprets for you a year's worth of security-related data.

- **Pay As You Go**: No initial expenditure; only event analysis incurs a cost, requiring no supplementary software.

Core Features:
Visualizes your environment and detects threats automatically.

- **Behavior Graph**: An interactive, consolidated, and single-window view of resources, activities, and relationships that are inferred from logs (CloudTrail, VPC Flow Logs, GuardDuty, Security Hub, EKS audit logs).

- **Locating Groups**: Unites associated security findings into clustered incidents for speedier interpretation.

- **Automated Investigations**: Using machine learning, we detect compromised IAM entities, anomalous behaviors, and indicators of compromise.

Integration:
Seamlessly connects with AWS security tools for easy management.

- Operates without interruption with GuardDuty, Security Hub, and Security Lake, amplifying the inter-service security workflow.

Cybersecurity Benefits:

Early threat detection and fast response keep your systems secure.

- Swift hazard recognition and reaction via pre-emptive scrutiny

- Complete visibility and automatic correlation of actions across resources

- Enhanced security stance with effective inquiries, rule adherence, and condensed time-to-remedy

Vital support is provided by Amazon Detective for cybersecurity teams so they can quickly and effectively investigate, understand, and mitigate threats within the AWS environment.

Amazon Inspector

Amazon Inspector is an automated vulnerability management system that continuously scans for holes in Amazon EC2 instances, AWS Lambda functions, Amazon ECR container images, and CI/CD integrations. Inspector identifies not only standard vulnerabilities but also unintended network exposures in these AWS components.

Key Benefits:

Automates scanning and risk scoring, so you stay ahead without manual effort.

- **Constant, Automated Scanning**: Real-time vulnerability detection without manual effort.

- **Centralized Management**: Central visibility and control through Delegated Administrator accounts.

- **Contextual Risk Scoring**: Ranks weaknesses in a system by assigning scores that make sense in a given context.

- **Comprehensive Dashboard**: User-friendly cover interface comprehensively across EC2, Lambda, ECR, and CI/CD pipelines. Monitoring is made easy.

- **Agile Scanning**: Enables both agent-based and agentless (preview) methods for optimal detection.

- **Software Bill of Materials (SBOM)**: Software Bill of Materials (SBOM) is a centralized management system that allows the user to export the SBOM in standard formats.

- **Seamless Integration**: The AWS integration is seamless. It operates with AWS Security Hub and EventBridge, allowing for automated security workflows.

Key Capabilities:

Secures containers, code, and the cloud with seamless CI/CD and AWS integrations.

- **Container Security**: Comprehensive vulnerability scanning goes beyond the basic Amazon ECR scans.

- **CI/CD Integration**: There are plugins for Jenkins and TeamCity that allow you to scan container images as part of your build process.

- **Exporting Findings**: Find detailed vulnerability reports and SBOMs in formats such as CSV, JSON, CycloneDX, and SPDX.

- **Notification and Logging**: EventBridge and CloudTrail are integrated for detailed logging and real-time alerts.

Cybersecurity Advantages:

Prioritizes what matters, cuts noise, and keeps your environment safer, automatically.

- **Improved Security**: Timely and proactive detection of weaknesses elevates the security stance.

- **Effective Oversight**: Having everything under one roof reduces the operating weight. And it makes everything simpler, especially the processes you go through when something goes wrong.

- **Prioritization of Risk**: Scoring that is placed in context allows a prompt and precise reaction to be made.

- **Sweeping Support**: When it comes to core AWS services, the support is well-rounded, which means vulnerability assessments are pretty much everywhere you look.

- **Automated systems**: Less manual work, fewer complexities, and lower chances of making mistakes. If you think about it, people are good at a lot of things, but there's a limit to how much we can do and how well we can do it when we're tired or distracted. Machines don't have those limits. They don't get tired. They don't get bored or lose focus, and they don't make mistakes.

Amazon Inspector delivers comprehensive, continuous, and automated vulnerability management, playing a key role in maintaining a secure AWS environment.

AWS Security Hub

AWS Security Hub is an automated cloud security posture management (CSPM) service that offers nonstop security evaluations, alert unification, and centralized oversight of AWS cloud environments. Compliance and threat management are greatly facilitated by Security Hub, which serves as a "single pane of glass" for viewing not only the AWS cloud resources under the direct jurisdiction of an organization but also the state of security compliance in those resources.

Key Capabilities:

Helps you stay in control of your cloud security with smart automation, clear insights, and tools that work the way you do.

- **Automated Continuous Monitoring**: Automatically checking the environment against AWS security best practices, regulatory standards (like PCI DSS), and even more detailed frameworks (like CIS and NIST), CloudCheckr gives you a pretty clear scoring system (0–100) to quickly assess what needs to be fixed.

- **Centralized Management**: Gathers security notifications from AWS and external tools into a single, cohesive interface. This permits a direct look into what is happening across our cloud ecosystem and makes it far easier to answer the question, "What is going on under the hood?"

- **Customization with Flexibility**: This allows for controls to be fine-tuned to fit the specific requirements of an organization, such as the criteria for unused resources or the policies for passwords.

- **Insightful Power**: Provides customizable dashboards that allow for the visualization of security trends, helping to identify patterns and enabling quick response to threats.

- **Standardized Data Format**: AWS Security Finding Format (ASFF) is utilized as a standardized data format to standardize alerts. This means that the way alerts are presented is consistent across different services. And that consistency allows the security operations center (SOC) to do analysis and take action.

- **Accounts and Regions Supported**: Provides a consolidated view that spans across accounts and regions in AWS. This is done while using a single controlling account that has administrative permissions.

- **Remediation and Integration of Automation**: With integrations that are truly seamless, this service works with not only Amazon EventBridge and AWS Lambda but also with a variety of third-party incident response tools. This allows for a full automation of security workflows and incident responses.

Cybersecurity Benefits:

Turns complex cloud environments into manageable, secure spaces, so you can focus on action, not just alerts.

- **Improved Security Stance**: Not just regular monitoring but constant, even obsessive, watching, in line with best practices, really reduces exposure.

- **Consolidated Insight**: Combining the results from the various accounts enables a secure, manageable atmosphere for all the parts of the system.

- **Efficient Security Operations**: Automation and standardized formats accelerate incident response and remediation.

- **Contextual Prioritization**: Risk scoring assists in the effective mitigation of prioritized, serious threats.

- **Scalable and Customizable**: Adapts to your organizational needs and integrates with diverse tools, enhancing your overall security infrastructure.

AWS Security Hub delivers a centralized, automated, and integrated approach to AWS security management, ensuring robust protection and streamlined operations.

AWS IoT Device Defender

AWS IoT Device Defender is a completely managed IoT safety service that uninterruptedly checks and observes your IoT configurations, spots safety risks, and allows for swift reactions to possible problems.

Key Features:

Keeps an eye on your IoT fleet so you don't have to, automating checks, alerts, and fixes to catch issues before they become problems.

- **Audit**: Checks IoT configurations (certificates, policies, IDs) against AWS best practices, identifying risks like shared identities or overly permissive access.

- **Rules Detection**: Monitors defined security metrics (e.g., open ports, failed logins) to detect abnormal device behavior based on custom user rules.

- **Alerting**: This is the most basic function of a security monitoring system. It takes care of real-time visibility for you. If anything suspicious happens, an alert will be sent to Amazon SNS, CloudWatch, or AWS IoT Console. You can choose where your alerts are sent. For real-time security visibility, you have three options for where to send your alerts.

- **Mitigation**: Provides built-in remediation actions, such as updating policies or certificates, and contextual device history to address identified issues quickly.

How It Works:

Runs regular audits and monitors device activity in real time. If something seems off, it flags it and can take action automatically if needed.

- Conducts audits of configurations on a regular basis, either on demand or according to a predetermined schedule

- Ongoing analysis of interactions between devices and the cloud, using rule-based detection to identify any irregularities

- Works with CloudWatch and SNS so you can keep an eye on security and automate routine tasks

Cybersecurity Benefits:

Protects what matters with always-on visibility, smart automation, and guardrails that keep your devices in line with best practices.

- **Continuous Monitoring**: Ongoing detection ensures prompt identification of IoT threats.

- **Automated Response**: Enables swift action through built-in mitigation strategies.

- **Enhanced Compliance**: Regular audits ensure adherence to AWS security best practices.

- **Proactive Protection**: Helps secure IoT environments from emerging threats and unauthorized access.

AWS IoT Device Defender delivers proactive, automated, and intelligent security for IoT deployments, significantly strengthening the protection of connected device ecosystems.

Logging, Audit, and Governance

Beyond just AWS Config, services like CloudTrail, CloudWatch, and Audit Manager work together to help you track changes, prove compliance, and keep your cloud behavior in check.

AWS Config

AWS Config is a fully managed service, which monitors and audits AWS resource configurations for security, troubleshooting, and compliance.

Key Features:

These are the main tools and capabilities AWS Config offers to help you monitor and manage your cloud resources.

- **Resource Inventory and Configuration History**: Provides comprehensive history of AWS resource configurations to audit and troubleshoot.

- **Config Rules**: Validate resources against predefined rules to ensure that they are in compliance; alert on compliance breaches on a dashboard.

- **Conformance Packs**: Assemblies of AWS Config rules and remediation procedures for simple roll-out across accounts and regions.

- **Proactive Rule Evaluation**: Detect non-compliance before provisioning resources.

- **Third-Party and On-Premises Recording**: Requires monitoring of outside resources using custom resource types.

- **Integration with AWS CloudTrail**: Correlates configuration changes with user activity for auditing and troubleshooting.

- **Centralized Compliance Monitoring**: Monitors compliance status in accounts and regions in AWS Organizations.

Cybersecurity Benefits:

Here's how AWS Config helps keep your environment secure and compliant, making life easier for your security teams.

- **Continuous Monitoring**: Scans automatically configurations for rule compliance

- **Automated Remediation**: Brings resources back into compliance with pre-specified actions

- **Enhanced Visibility**: Provides fine-grained configuration history and change tracking

- **Audit Support**: Enables complete audits with historical data and CloudTrail log correlation

- **Scalability and Flexibility**: Compliant rules and conformance packs for various compliance needs

- **Proactive Security**: Prevents non-compliant resources from being started

AWS Config offers continuous monitoring, automated compliance verification, and full auditing capabilities, enhancing security and governance within your AWS environment.

AWS CloudTrail

AWS CloudTrail is a managed service for auditing, monitoring, and troubleshooting that records user activity and API calls on AWS services. It provides comprehensive visibility into AWS account activity for security, compliance, and operational efficiency.

Key Features:
Here's a quick look at what CloudTrail can do to help you keep an eye on everything happening in your AWS setup.

Event Types:
CloudTrail keeps track of different kinds of activity so nothing slips through the cracks.

- **Management Events**: Control plane actions (e.g., creating or deleting resources)

- **Data Events**: Data plane actions (e.g., reading or writing objects in S3)

- **Insights Events**: Detects abnormal API call activity and error rates

Event History:
Find out how long your activity logs are saved and what's running behind the scenes by default.

- Stores 90 days of management events by default

- Always on in all AWS accounts

Trails:
This is how CloudTrail gathers and sends your logs, even across multiple accounts and regions.

- Collects and forwards activity logs to S3, CloudWatch Logs, and EventBridge

- Provides multi-account and multi-region logging

CloudTrail Lake:
Think of this as a powerful tool that stores all your logs and lets you search them easily whenever you need.

- Managed data lake for storage, querying, and analysis of logs

- Provides immutable storage and SQL-based query

- AWS and non-AWS sources supported

Security and Integrity:
CloudTrail makes sure your logs stay safe, secure, and untampered with.

- Logs are encrypted by default and can also be secured with additional AWS KMS keys.

- Integrity validation keeps logs tamper-free and unchanged.

- **Multi-cloud and Multi-source Integration**:

  - Supports integration with AWS Config, AWS Audit Manager, and third-party solutions

Cybersecurity Benefits:
Here's why all this logging and monitoring really matters for keeping your environment secure and compliant.

- **Comprehensive Auditing**: Monitors all user interactions and API calls for proper monitoring.

- **Enhanced Security**: Detects anomalies based on CloudTrail Insights.

- **Compliance Support**: Delivers comprehensive records required for audits and compliance.

- **Forensic Analysis**: CloudTrail Lake supports thorough investigations with query capability.

- **Flexible Logging**: Multi-account and multi-region support ensures consistent visibility across environments.

- **Data Integrity**: Guarantees that logs are protected from tampering.

AWS CloudTrail provides secure logging and monitoring capabilities essential to security, compliance, and operational integrity of AWS environments.

Amazon CloudWatch

Amazon CloudWatch is a monitoring service for AWS resources and applications, offering visibility into performance, resource utilization, operational health, and security (think of CloudWatch as your eyes and ears inside AWS).

Key Features:
Here's a quick look at what CloudWatch can do to keep your system running smoothly.

Monitoring and Logging:
It gathers info from a variety of AWS services so you always know what's going on.

- Gathers and monitors metrics from AWS resources, applications, and custom metrics

- Logs data from EC2 instances, Lambda functions, DynamoDB, RDS, EKS, ECS, and others

Logs Insights and Analysis:
Dig into your logs easily and spot any weird behavior before it becomes a problem.

- Interactively search, visualize, and analyze logs with CloudWatch Logs Insights.

- Detect anomalies using AI/ML models with CloudWatch Anomaly Detection.

- Identify top contributors to performance issues with Contributor Insights.

Application Monitoring:
See how your apps and containers are performing, all in one place.

- Amazon CloudWatch ServiceLens integrates metrics, logs, and traces (via AWS X-Ray) for end-to-end application monitoring.

- Container Insights supports EKS, ECS, and Fargate monitoring.

User Experience Monitoring:
Keep track of what your users actually experience, whether it's real users or test runs.

- Digital Experience Monitoring (DEM) offers synthetic monitoring and Real User Monitoring (RUM) for end-to-end visibility.

- Internet Monitor monitors internet availability and performance between AWS applications and end users.

Dashboards and Alarms:
Build your own dashboards and set up alerts to catch issues early.

- Customizable dashboards for visualization of metrics and logs.

- Define thresholds and alarms and trigger automated responses via SNS, Lambda, or Auto Scaling.

Security and Compliance:
CloudWatch helps you keep your data safe and meet security requirements.

- Integrated with IAM for access management.

- Log data is encrypted by SSE and can be further protected using KMS keys.

- Log anomaly detection helps identify unusual patterns ahead of time.

Cross-Account and Multi-region Support:
Watch over your whole AWS setup, no matter how many accounts or regions you have.

- Monitor applications across AWS accounts and regions with ease.

Data Protection and Privacy:
It automatically finds and hides sensitive info, so you don't have to worry.

- Log data protection automatically detects and masks sensitive information.

Cybersecurity Benefits:
Here's how CloudWatch helps you stay ahead of threats and keep things secure.

1. **Proactive Threat Detection**: Anomaly detection in real time and automatic alerts give instant visibility into potential threats.

2. **Compliance and Auditing**: Comprehensive logs facilitate compliance with regulations and exhaustive auditing.

3. **Automated Response**: Initiate automated workflows for quick response to issues detected.

4. **Secure Log Management**: Maintains data privacy and integrity with encryption and anomaly detection.

5. **Centralized Monitoring**: Single-pane-of-glass visibility across all AWS accounts and regions for consistent security management.

Amazon CloudWatch offers extensive monitoring, alerting, and anomaly detection functionality that enhances both operational efficiency and cybersecurity posture.

AWS Audit Manager

AWS Audit Manager simplifies and automates audit and compliance processes by automatically collecting evidence from your AWS account. It provides preconfigured frameworks based on industry standards (e.g., PCI DSS, HIPAA, GDPR) with the option to customize controls to fit individual requirements.

Key Features:
Here's what AWS Audit Manager brings to the table to make compliance easier and more reliable.

- **Prebuilt Frameworks**

- Ready-made compliance templates help you get started quickly, with room to tweak them to your needs.

  - AWS resource mappings to control obligations for standards like PCI DSS, GDPR, HIPAA

  - Easily customizable to fit individual compliance requirements

- **Automated Evidence Collection**

  It keeps gathering compliance evidence automatically, so you're never caught off guard.

  - **Ongoing Evidence Collection**:

    - Gathers evidence from AWS CloudTrail, AWS Config, AWS Security Hub, and other services on an ongoing basis

    - Automatically maps evidence to control requirements

- **Simplified Collaboration**

  Makes it easy to share the load by involving experts and teams in your audit process.

  - Offload control reviews to subject matter experts.

  - Allow team-based review workflows for audits.

- **Centralized Evidence Storage**

  All your audit data is stored safely in one place with tight control over access.

  - Evidence stored securely with read-only access for end users

  - Report checksums supplied to guarantee evidence integrity

- **Custom Frameworks and Controls**

  You can build your own compliance rules and controls if your needs are a bit different.

  - Create custom frameworks and controls for specific governance or compliance requirements.

  - Support for automated and manual evidence collection.

- **Integration with AWS Services**

  Works smoothly with other AWS tools to give you a full view of your security and compliance.

  - Works with AWS Security Hub, AWS Config, AWS CloudTrail, and AWS Control Tower for end-to-end visibility

  - Supports event-driven apps with Amazon EventBridge

- **Reporting and Documentation**

  Generates ready-to-go audit reports and keeps evidence on hand when you need it.

  - Delivers audit-ready reports with summaries and evidence for compliance requirements

  - Stores evidence for up to two years, enabling long-term compliance visibility

Cybersecurity Benefits:

Here's how Audit Manager helps keep your compliance on track and your audits stress-free.

1. **Continuous Compliance Monitoring**

   - Ensures compliance with industry standards via automated evidence collection and assessment

2. **Scalable and Customizable**

   - Supports multiple accounts and regions for end-to-end coverage.

   - Custom controls can be created to address unique security requirements.

3. **Integration with Security Tools**

   - Close integration with AWS Security Hub, AWS CloudTrail, and other services enhances security posture.

4. **Evidence Integrity and Chain of Custody**

   - Robust evidence management with integrity checking

5. **Greater Efficiency**

   - Automates evidence collection, reducing manual effort and improving audit readiness

AWS Audit Manager is a valuable service for customers seeking simplified, automated, and scalable compliance management in AWS.

Data Protection and Cryptography

Protect your data and privacy using AWS services that provide strong encryption, secure key management, and comprehensive access controls.

AWS Key Management Service (KMS)

AWS KMS is a service that allows you to create, manage, and control cryptographic keys used to encrypt your data. It allows secure encryption and digital signing in AWS services and applications.

Key Features:

Here's what makes AWS Key Management Service (KMS) a powerful tool for managing your encryption keys securely and efficiently.

1. **Centralized Key Management**

    - Manages keys on all AWS services from a single location

    - Supports symmetric, asymmetric, and HMAC keys

2. **Scalability and Flexibility**

    - Easily integrates with AWS services through APIs, SDKs, CLI (command line interface), or console

    - Automatic key rotation and deletion management

3. **Security and Compliance**

    - FIPS 140-2–validated HSMs for key protection

    - Logging in detail through AWS CloudTrail for auditability and compliance

4. **Integration with AWS Services**

    - Seamless integration with services like S3, EBS, Lambda, DynamoDB, and others

    - Envelope encryption to reduce network load and enhance performance

5. **Key Types**

    - **Customer-Managed Keys**: Total control over policies, lifecycle, and permissions

    - **AWS-Managed Keys**: Automatically managed by AWS, used for specific services

- **AWS-Owned Keys**: Owned by AWS exclusively, not visible or controllable to users

6. **Key Rotation and Deletion**

   - Automatically supports rotation or manual rotation of keys

   - Automated key deletion with a timed waiting period

7. **Data Encryption Methods**

   - Direct API usage

   - Usage integration with AWS services

   - AWS Encryption SDK for client-side encryption

Why Use AWS KMS from a Cybersecurity View:

From a security perspective, AWS KMS helps protect your data with strong encryption, strict controls, and full auditability.

1. **Improved Data Protection**

   - Securing data in transit and at rest using strong encryption

2. **Regulatory Compliance**

   - Complies with standards such as PCI DSS and supports audit trails

3. **Strong Security Controls**

   - Highly controlled keys with highly managed IAM policies

4. **Scalability and Performance**

   - Scaling effectively as key management needs grow through envelope encryption

5. **Audit and Monitoring**

   - Tracks key usage and management activity with AWS CloudTrail integration

AWS KMS provides a scalable, secure, and compliant key management system for companies intending to strengthen their data security and encryption abilities.

AWS CloudHSM

AWS CloudHSM is a hardware security module (HSM) that is cloud-based and is designed to meet security and compliance needs by offering secure key management with dedicated HSM instances in the AWS cloud environment.

Key Benefits:

Here's what makes AWS CloudHSM a strong choice for secure key management and compliance.

1. **Secure Key Management**

   - Holds cryptographic keys in tamper-resistant hardware, accessible only to you

2. **Compliance and Regulation**

   - Meets FIPS 140-2 Level 3 standards, required for high-security applications

3. **Flexibility and Integration**

   - Supports database encryption, DRM, PKI (public key infrastructure), transaction processing, etc.

   - Integrates with AWS KMS and other AWS services

4. **High Availability and Durability**

   - Synchronizes HSMs between Availability Zones with daily encrypted backups

5. **Scalability**

   - Clusters scale up to 28 HSMs for high-performance demands (limit as of May 2025; this quota may change as AWS updates its service offerings).

How It Works:

A quick look at how you set up and use CloudHSM to protect your cryptographic keys.

1. **Create a Cluster**

   - Several HSMs can be spread out over Availability Zones.

2. **Initialize**

   - Configure a client on your EC2 instance to securely connect.

3. **Perform Operations**

   - Use standard APIs (PKCS#11, Java JCE, OpenSSL, Microsoft KSP/CNG) to perform cryptographic operations.

Security and Compliance:

What makes CloudHSM trusted for keeping your keys safe and meeting strict regulations.

- Single-tenant access ensures only you control your keys.

- AWS does not have access to your keys; hardware and firmware are only managed.

- Certified to FIPS 140-2 Level 3 to meet stringent regulatory demands.

- Comprises tamper detection and monitoring through CloudWatch.

Why Utilize AWS CloudHSM for Cybersecurity:

Why this service is essential for securing sensitive data and meeting your security goals.

- **Improved Data Security**: Dedicated HSMs minimize key exposure vulnerabilities.

- **Regulatory Compliance**: Compliant with strict requirements such as FIPS 140-2 Level 3.

- **Full Control**: You alone control your keys – no access to AWS.

- **Secure Integration**: Provides standard cryptographic APIs for interoperability.

- **Reliability**: Highly available with automated sync and load balancing.

AWS CloudHSM provides secure, scalable, and compliant cryptographic key management for sensitive data to meet regulatory requirements.

AWS Secrets Manager

AWS Secrets Manager is a fully managed service that securely stores, manages, and retrieves secrets such as database credentials, API keys, and other sensitive information. It offers centralized management, automated rotation, auditing, and monitoring to reduce the risk of unauthorized access.

Key Features:
Discover how AWS Secrets Manager securely handles your sensitive information with automation and strong encryption.

1. **Centralized Secret Management**

   - Store and retrieve secrets such as database credentials, API keys, SSH keys, and more.

   - Replace hardcoded secrets with programmatic retrieval using APIs.

2. **Automated Secret Rotation**

   - Automatically rotate secrets on a schedule or on demand.

   - Enforces security best practices and regulatory compliance.

3. **Enhanced Security**

   - Encryption at rest with AWS KMS keys

   - Encrypted transmission through TLS

   - Fine-grained access control through AWS IAM policies

4. **Compliance and Auditing**

   - Monitor and audit secret usage with integration with AWS CloudTrail, CloudWatch, and Amazon SNS.

   - Generates logs for compliance and regulatory reporting.

5. **Scalability and Flexibility**

   - Supports many use cases such as database credentials, SaaS applications, third-party API keys, and more

   - Easily integrates with AWS services and custom applications

6. **Cost-Effective**

- Eliminates expenses of self-managing a secrets infrastructure

- Presents a scalable, pay-as-you-go pricing model

7. **Security Details**

- Utilizes envelope encryption (AES-256) under AWS KMS management

- Enables creation and management of custom access policies for secrets

- Securely stores secrets and provides lifecycle management

Why Use AWS Secrets Manager from a Cybersecurity Perspective:
AWS Secrets Manager is a smart choice to protect credentials, reduce risk, and keep your secrets safe and compliant for AWS ecosystem.

- **Improved Data Protection**: Encrypts secrets in transit and at rest

- **Automatic Rotation**: Reduces risk of credential compromise through automatic rotation of secrets

- **Centralized Management**: Simple secret lifecycle management and increased visibility

- **Compliance Support**: Integrates with logging and monitoring systems for compliance

- **Less Human Error**: Fetches secrets programmatically without plaintext exposure

AWS Secrets Manager enhances security with automatic secret rotation, detailed audit trails, and simple secret management through centralized control.

Amazon Macie

Amazon Macie is a data security service that uses machine learning and pattern matching to discover and protect sensitive data stored in Amazon S3. It provides visibility into data security risks, enabling automated protection.

Key Benefits:

Here's what makes Amazon Macie a smart choice for managing and protecting your sensitive data in the cloud.

1. **Automated Sensitive Data Discovery**

   - Identifies personally identifiable information such as names, addresses, and credit card numbers

   - Consistently tracks Amazon S3 data through the use of machine learning and pattern matching

2. **Simplified Management**

   - Set up with a single click or make an API call.

   - Using AWS Organizations to support multiple accounts.

3. **Cost Efficiency**

   - Charges based on evaluated buckets, monitored objects, and inspected data volume

   - Presents a 30-day free trial

4. **Custom Data Type Support**

   - Use regular expressions to define one-of-a-kind or proprietary data types.

5. **Bucket Exclusion**

   - Exclude specific S3 buckets from automated discovery via console or API.

6. **Detailed Metadata for Data Map Enrichment**

   - Offers a glimpse into public access, encryption type, shared status, total storage, classifiable volume, and sensitivity score

Why Use Amazon Macie from a Cybersecurity Perspective:

From security to compliance, here's why Macie is essential for keeping your data safe and meeting regulations.

- **Enhanced Data Security**: Ongoing surveillance of delicate data.

- **Regulatory Compliance**: Ensures compliance with GDPR, HIPAA, and CCPA.

- **Cost-Effective Management**: Scalable security without manual intervention.

- **Complete Clarity**: In-depth visibility into the protection of your data.

- **Detection That Can Be Tailored**: Create unique data types to meet distinctive requirements.

- **Automation and Ease of Use**: Simple setup across multiple accounts. Integrate effortlessly with a variety of AWS services.

- Amazon Macie is critical for data security and compliance, ensuring that sensitive information stored in Amazon S3 is properly found and protected.

AWS Certificate Manager

AWS Certificate Manager (ACM) simplifies provisioning, management, and deployment of SSL/TLS certificates for publicly facing websites and private applications. By automating some of the most crucial processes, such as purchasing, validation, renewal, and deployment of certificates, ACM reduces manual efforts and makes secure data transfer easier.

Key Benefits:

Discover how AWS Certificate Manager (ACM) makes managing SSL/TLS certificates easy, secure, and cost-effective.

1. **Simplified SSL/TLS Management**

   - Automatically provisions, deploys, and renews certificates, preventing service downtime due to expired certs

2. **Enhanced Safety**

   - Encrypts data in transit both between clients and servers, thereby safeguarding sensitive information against manipulation and unauthorized access

3. **Certificates – Public and Private**

   - It provides free public certificates for services like Elastic Load Balancing, CloudFront, and API Gateway.

   - Manages private certificates of internal resources using AWS Private CA.

4. **Cost-Effective**

   - Public and private certificates used exclusively with ACM-integrated services are free.

5. **Seamless AWS Integration**

   - Centralizes the deployment and management of certificates across AWS services like CloudFront, ELB, and API Gateway

6. **Automated Renewals**

   - Continuous certificate monitoring and renewal, reducing manual handling and potential downtime

Why Use ACM from a Cybersecurity Perspective:
Understand why ACM is essential for protecting your data in transit and meeting compliance standards effortlessly.

- **Secure Communications:** Ensures data being sent is encrypted, hence meeting regulatory and compliance needs

- **Automated Lifecycle Management:** Eliminates human error by automating certificate renewal and provisioning

- **Centralized Control:** Allows administration of certificates in one console, improving visibility and governance

- **Regulatory Compliance:** Helps satisfy encryption requirements for data in transit across industries like finance and healthcare

AWS Certificate Manager is crucial for organizations seeking straightforward, automated, and secure SSL/TLS certificate management across their AWS environments.

AWS Payment Cryptography

AWS Payment Cryptography is a managed service that takes the place of specialized payment HSMs previously used for securely processing credit, debit, and other forms of electronic payments. It manages keying and cryptographic functions specifically related to payments in the cloud, and it does so in a way that adheres to the strict security requirements set forth by the PCI Security Standards Council and EMVCo (EMVCo is a consortium of the following companies: Visa, Mastercard, JCB, American Express, China UnionPay, and Discover).

Key Benefits:
Here's how AWS Payment Cryptography makes payment security simpler, stronger, and more cost-effective.

1. **Eliminates On-Prem HSM Overhead**

   - No specific devices to acquire or maintain

   - Lowers operational and infrastructure expenses

2. **Payment-Specific Key Management**

   - Aligns with PCI PIN Security, P2PE (Point-to-Point Encryption), and other payment standards

   - Provides key creation, distribution, and cryptographic operations that are driven by an API

3. **Scalability and High Availability**

   - HSMs provisioned on demand to manage high transaction volumes.

   - HSM management for multiple tenants; the customer manages the lifecycle of hardware.

4. **Security and Compliance**

   - Employs HSMs that are managed by AWS and are in compliance with PCI.

   - Plaintext keys never leave the HSMs and are protected via dual control and continuous audits.

5. **Integrated Ecosystem**

- Enhances AWS KMS and AWS CloudHSM with payment-specific cryptography

- Decreases the number of manual key exchanges (such as those involving ANSI TR-34 (security standard defining how to securely distribute symmetric cryptographic keys in payment card transactions using asymmetric methods)) through the use of asymmetric cryptography

How It Works:

A quick look at how AWS handles payment keys securely in the cloud, following strict industry rules.

- **Payment HSMs in the Cloud**: Under stringent PCI PTS HSM rules, AWS organizes and oversees the HSM hardware (under the shared responsibility model).

- **Asymmetric Key Exchange**: Reduces the necessity for sharing keys by hand, although it is possible to do so offline if really required.

- **Shared Responsibility Model**: AWS secures HSM hardware; customers handle imported/exported keys and ensure PCI compliance for any returned cardholder data.

Why Use AWS Payment Cryptography from a Cybersecurity Perspective:

Understand why this service is a smart choice for keeping payment data safe and compliant.

- **Elevated Data Security**: Guarantees that delicate payment encryption keys stay within secure HSM confines. Payment keys in HSMs enhance data security, thus ensuring that payment data is always secure.

- **Compliance with Regulations**: Aids in meeting strict regulations (PCI DSS, 3DS, PIN Security) with little burden.

- **Decreased Risk**: Eliminates on-prem HSM complexities; robust auditing and multiparty controls prevent unauthorized key access.

- **Efficient Key Management**: An approach to encryption and decryption operations that is secure, streamlined, and API-driven.

AWS Payment Cryptography enhances payment security by delegating cryptographic functions to a fully managed, PCI-compliant service, thereby minimizing manual processes and operational risks while upholding stringent compliance standards.

AWS Private Certificate Authority

AWS Private CA is a managed service for creating and operating your own private PKI (public key infrastructure) within AWS. It eliminates the cost and complexity of running your own certificate authority infrastructure.

It issues private certificates for securing internal communications among servers, IoT devices, apps, and users, typically for non-public DNS names or IP addresses.

Key Highlights:

Here are the main features that make AWS Private Certificate Authority a powerful tool for managing your internal certificates with ease and security.

1. **Private CA vs. Public CA**

    - Certificates issued by private CAs are limited to internal networks and customized naming. They are not bound by the public CA constraints.

    - Only resources with valid public DNS names can be identified by public certificates.

2. **Core CA Concepts**

    - **Root CA**: The trust anchor at the top of the hierarchy that is only rarely used to issue certificates for end entities.

    - **Subordinate Certificate Authorities (CAs)**: Intermediates that issue end-entity certificates. CA hierarchies provide security by isolating the root CA and delegating issuing tasks to subordinate CAs.

    - **Certificates**: Certificates are digital forms of verification that identify an entity's public key. Private certificates work best when used with internal resources or with custom use cases for which public certificates do not provide adequate support.

3. **Centralized Certificate Lifecycle Management**

- **Capability**: AWS Private CA simplifies the management of private certificates by automating issuance, renewal, and revocation processes.

- **Features**:

  - Unified console for creating, storing, and managing certificates

  - Integration with AWS Certificate Manager (ACM) for seamless deployment across AWS services

  - Support for certificate revocation mechanisms like Certificate Revocation Lists (CRLs) and Online Certificate Status Protocol (OCSP)

4. **Flexible CA Hierarchy Design**

- **Capability**: AWS Private CA enables organizations to create hierarchical PKI structures tailored to their needs.

- **Features**:

  - Support for root and subordinate CAs

  - Hybrid setups combining cloud-based and on-premises CAs for extended flexibility

  - Secure root CA management with restrictive access controls and FIPS 140-2 hardware-protected private keys

5. **Secure and Scalable Operations**

- **Capability**: AWS Private CA provides high availability and scalability while adhering to robust security standards.

- **Features**:

  - Short-lived certificate mode for certificates valid up to seven days, reducing revocation overhead

  - General-purpose mode for certificates with configurable validity periods

- Secure HSM-backed key storage compliant with FIPS 140-2 standards to protect sensitive keys

- Cross-account CA sharing via AWS Resource Access Manager (RAM) to avoid redundant CAs across accounts

6. **Customizable Certificates**

- Fully customizable certificates tailored to organizational identity or data protection requirements, including support for non-standard extensions

7. **API-Based Automation**

- Automate certificate management using AWS SDKs, CLI tools, or CloudFormation templates

8. **Audit and Compliance**

- Integrated with AWS CloudTrail for auditing CA activity and ensuring compliance with industry regulations

Why Use AWS Private Certificate Authority from a Cybersecurity Perspective:
AWS Private CA helps you build a strong security foundation by keeping your internal communications trusted and protected without the hassle of managing your own infrastructure.

- **Stronger Internal Trust**: Issues private certificates that secure internal apps, devices, and services, reducing risks of impersonation or data interception.

- **Improved Security Posture**: Centralized certificate management enforces consistent policies and timely renewals, preventing expired or vulnerable certificates.

- **Compliance Made Easier**: Supports audit requirements by integrating with AWS CloudTrail, providing detailed logs of certificate activity.

- **Reduced Operational Overhead**: A fully managed service eliminates the complexity of running your own PKI infrastructure, freeing your team to focus on core security tasks.

- **Flexible and Scalable**: Easily adapts to your growing environment with scalable and customizable PKI hierarchies.

With AWS Private Certificate Authority, you get a secure, scalable, and easy-to-manage solution that takes the complexity out of private certificate management helping your organization maintain trust and compliance effortlessly.

What You Have Learned

Here's a quick summary of the key topics we covered in this chapter:

- **Shared Responsibility Model**:

  - Understanding who is responsible for what in cloud security is fundamental.

  - Cloud providers (such as AWS, Azure, GCP) are responsible for securing the *infrastructure* (physical data centers, hardware, network).

  - Customers are responsible for securing their *data, applications, configurations, and access controls* within the cloud.

  - **Analogy**: AWS secures the "building" (infrastructure), while you secure your "office" (data/apps).

- **Threat Landscape**:

  It's important to know the types of threats your cloud environment faces.

  - Key threat actors include hackers, cybercriminals (ransomware, fraud), insider threats, script kiddies, and hacktivists.

  - Threats evolve constantly, requiring proactive monitoring and layered defenses.

- **AWS Cybersecurity Services**:

  AWS offers a range of tools to help you secure your cloud environment effectively.

  - **IAM**: Granular access control via IAM policies, roles, and identity federation (IAM Identity Center, Cognito)

- **Networking Security**: VPC isolation, PrivateLink, firewalls (Network Firewall, WAF, Shield), DNS filtering (Route 53 Resolver)

- **Threat Detection**: GuardDuty (anomaly detection), Inspector (vulnerability scanning), Detective (incident investigation)

- **Logging and Governance**: CloudTrail (audit trails), Config (compliance checks), Audit Manager (evidence collection)

- **Data Protection**: KMS (encryption), Secrets Manager (credential rotation), Macie (sensitive data discovery)

- **Zero Trust**: Verified Access (VPN-free secure app access)

- **Best Practices**:

  - Following proven security practices will help keep your cloud workloads safe and compliant.

  - Enforce **least privilege** (IAM), encrypt data (KMS), automate security (Firewall Manager), and monitor continuously (CloudWatch, Security Hub).

  - Use **automated compliance tools** (AWS Config, Audit Manager) to meet standards like PCI DSS, HIPAA, and GDPR.

Summary

The chapter stresses that ensuring cloud security is a shared endeavor: AWS looks after the infrastructure, but it is the customer's job to safeguard the data and configure everything in a secure manner. Given the threat landscape that keeps evolving, with hackers and outsiders as well as malicious insiders to do harm, it has become vital for organizations to take up strong, effective, and mostly proactive measures. AWS provides defenses at every layer: Identity and Access Management, networking protections (VPC, WAF, Shield), and threat detection (GuardDuty, Inspector), not to mention data protection (KMS, Macie). By applying these services, effectively logging and auditing with CloudTrail and Config, automating defenses, and following best practices, businesses can build secure, compliant cloud environments that stay one step (or two steps) ahead of the threat actors.

CHAPTER 3

Understanding Attacker Tactics and Framework-Aligned Defense Strategies in the Cloud Era of AI

In today's world threats to cybersecurity are everywhere and getting more complex all the time. Knowledge of attacker "tactics, techniques, and procedures" (TTPs) is essential to a strong defense. This chapter describes these TTPs in detail, spotlighting the reconnaissance threat actors do and the access they achieve in order to move through networks and either take out or make off with vital data. The work threat actors do at each stage from the very first sign of reconnaissance to the last, big act of impact is discussed so that you can have both the technical and the strategic picture of modern cyber operations.

We will start with an introduction to TTPs and explain why understanding them is crucial. Then we'll look at the overview of the changing cyber threat landscape and the foundational security frameworks that help organizations steer clear of those threats. From the leading cybersecurity frameworks, such as the NIST Cybersecurity Framework (**CSF**), to **OWASP (Open Web Application Security Project)** guidelines, each provides a structured approach to thinking about and implementing robust defense strategies. The logical flow of an attack unfolds across the following sections. They begin with **reconnaissance** – the detailed methods and means by which an attacker discovers all

© Syed Rehan 2025
S. Rehan, *Cybersecurity with AWS*, https://doi.org/10.1007/979-8-8688-1554-6_3

that is necessary to mount an effective initial access attempt. At this stage, the threat actor collects intelligence not only on the target but also on the types of systems they use, in order to better tailor access attempts to the specific target.

Next comes **initial access**, the actual entry into the target environment. Here, we outline common tactics and techniques threat actors use to gain that critical initial foothold, such as phishing. We will discuss some less common but still effective methods, like using a compromised third-party vendor (a supply chain attack). The chapter ultimately concludes with more general defensive insights, concentrating on three main areas: "**defensive strategies**," "**threat intelligence**," and "**incident response**." Given that the necessary foundation for an effective cyber defense is proactive layered security, we examine how human and machine intelligence can be used for comprehensive monitoring and almost immediate detection of attacks.

Once a cyber-attack is underway, the next goal is to reduce the attack surface and the number of viable options an attacker has to succeed. The chapter in its final sections also offers a look ahead at emerging threats like those posed by generative AI.

When organizations gain proficiency in these tactics, techniques, and procedures, they can better predict and spot ongoing assaults. More important, though, is the effect this mastery has on the cybersecurity posture of the organizations that accomplish it. By internalizing the knowledge gained through working with threat actor TTPs, an organization can better reinforce its defenses against the ever-evolving threat landscape.

Before delving extensively into the chapter, it is pertinent to examine several specialized cybersecurity teams that organizations engage to thwart, defend against, mitigate, and analyze cyber incidents. Frequently, these teams are designated as the "**Red Team**," "**Blue Team**," and "**Purple Team**":

- **Red Team**: A team of security experts simulating realistic attacks to test the defenses of an organization, thinking and behaving like real threat actors (adversaries) to highlight vulnerabilities and show how an attack could be carried out successfully.

- **Blue Team**: Consists of defenders responsible for daily protection, detection, and response activities. They monitor systems, analyze threats, and continuously refine the organization's security posture in order to minimize potential damage from cybersecurity attacks.

- **Purple Team**: The collaborative cybersecurity function of the Purple Team is designed to bridge the gap between the **Red Team** (simulating attackers) and the **Blue Team** (the defenders). In contrast

to operating in solitude, the Purple Team shares knowledge and
serves as an intermediary between the Red Team and the Blue Team.
The real goal here is to take the intelligence gained through the
Red Team's activities and use it to make the Blue Team's defensive
measures much more effective.

Overview of TTPs

TTPs are the foundational building blocks of a threat actor's approach. They describe
what a threat actor does (tactics), how they do it (techniques), and the specific
implementations (procedures) used during a cyber-attack. They are closely related and
represent the three "what's" of an attack. Tactics are the overarching goals of an attack
and the general means by which those goals are pursued. Techniques are the specific
methods used to achieve those tactical objectives. Each technique is associated with a
set of procedures, the "how-to" part of an attack, detailing exactly how the technique is
executed.

What a cyber-attacker does, what methods they use, and what specific actions they
take to pull off an attack are what TTPs describe.

When a malicious activity happens, security teams use tactics, techniques, and
procedures (TTPs) to analyze and categorize it. A malicious activity can be in the early
stages or in full tilt, but TTPs help give it an understandable context. For example, if
a security team sees a surge in failed logins, they might also note that user account
passwords are being brute-forced. But what's the context? If, on the same day, defenders
observe unusual lateral movement where an attacker moves between systems within the
network to gain further access or escalate privileges, that's a big clue. And all this is TTP
stuff: contextualizing what could be seen as random chaos, giving order to nature.

Importance of Understanding TTPs

Tactics, techniques, and procedures (TTPs) refer to the observable patterns and
behaviors used by threat actors when carrying out cyber-attacks. When organizations
understand and can analyze these attacker TTPs, they gain the ability to shift from
a reactive to a more proactive and intelligence-driven security posture. This shift
happens in several ways. First, by studying threat actor TTPs, security teams gain

critical insight into how adversaries operate – what goals they pursue (tactics), how they go about achieving them (techniques), and the specific steps taken (procedures). This understanding makes investigations within the security operations center (SOC) more focused and effective. With that intelligence, defenders can develop tailored countermeasures and targeted mitigation strategies, moving beyond traditional perimeter defenses to a more resilient and adaptive security approach.

The Evolution of Cyber Threats

As digital technology and connectivity have expanded, so too have cyber threats evolved in scale, sophistication, and scope. At first, threats involved basic phishing emails, exploiting weak passwords, and hitting simple security vulnerabilities. But threat actors have gotten smarter. And even if the bad guys are using the same old tricks (like using email to fish for sensitive information), they're employing way more advanced techniques to circumvent traditional security controls.

Today's threat actors, which include cybercriminals, hacktivist groups, and nation-state-sponsored attackers, employ a blend of traditional and modern tactics to breach systems. Many are highly organized and well-funded and operate under sophisticated covers. Some, such as advanced persistent threat (APT) groups backed by governments, conduct ongoing cyber-espionage campaigns. These actors are deeply engaged in studying and refining tactics, techniques, and procedures (TTPs) – the core behavioral patterns that define how attacks unfold. Their motivation? Gaining a tactical edge. By continuously evolving their methods, threat actors effectively produce their own intelligence updates within their own knowledge groups, helping them stay ahead of defenses and fuel the next wave of cyber-attacks.

Understanding Cybersecurity Frameworks

To help organizations systematically manage cyber risks, several leading frameworks have been developed, each offering structured guidance for strengthening cybersecurity. Among these, the **NIST Cybersecurity Framework (CSF)** stands out as a foundational model augmented by the **NIST SP (Special Publication) 800 series**.

NIST Cybersecurity Framework (CSF)

The National Institute of Standards and Technology (NIST) created the Cybersecurity
Framework (CSF) in answer to US Executive Order 13636 (Improving Critical
Infrastructure Cybersecurity). The CSF was first rolled out in 2014 and presents
a voluntary, risk-informed method for managing and diminishing the odds and
consequences of cybersecurity events that can affect critical infrastructure.

Who can use this framework?
While the CSF was designed with a US critical infrastructure audience in mind, it's clear
language and even clearer concepts have made it a hit across public and private sectors
around the world.

Essential Functions

The CSF is structured around five core functions. Every function encompasses particular
objectives that any organization regardless of its size, sector, or type should accomplish
to address cybersecurity adequately.

1. **First Function: Identify** is foundational. By understanding the
   business context, as well as the assets under its protection and
   the associated cybersecurity risks, an organization can focus on
   the right things. This context enables better decision-making in
   allocating resources and in cybersecurity governance.

2. **Second Function: Protect** is about having in place and in action
   appropriate safeguards so that the critical services and assets that an
   organization needs to protect can withstand most types of threats.

3. **Third Function: Detect** is about having the right mechanisms in
   place to identify cybersecurity events when they occur. The Detect
   function is closely tied to the real-time state of an organization's
   security posture.

4. **Fourth Function: Respond** is about taking the right actions
   in a timely manner when something has gone wrong despite
   preventive measures.

5. **Fifth Function: Recover** is about being able to get back to
   business as usual once a cybersecurity incident has occurred.

Implementation Tiers

These tiers reflect how mature and proactive an organization is in handling cybersecurity from reactive fixes to adaptive, intelligence-driven defenses.

- **Tier 1 (Partial)**: Reactive and ad hoc risk management processes.

- **Tier 2 (Risk-Informed)**: Some awareness of risks, but management is not fully integrated.

- **Tier 3 (Repeatable)**: Formal policies and procedures are in place and consistently executed.

- **Tier 4 (Adaptive)**: A continuous improvement culture with active threat intelligence usage and real-time collaboration between different departments.

Framework Profiles

Understand where you are, where you want to be, and what's needed to close the gap in your cybersecurity journey.

- **Current Profile**: This demonstrates the present-day cybersecurity activity within the organization and shows the risk posture it has accepted.

- **Target Profile**: This describes the organization's true north, the way it wishes to look and act regarding cybersecurity when it grows up.

- **Gap Analysis**: This is what you do when you compare the Current Profile with the Target Profile. When you do this right, you come up with a list of enough issues with sufficient priority that you can guide your budget better.

NIST SP 800 Series

The National Institute of Standards and Technology's Special Publication 800 series offers detailed and directive guidance on computer and information security for federal agencies. These publications have become the de facto best practices for the private sector, too, because of their thoroughness and practicality.

NIST SP 800-53 (Security and Privacy Controls for Information Systems and Organizations)

Offers a catalog of security and privacy controls for federal information systems. It has an extensive reach and is almost universally used and trusted in both the public and private sectors. The controls are organized into families (e.g., Access Control, Audit and Accountability, Configuration Management) and specify what an information system must do to be secure and protect privacy.

NIST SP 800-37 (Risk Management Framework or RMF)

Presents a detailed, stage-by-stage procedure for classifying information systems, choosing and enacting security measures, judging their efficacy, clearing system operations, and keeping an eye on them all the while. Integrates well with the controls in SP 800-53.

NIST SP 800-171 (Protecting Controlled Unclassified Information in Non-federal Systems)

Establishes the confidentiality security demands for controlled unclassified information (CUI). Typically needed by contractors working with US federal agencies.

NIST SP 800-61 (Computer Security Incident Handling Guide)

Offers a framework for dealing with various types of incidents. Stresses that the best time to handle an incident is before it happens and the best way to do that is to have a plan that is practiced and well understood by all personnel.

Advantages of Using NIST SP 800 Series Standards

Here's why the NIST SP 800 series is a trusted framework that fits organizations of all sizes and needs:

- **All-Encompassing**: Covers all necessary areas including technical, operational, and managerial controls

- **Scalable**: Works for organizations of any size and allows them to adopt controls that fit their particular risk profile and maturity level

- **Highly Respected**: Frequently cited and referenced in regulatory frameworks and in the development of commercial standards

Understanding Web Application Security Risks

Web applications are prime targets for cyber-attackers, making it essential for developers and security professionals to stay informed about the most critical security threats. The Open Web Application Security Project (OWASP) is a widely respected non-profit organization that provides practical, community-driven insights into these risks.

Among its most influential resources are the OWASP Top 10 and OWASP API Security Top 10 – two cornerstone frameworks that guide secure development and assessment practices across the web and API ecosystems.

OWASP Top 10

Summary: The Open Web Application Security Project (OWASP) puts together this list of the most dangerous web application security risks.

Why You Should Care: This list is used quite often as a baseline when security testers go in and assess how vulnerable an application might be.

Common Vulnerabilities:

1. Injection (e.g., SQL injection)

2. Broken authentication

3. Sensitive data exposure

4. XML external entities (XXE)

5. Broken access control

6. Security misconfiguration

7. Cross-site scripting (XSS)

8. Insecure deserialization

9. Using components with known vulnerabilities

10. Insufficient logging and monitoring

OWASP API Security Top 10

As the world of business relies more and more on APIs, these interfaces are becoming fertile ground for hackers to exploit. They've taken to using common API misconfigurations and weaknesses to their advantage – tactics that are now responsible for some of the largest data breaches we hear about.

Common API Risks:

1. Broken object-level authorization

2. Broken user authentication

3. Excessive data exposure

4. Lack of resources and rate limiting

5. Broken function-level authorization

6. Mass assignment

7. Security misconfiguration

8. Injection

9. Improper assets management

10. Insufficient logging and monitoring

Why Does OWASP Matter?

OWASP provides up-to-date practical advice. Each item on their Top 10 lists describes a web security problem, gives recommendations on how to fix it, and offers "at-a-glance" visuals so that you can quickly understand what the issue is.

OWASP regularly updates its lists to reflect changes in the threat landscape. Because our threat landscape constantly evolves, having a cutting-edge list of the current top ten web security risks is invaluable.

The Top 10 has been adopted across industry sectors. We see its influence in compliance checks, bug bounty programs, and penetration tests. Knowing the OWASP Top 10 often seems like a prerequisite for working in web security.

Choosing and Integrating Several Frameworks

Organizations are required to choose which frameworks to adopt based on their **risk appetite**, specific **data needs**, and any **industry** or **regulatory mandates**. More often than not, suggestion usually is to combine multiple frameworks mapping controls across standards like the **NIST Cybersecurity Framework** and **ISO 27001** to minimize duplication. This harmonization enables a single control set to satisfy various compliance obligations (e.g., PCI DSS, GDPR) and, at the same time, adhere to best practices (e.g., NIST SP 800-53). Regular audits allow a look at compliance and performance, with the chosen frameworks necessitating continual updates required to address emerging threats like zero-day exploits, ransomware, and advanced persistent threats (APTs).

ISO/IEC 27001

The ISO/IEC 27001 standard specifies the requirements for setting up and continually improving an Information Security Management System (ISMS). It is published by the International Organization for Standardization (ISO) and the International Electrotechnical Commission (IEC).

> **Risk Assessment**: Identify what you have, what can happen to it, and how to stop it from happening.

> **Annex A Controls**: Decide how to organize your security, considering physical, technical, and various other controls the standard makes you think about.

> **Certification**: Have an external audit organization look at what you've done mapping to the requirements. If they find you compliant, you can then become ISMS compliant, and that often helps with vendor management and contracts.

Benefits: The standard is well-known, even to people who don't know much about information security. It places a strong emphasis on good governance, with a focus on continual improvement. Meeting it gives good confidence to stakeholders that you have a serious security effort underway.

PCI DSS (Payment Card Industry Data Security Standard)

The aim of this standard is to protect cardholders from being defrauded because of their credit cards. This applies to any organization that deals with payment card information in any form, including storage, processing, or transmission.

The core requirements for PCI DSS are as follows:

- Construct and uphold a secure network and systems.

- Protect the data of cardholders.

- Maintain a vulnerability management program.

- Implement strong access control measures.

- Regularly monitor and test networks.

- Maintain a security policy that is written in clear and concise language.

There are different levels of compliance, which are determined primarily by transaction volume and which come with different requirements for reporting and auditing.

GDPR (General Data Protection Regulation)

In 2018, the GDPR came into effect and is now applicable in every corner of the world to every kind of organization that deals with the personal data of EU residents. The act enforces basic principles that many in the privacy community might consider no-brainers: be lawful, fair, and transparent; minimize data you collect and keep; use strong security safeguards; and, in the event of a data breach, notify everyone promptly within

72 hours. There are indeed several no-fine kinds of provisions in the act. But the kind that we might care about most comes at the end in the form of a fine that can reach 4% of your annual global revenue or €20 million.

HIPAA (Health Insurance Portability and Accountability Act)

In the United States, HIPAA safeguards delicate patient medical information by controlling how it is used and shared. The law has several parts; the most significant for protecting health information are the Privacy Rule and the Security Rule. The Privacy Rule governs how health information can be used and shared with others. It requires health organizations to have appropriate privacy policies and to train staff on those policies so that everyone knows what information is private and what information can be shared.

Understanding the Attacker's First Move: Reconnaissance in Cybersecurity

Every cyber-attack begins with information gathering. Before launching an attack, adversaries spend time learning about their target's environment, identifying weak points, and planning the most effective path in. This phase known as reconnaissance is critical for threat actors to build a blueprint of the target's infrastructure. By understanding the techniques used in this phase, defenders can proactively secure assets and reduce exposure. The following sections break down key reconnaissance methods used against traditional networks and cloud environments like AWS, Azure, or GCP.

Reconnaissance

Understanding how attackers gather information is the first step in spotting potential vulnerabilities.

Open Source Intelligence (OSINT)

Collecting data that is readily available to the public is the basis for open source intelligence, or OSINT. That data comes from a variety of sources such as websites, social media, and public repositories, and it offers a window into an organization. But in the hands of a threat actor, simply available public information can be weaponized. For example, the 2020 Ubiquiti hack used a combination of OSINT and social engineering to penetrate the organization. One of the necessary prerequisites for effectively using OSINT is the audacious infiltration of an organization's public-facing assets. Both Ubiquiti's experience and a number of other high-profile hacks demonstrate the use of OSINT to significant effect.

Network Scanning and Enumeration

Network scanning and enumeration involve identifying active hosts, open ports, and running services, insights an attacker would use to discover network vulnerabilities. This will typically include host discovery, port scanning (e.g., HTTP on port 80, HTTPS on 443, SSH on 22), and service enumeration, with the goal of pinpointing software versions. In AWS, ephemeral IPs and restrictive security groups can limit traditional scans. To protect, security group and network ACL least-privilege rules must be enforced; logs (CloudTrail, VPC Flow Logs, GuardDuty) must be monitored; IDS/IPS solutions must be deployed to detect suspicious traffic.

Cloud Reconnaissance in AWS

When threat actors recon an AWS environment, they typically look for vulnerabilities in services like S3 buckets, IAM roles, and EC2 instances. If these services are not properly secured or left exposed, they can potentially expose large amounts of sensitive information.

Notable Targets:
Here are some common AWS resources attackers often focus on.

- **S3 Buckets**: Publicly accessible or insecurely configured buckets.

- **IAM Roles and Policies**: Roles with overly permissive permissions or credentials hardcoded in code.

- **EC2/Serverless Services**: Instances and Lambda functions that can be enumerated or exploited.

- **Metadata Service**: If misused, it can leak temporary AWS credentials.

To Protect Yourself:

Here are key steps to help secure these critical resources and reduce risks.

- Block public access on S3 and make sure you're using strict policies (we will see this in a later chapter).

- Harden IAM policies (avoid overly broad permissions).

- Enable CloudTrail and VPC Flow Logs to monitor and detect unusual activity.

- Upgrade to IMDSv2 (Instance Metadata Service version 1). (IMDSv2 is a secure, token-based metadata service that helps prevent unauthorized access to instance metadata. It protects against attacks like **SSRF** – Server-Side Request Forgery – which tricks servers into making unintended requests, often exposing sensitive data.) IMDsv2 adds an extra layer of security to the metadata service.

Key Takeaways

Here are the main points to remember for keeping your cloud environment secure:

- **OSINT** gives attackers free info; minimize what you reveal online.

- **Network scanning** finds weak entry points, locks down services, and monitors unusual traffic.

- **Cloud reconnaissance** focuses on misconfigurations (e.g., open S3 buckets, over-permissive IAM). Implement strict permissions and logging.

If you grasp how threat actors carry out reconnaissance, you can find and fix the weak spots in your security. You can achieve this even before the bad guys get to work on poking and prodding your defenses to see where they give way.

Initial Access

The initial access stage is when an adversary first breaks into a targeted environment and succeeds in the penetration. To get in, adversaries use a range of techniques from social engineering to software supply chain sleight-of-hand to get the software they need into the hands of unsuspecting users. The most common techniques are easy to understand and therefore easy to defend against. The hard part is that defenders must understand these common techniques inside and out to keep the adversaries at bay. Here are the most common ways adversaries achieve initial access:

- Phishing and social engineering

- Exploitation of public-facing applications

- Supply chain attacks

- AI-driven phishing

Phishing and Social Engineering

One of the most common ways for attackers to gain initial access to a system is through phishing. This tried-and-true method involves deceiving users into carrying out certain actions most often, clicking a link or entering information into a form that will give the attackers the kind of access they need. Phishing works not because of any particular technical sophistication on the part of the attackers but because of the low-tech, reliable ways it exploits human nature.

Common Phishing Variants:
Learn about the different tricks attackers use to steal information and how they target people.

- **Spear Phishing**: Tailored attacks aimed at individuals or organizations, informed by open source intelligence (OSINT).

- **Whaling**: Targeting high-profile individuals, usually top management, such as CEOs or CFOs, with the hope of conducting financial transaction fraud.

- **Vishing/Smishing**: In this variant, the phishing payload or request for sensitive information is delivered via a phone call or SMS.

Best Practices for Defense:

Here are simple steps you and your team can take to spot, stop, and stay safe from phishing attacks.

- **Security Awareness Training**: Keeping staff informed through regular training, helping them recognize and therefore avoid suspicious emails with unknown links or attachments.

- **Email Security Gateways:** Filter technologies block known malicious domains, attachments, and links.

- **Multi-factor Authentication (MFA):** Even if credentials are stolen, MFA provides an additional layer of verification.

- **Real-Time Reporting**: Allow employees to report any suspected phishing emails so the security team can act in a timely manner.

Exploitation of Public-Facing Applications

Publicly accessible web applications and network services are frequent targets for online adversaries. They attempt to exploit well-known vulnerabilities such as flaws in unpatched software, errors in system configuration, or even newly discovered security holes to gain access to internal networks. Once inside, the intruders can cover their tracks, steal data, or do just about anything that a rogue element might wish to do.

Common Ways to Exploit Systems:

Here are some of the most common tricks attackers use to break into apps and systems.

- **Injection Attacks (SQL Injection, Command Injection):** Bad actors insert harmful code or commands into user inputs to mess with the app or its databases.

- **Cross-Site Scripting (XSS):** Hackers put malicious scripts on web pages other users see, which can steal session tokens or do things pretending to be the victim.

- **Remote Code Execution (RCE):** Attackers use weak spots in apps or servers to run whatever code they want.

- **Deserialization Vulnerabilities**: Cybercriminals take advantage of how apps handle serialized data letting them run code when the data gets deserialized.

How to Protect Yourself:

Here are simple and effective ways to defend your applications and infrastructure from these threats.

- **Safe Coding Methods**: Use guidelines like the OWASP Top 10 to develop and test web apps.

- **Consistent Update Management**: Keep OS, web server, and app frameworks up to date.

- **Web App Firewalls (WAFs)**: Spot and stop fishy requests.

- **Weakness Checks and Security Tests**: Often check outward-facing assets to find and fix weak spots.

Supply Chain Attacks

The software or services that organizations rely upon are the targets of supply chain attacks. These are not direct assaults against the organizations themselves but are instead aimed at the vulnerable intermediate targets upon which many organizations rely. Once the attackers have access to the service or the software, they can then use it as a means of access to the real target – the organizations that use the now-compromised service or software. One of the simplest and most effective methods for using the compromised code or service to gain access to an organization's systems is to update the existing code in a way that is not detected by the organization's personnel.

Supply Chain Attack Strategies:

Here's how attackers often sneak in through your vendors, tools, or updates to compromise your systems.

- **Software Update Tampering**: Bad actors sneak into a trusted vendor's distribution system to send out infected software updates.

- **Package Impersonation**: In the world of open source, hackers might upload harmful packages pretending to be real dependencies.

- **Third-Party Breaches**: Getting in through protected networks of partners that link to the main target.

Top Ways to Protect Yourself:

Here are proactive steps you can take to secure your software supply chain and reduce exposure to third-party threats.

- **Vendor Risk Management**: Check vendors, make them follow secure development practices, and ask for security certificates (like ISO 27001).

- **Software Bill of Materials (SBOM)**: Keep a record of all parts, libraries, and dependencies used in products or services to spot risky or harmful elements quickly.

- **Code Signing and Integrity Checks**: Make sure software updates and dependencies are real and unchanged by using digital signatures.

- **Segmentation**: Restrict third-party access to important parts of the network to lessen the spread if someone breaks in.

AI-Driven Phishing

Bad actors have begun to use generative AI tools (e.g., large language models (LLMs)) to more convincingly craft highly customized phishing lures. These advanced phishing campaigns are much harder to detect because they can almost perfectly replicate an organization's style, tone, and branding while maintaining near flawless grammar and contextual relevance.

How AI Makes Phishing More Effective:

AI is making phishing attacks smarter, more convincing, and harder to detect by mimicking personalization and scale at lightning speed.

- **Personalized Context**: AI has an impact on phishing by using public info (like social media profiles and company websites) to tailor email content, references, or even code syntax.

- **Attacks on a Larger Scale**: Generative AI lets attackers create many phishing templates while keeping the language quality high.

- **Quick Changes**: AI can update content based on how users respond or how well previous campaigns worked.

Ways to Defend:

To stay ahead of AI-powered phishing, we need smarter defenses from intelligent detection to better training and response plans.

- **AI-Based Detection**: Use machine learning tools trained to identify patterns typical of AI-generated phishing attempts like subtle language markers or questionable attachments/links.

- **Adaptive Email Filters**: Put in place security solutions that examine message content sender reputation and past communication patterns to spot unusual activity.

- **Contextual Training**: Bring security awareness training materials up to date to teach employees about the growing complexity of AI-driven attacks.

- **Incident Response Playbooks**: Have plans ready to look into and reduce the impact of AI-driven phishing scenarios, including steps to analyze evidence, link threat information, and inform users.

Key Takeaways

Here's a quick recap of what matters most when facing modern threats from human-targeted scams to advanced AI-driven attacks:

- **Phishing and Social Engineering**: These target human trust and slip-ups. Educating users and having strictly security-reinforced email protection is super important.

- **Public-Facing Application Exploitation**: This shows why it's super important to make public-facing apps secure from the start by working backward and making security ingrained from foundation, keep apps updated, and use application and web firewalls.

- **Supply Chain Compromises**: These show that even with great internal security, things can go south if the third parties you trust get hit with a cybersecurity attack.

- **AI-Powered Phishing**: This type of phishing is getting trickier; to defend we need to be smarter and use AI-boosted ways to catch and deal with these attack vectors.

Execution

When someone gains initial access to a system, they usually work to get more privileged access so that they can carry out their objectives without being stopped. Some of those objectives might be to steal sensitive information or to destabilize systems. But in many cases, adversaries are working to make money, and the execution phase is where they try to do that.

Malware and Ransomware

Malicious software, or malware, is a catchall term used to describe any software that's designed to harm a computer user. A person can be harmed in several ways, however. Malware can make a computer inoperable, but it can also cause a user to lose control of their data. Recent years have seen a surge in ransomware, a type of malware that seizes control of a victim's data and demands payment (often in the untraceable form of cryptocurrency) to free it.

Malware Delivery Methods:
Let's look at how malware typically sneaks into systems from suspicious clicks to invisible memory-based attacks.

- **Email Attachments**: Attackers often opt for this route with a side of social trickery like phishing.

- **Drive-By Downloads**: Bad actors sneak malware onto suspicious websites or sketchy ads. Unsuspecting users get the malware just by visiting the website or clicking stuff.

- **Fileless Attacks**: This sneaky malware hangs out in your computer's memory. It doesn't mess with your hard drive, so spotting it is tricky.

Protective Measures:
Now that you know how malware gets in, here's how you can stay one step ahead and protect your environment.

- **Guarding the Endpoints**: Use top-tier EDR (Endpoint Detection and Response)/XDR (Extended Detection and Response) services to spot threats on the fly (which integrates data across multiple security layers). You'll have a variety of options from AWS Marketplace, along with AWS's own services to augment them.

- **Dividing the Network**: Keep viruses at bay by setting up barriers around key systems and getting strict with user access.

- **Backup Habit**: Save your data with backups that hackers can't touch; think offline or read-only to make a ransomware strike less impactful.

- **Update Routine**: Keep software and operating systems up to date to reduce the chance of exploitation via known vulnerabilities.

Living off the Land

Living off the Land (LotL) refers to the practice of using legitimate, pre-installed tools and processes within a target environment to further an attack. Because attackers use tools already considered "safe" by the system (e.g., PowerShell, Windows Management Instrumentation (WMI) in Windows), their activities blend in with normal operations, making detection more difficult.

Common Techniques:

Attackers often exploit trusted system tools to blend in and avoid detection during cyber intrusions.

- **PowerShell Scripts**: Running malicious scripts through PowerShell, which is typically whitelisted in many enterprise environments

- **Remote Desktop Protocol (RDP)**: Exploiting valid credentials and native services to move laterally, gather information, or exfiltrate data

- **Windows Management Instrumentation (WMI)**: Manipulating WMI for system reconnaissance and remote command execution

Defensive Measures:

Proactive security practices help detect and block abuse of legitimate administrative utilities before damage is done.

- **Least-Privilege Access**: Restrict user privileges so built-in administrative tools can't be easily abused.

- **Application Whitelisting/Allowlisting**: Limit which executables and scripts can run, even for trusted utilities.

- **Behavioral Monitoring**: Detects anomalies such as unexpected command-line arguments or script usage patterns that deviate from normal workflows.

- **Audit and Logging**: Monitor logs for suspicious use of administrative tools, especially outside regular business hours or from unusual locations.

Cloud-Aware Malware (Ransomware or Crypto-miners)

As businesses move their most important tasks to the cloud, bad actors have evolved right alongside them. Today's malware is "cloud-aware." That means it's built with the cloud infrastructure – whether its Amazon Web Services, Microsoft Azure, or Google Cloud Platform – in mind. These are not just cloud platforms we use day to day; instead, they're high-performance computing platforms that are ideal for hacking and evasion. Today's cloud-aware malware can efficiently go to work on the cloud, earning its keep by effectively moving laterally through the virtual infrastructure.

Tactics for Cloud-Aware Malware:

Modern malware is evolving to exploit cloud-specific tools and configurations; here are some key tactics attackers use once inside a cloud environment.

- **Credential Harvesting**: Stealing or brute-forcing cloud service credentials to deploy malicious containers or virtual machines.

- **Privileged IAM Roles**: Once inside a compromised environment, threat actors leverage over-privileged identity and access management (IAM) roles to encrypt critical cloud storage, spin up crypto-mining instances, or even abuse expensive GenAI LLM access to power fraudulent chatbots, an increasingly common tactic.

- **Resource Enumeration**: Automatically run scripts that scan the hacked cloud account for any available services (such as S3 buckets and EC2 instances) that might yield useful data or usable computing power.

Defensive Measures:

In the face of increasingly sophisticated threats, implementing layered and proactive defenses is crucial. Defensive strategies in the cloud must go beyond basic perimeter controls and encompass everything from secure configurations and access management to real-time monitoring and automated responses. The following are key defensive measures, with a particular focus on AWS-native tools, and best practices that can help fortify your cloud environment against modern cyber threats.

- **Cloud Security Posture Management (CSPM)**: Keep a watchful eye on the configurations at all times to make certain that they conform to the best practices in access control, network security, and encryption and utilize AWS-provided security services such as AWS Security Hub and adapt organization-wide AWS best practices for security, identity, and compliance.

- **IAM Hardening**: Uphold the least-privilege principle, and implement strong credential management. Use short-lived tokens and multi-factor authentication and utilize AWS IAM Access Analyzer.

- **Cloud Monitoring and Logging**: Use AWS services such as Amazon GuardDuty, AWS CloudTrail, and Amazon Detective to detect unusual activities like anomalous instance provisioning or suspicious API calls and centralize your logging into a single source such as AWS Security Hub or use Amazon Security Lake, which adheres to OCSF (Open Cybersecurity Schema Framework).

- **Automated Incident Response**: AWS has a newly launched service in 2024, which is called AWS Security Incident Response, which will help you automate triage and respond to threats within your AWS environment; however, another option you can also leverage would be augmenting AWS services such as AWS Security Hub, Amazon GuardDuty, and AWS Systems Manager along with Amazon EventBridge and AWS Lambda for incident response automation and to make API calls to shut down the threat vector for custom applications you are running inside AWS.

Key Takeaways

Let's recap the most important threat types and how you can defend against them effectively:

- **Malware and Ransomware**

  There are many avenues malware or ransomware can infect your environment such as through malicious emails, infected downloads, or compromised websites. Having strong endpoint security (i.e., antivirus or EDR) is crucial, and keeping offline backups means you won't be left helpless if your files get encrypted in the form of a ransomware attack.

- **Living off the Land (LotL)**

  Here, attackers use the same everyday tools your team relies on – think PowerShell or remote desktop utilities. Because these tools seem "legit," it can be tough to spot bad behavior. Keeping an eye on unusual activity and tightly controlling who has access to powerful tools can help catch these stealthy attacks.

- **Cloud-Aware Malware**

  As more services move to the cloud, malware is evolving to exploit that. Adversaries may target your AWS environment by stealing credentials or misusing your cloud resources to mine cryptocurrency or encrypt data. Continuous monitoring and strict oversight of user permissions (especially IAM roles) can stop an attacker before they do real damage.

Whether it's classic malware, stealthy built-in-tool attacks, or sophisticated cloud hacks, understanding how each method works is key. When you do, you can design defenses that head off small breaches before they spread, keeping your systems and your organization resilient in the face of cyber threats.

Persistence

An attacker's ability to sustain long-term, stealthy access to a hacked system or infrastructure is known as persistence. Even things like system reboots, security patches, or changes to the environment that shouldn't affect access in a normal system usually don't affect the attacker's access to a compromised system when they have something in place to ensure that access is maintained. Indeed, in the aftermath of a security incident, a Red Team might be used to ascertain what the Blue Team might have missed during the incident response.

When we talk about persistence in the context of cybersecurity, we're very much focused on the threat that advanced persistent threats (APTs) pose. A couple of classic APTs that we read about frequently are Stuxnet and Conficker. Both are long-lived, maintain access to a compromised system, and can't be easily evicted.

Backdoors

Backdoors are secret entry points in applications, systems, or network devices that give attackers access to the application while bypassing normal authentication or security checks.

Examples include

- **Application Backdoors**: Code injected by attackers to access an application

- **OS/Kernel-Level Backdoors**: Modifying core system components to allow access to the system

- **Key Characteristics**:

- **Stealth**: They don't want you to find them.

- **Redundancy**: They have a backup plan in case you find them.

Defense Techniques:

Stay ahead of backdoors by combining proactive monitoring, smart isolation, and real-time threat detection strategies.

- **File Integrity Monitoring**: Pay close attention to any alterations made to essential system files, command files, and configuration scripts. This is vital to maintain the integrity of a system suspected of harboring a backdoor.

- **Network Segmentation**: Keep essential systems away from the general traffic of your internal network and external networks. This can prevent C2 (command-and-control) servers used by attackers to communicate with compromised systems from having any dialogue with the backdoored system waiting for orders.

- **Endpoint Detection and Response**: This constantly watches workstations, servers, and system processes; anything that seems a little "off" may be an indication of a backdoor. Flag it, analyze it, and remediate it.

Rootkits

Rootkits are sophisticated and usually stealthy tools of malware. They are designed to hide nasty little things like malicious processes, files, or system changes. They can burrow deep into your operating system at the kernel level or, if they wish to be even stealthier, at the user level. They have been known to embed themselves in the firmware of computers. In some cases, the rootkit is so well hidden that undetectable malware can run using it while the user thinks everything is functioning normally because the computer shows no outward signs of infection and has not exhibited any of the usual symptoms of malware.

Defensive Techniques:
To guard against rootkits and other deep threats, a mix of hardware security, system integrity checks, and forensic tools is essential.

- **Secure Boot**: Allows only trusted firmware and software components to be loaded at startup, which reduces the opportunity for rootkit installation.

- **Kernel Integrity Monitoring**: Consistently checks the critical structures in the Linux kernel, as well as its system calls, to ensure that they remain intact.

- **Hardware-Based Security**: For example, Intel's TXT or AMD's SEV. Can furnish extra trustworthy execution environments where active attempts to tamper with the kernel are likely to be detected.

- **Manual Forensics**: Sometimes the only way to find sophisticated rootkits is to do offline forensic examination or using memory dumps, performed outside of the infected operating system.

Credential Access

Gaining access to the target environment starts with credential access, getting hold of usernames and passwords. Hackers may also go after access tokens, keys, or even secrets embedded in applications. Many targets have a public-facing front door such as a website. They will use this to get inside and still be on the side of the environment that's open to them. When hackers obtain credentials, they use them to go past the front door and enter the interior of the environment.

Common Methods Used to Acquire User Credentials:

Attackers use a variety of clever and persistent techniques to steal user credentials. Here are some of the most common ones you should watch out for.

- **Keylogging**: Is malware that records keystrokes to capture usernames and passwords. There are some very effective keyloggers in the wild today, and some are even bundled with other malware as "remote access tools."

- **Credential Dumping**: Is the process of extracting a user's credentials from memory, files, or registry hives (e.g., using Mimikatz to pull plaintext passwords or hashes from LSASS on Windows systems). Windows systems, in particular, are notorious for storing weakly protected passwords in memory and on disk.

- **Brute Force and Password Spraying**: Are methods to gain access by guesswork. Brute force involves systematically guessing weak passwords. A password is a weaker form of a credential. When a brute-force attack is not successful, a password spray attack is used.

- **Session Hijacking**: Applies to web-based applications where an attacker will steal active session tokens or cookies, bypassing the need to log in altogether.

How to Defend Against Threats:

Here are simple but powerful steps you can take to protect your systems and data from common cyber threats.

- **Establishing Multi-factor Authentication (MFA)**: An attacker's attempts to gain access can still be thwarted even if they have the password because they would still need a second factor (e.g., token, push notification) to get through to the other side.

- **Enforcing the Principle of Least Privilege**: When user and system access rights are limited to strictly what is necessary for function, the potential impact of exposed credentials is substantially lowered.

- **Storing Secrets Securely**: Passwords should be hashed and salted, and even then, they should not be stored in code repositories, unsecured "vaults," or configuration files.

- **Monitoring and Alerting**: If you have an incident, you need to know about it, and as fast as is feasible, so that the Blue Team can go to work and try to contain the incident.

- **Password Rotation**: The easiest form of defense you can deploy is regularly rotating passwords (or leveraging password-less solutions, i.e., passkeys and others), which can limit the usefulness of stolen credentials.

Persistent Cloud Access (AWS, Azure, or GCP)

As more organizations adopt cloud infrastructure, attackers have adapted their persistence methods to exploit the weaknesses of these platforms. Persistent cloud access often involves the misconfiguration of cloud resources or IAM roles (AWS or GCP), or for Azure it would be Azure Active Directory in the form of role-based access control (RBAC), which allows attackers to maintain a foothold when other credentials are revoked.

Rogue IAM Roles:

Rogue IAM roles occur when attackers create or modify AWS or GCP roles to maintain access or elevate their privileges.

- **Creating New Roles**: Attackers create roles with broad permissions
  and attach them to existing AWS services so that they can assume
  those roles without being detected.

- **Modifying Existing Roles**: An attacker might quietly increase
  privileges or trust policies for a role that already exists in the
  environment.

Defense Strategies:

Here are practical steps to keep your AWS environment secure by controlling access,
monitoring activity, and cleaning up unused permissions.

- **IAM Governance**: Limit who can create or modify roles and enforce a
  strict approval process.

- **Least Privilege**: Set granular permissions so that roles are granted
  only the minimal number of permissions they need in order to
  perform legitimate business tasks.

- **Logging and Monitoring**: Use AWS CloudTrail to log all IAM actions
  like CreateRole and AttachRolePolicy, and alert any unusual changes.

- **Detect and Revoke**: Regular auditing of all roles and revoking
  unused or over-privileged roles.

Misconfigured S3 Bucket Policies:

Amazon S3 (Simple Storage Service) buckets in AWS can be accidentally configured to
allow public read/write, effectively turning them into a gateway for malicious activity.
By default AWS creates the buckets secured to avoid these incidents, but with accidental
configurations we can create havoc.

- **Attackers Can Plant Malicious Files**: Upload payloads, backdoors,
  or scripts that can be accessed or executed by other compromised
  assets later.

- **Harvest Sensitive Data**: Leverage read access to exfiltrate data or
  simply store stolen data for future retrieval.

- **Evade Detection**: Leverage S3's storage for malicious artifacts
  masquerading as legitimate business data.

Defense Strategies:

Here are practical ways to protect your S3 buckets and keep your data secure.

- **Strict Bucket Policies**: Turn off public access at the account level if possible and define resource-based policies explicitly to restrict who can access or upload content.

- **Encryption**: Encrypt data at rest with AWS KMS or custom keys to prevent unauthorized reading in case the bucket is accidentally exposed.

- **Access Logging and Inventory**: Continuously monitor which buckets are publicly accessible. AWS Config and S3 Access Logs can detect and alert on changes.

- **Lifecycle Management**: Automatically remove or archive data after a certain period, reducing the window of time that malicious files remain accessible.

Defenses for Persistence

Multi-layered security means four things:

1. First, we need to ensure that the several segments of our network contribute to an overall system that is very difficult to break into and through.

2. Second, we need to fortify our endpoints and make them as close to impenetrable as possible.

3. Third, we must ensure that our identity protection system functions with, in effect, fortifying our firewall.

4. Routine patching of both on-prem and cloud systems to close off as many of the loopholes attackers exploit for persistence.

These four layers function best when they are combined and work in augmentation.

Proactive Threat Hunting

To do true proactive threat hunting, one must analyze system behavior and use threat intelligence to stay tuned in to the most current adversary tactics, techniques, and procedures.

This involves looking for any of a number of indicators, such as unusual service creation, high-privilege account activity at odd hours, or unexplained spikes in network traffic. Indicator analysis also gives one a better feel for what is "normal."

- **Molding the Security Culture and Governance**: Keep the train rolling. Ensure that developers, cloud administrators, and all other relevant personnel are continuously trained on security, including the latest configurations, threats, and attack vectors.

- **Policy and Compliance**: Align with clear and robust industry standards and best practices that emphasize strong identity management and monitoring, change control, and incident response.

- **Lean on Executive Support**: Getting the board on your side is crucial; their support lends weight and authority to crucial governance decisions and also helps secure necessary resources.

The long-term nature of threat actors' persistence means they can sit in your environment and watch for opportunities to strike, much like a floodlight-wielding security guard standing on a catwalk above the basement steps. Attackers would most likely use many different ways to maintain control once they are inside. In part, this is because maintaining control is the primary operational objective of these threat actors (adversary). When we talk about an attack's impact, we usually think about the point at which the attack is first discovered. But if the attacker is inside and undetected, they have achieved a pretty significant impact for that attack.

By proactively identifying and closing off persistence pathways, organizations can significantly reduce the overall impact and duration of a cyber intrusion, ultimately strengthening their overall security posture.

Privilege Escalation

When attackers get in, they typically want to go up the levels of access the most. And to do that, they look for weaknesses to exploit. Sometimes, these weaknesses are in the security stuff itself and not in whatever systems the attackers are getting into. For example, AWS IAM might be misconfigured. Or maybe instance metadata is insecure and can be abused to gain more access. Attackers might also exploit other parts of the system to do this cleanly.

Evading Detection

After gaining access, the attackers put in a lot of effort to ensure they aren't detected and do this in a number of ways. First, they may try to cover their digital tracks by eliminating any evidence of their presence. Even if they might leave behind some clues, they employ anti-forensic techniques to make those clues less obvious. Next, they may disable any security tools that could alert the "defenders" to something suspicious going on. On AWS, specifically, attackers might try to obfuscate their activities by going after CloudTrail logs or even delete CloudWatch Logs log groups – running this in tandem with the discovery process (see below) – and hinder forensic analysis.

Credential Theft

Acquiring credentials through theft or guesswork is a primary component of many attacks. For example, attackers might gather login details by means of phishing or other direct methods. They also employ brute-force tactics to gain entrance through the password itself. Even without the intelligence gathered from direct methods, there are constantly scanning bots looking for exposed credentials in public GitHub repositories. Those "golden" keys can unlock a vast number of services for unauthorized users.

Discovery

Gaining an initial foothold in a target system is a big step for an attacker. Yet even after achieving that, the threat actor's main goal is to learn as much as possible about the environment they've infiltrated. They'll do everything they can to figure out what's running on the network and its hosts and whether there's an Active Directory or another kind of domain. In AWS, they'll enumerate multiple resources both to understand the architecture and to find the most valuable targets for their next movement.

Lateral Movement

When attackers gain an initial access point, they will often attempt to dig deeper. To do this, they might use existing accounts to blend in or exploit supposed trust relationships between machines. Ultimately, they're trying to reach deeper into the environment to gain control over other parts of it.

Pivoting and Traversal Techniques

When attackers compromise a single system, they often use it as a stepping-stone to move laterally across the network, a tactic known as pivoting. This allows them to explore and exploit other systems within the same environment. To do this, they may use techniques such as proxies or VPN tunnels to bypass segmentation controls, effectively undermining the network's security boundaries and accessing sensitive areas that were thought to be isolated.

Remote Service Exploitation

Exploitation of remote services is a major way that system hackers gain entry into and control over vulnerable systems.

They work at it the same way an intruder would, taking the path of least resistance when trying to break into a building. Once inside, they try to move around and get access to as many rooms as they can. And if they can set up unmonitored access in a remote way (like through a door that looks locked but isn't), they do that, too.

When it comes to exploiting remote services, the first step is to identify and target them. Then it's on to breaking in, using whatever methods they've got (or can find). Finally, they probe for more sensitive systems and data, using whatever they can to take control and establish a long-term presence.

Collection

After establishing a foothold within a target system, many attackers move on to the next phase of their operations: collection. The collection can take many forms, but it often involves the long-term, clandestine assembly of truly sensitive or high-value items. This can be any document, email, or another piece of intellectual property that might help the thieves bolster their position or punch a way through to another target.

Data Collection Techniques

Techniques for gathering data attackers use – either manual or automated methods –
to search for sensitive files, databases, and any credentials that might be safely stored
somewhere. To unearth this data, they might systematically comb through shared drives
or cloud storage, hunting for anything that might be easily accessible and worth the
trouble of accessing it.

Keylogging and Screen Capture

To gather sensitive information, attackers may install keyloggers – malicious tools that
silently record every keystroke a user types, including passwords and confidential
messages. Additionally, they might use screen capture techniques to take periodic
or triggered screenshots of the victim's desktop. These methods can reveal personal
communications, login credentials, and strategic documents, making them highly
effective for data theft and espionage.

Exfiltration

When the assailants have the data they desire, their aim is to remove it from the network
without creating any undue suspicion. Exfiltration is the process of sending the stolen
information to an outside location, from which it can be easily accessed later.

Exfiltration of Data

Attackers can steal sensitive data from secure systems through a variety of methods.
Common techniques include transmitting files over encrypted HTTPS connections,
uploading them to cloud file-sharing platforms, or physically removing data via USB
drives. More advanced and stealthy attackers often rely on "low and slow" tactics,
transferring small amounts of data over time to avoid detection by security systems.
These gradual leaks are harder to trace and can go unnoticed for extended periods.

Covert Channels and Tunneling

Covert channels are secret communication paths used by attackers to bypass traditional security controls and remain undetected. These channels allow data to be exfiltrated or commands to be sent without triggering alarms, often by hiding within legitimate network traffic.

Think of it as a hidden backdoor; unlike the ones administrators create for maintenance, these are installed without consent and operate invisibly. Tunneling techniques further aid attackers by encapsulating malicious traffic inside allowed protocols, making their presence hard to detect while they quietly move data in and out of your network.

Impact

Ultimately, a cyber-attacker's goal is to significantly disrupt business operations or inflict serious damage. This could include financial losses, reputational harm through negative publicity, or even interference with physical infrastructure especially in sectors critical to the economy, such as banking, energy, or healthcare. The intent is often to destabilize, extort, or weaken the target organization in a way that has lasting consequences.

Denial of Service Attacks

A Denial of Service attack deliberately floods a server, application, or network with an overwhelming volume of traffic or resource-intensive requests so that legitimate users can no longer reach it. When the assault originates from a large botnet of compromised machines, it is called a Distributed Denial of Service (DDoS). Prolonged outages caused by DoS/DDoS campaigns can cripple online services, disrupt operations, and rack up significant financial losses for the targeted organization.

Destructive Attacks

Destructive attacks represent the gravest threat a hacker can pose to an organization. They can take several forms, but the most common is to encrypt important data and demand a ransom. Ransoms have become a lucrative business for hackers. Some hackers try to top each other by demanding ever-growing ransoms, but it's important to note that ransoms are frequently NOT paid, and even if they are, you're not guaranteed any data back.

Defensive Strategies

Because modern attackers can pivot quickly from reconnaissance to disruption, a single security control is never enough. To withstand today's multi-vector campaigns, organizations must layer complementary protections that address people, process, and technology.

Robust, multi-layered defenses therefore combine the familiar firewalls, intrusion detection or prevention systems (IDSs/IPSs), endpoint security with architectural safeguards such as network segmentation, least-privilege access, and a Zero-Trust model that continually re-verifies every request. Continuous monitoring for anomalies and regular "security calibration" (patching, configuration reviews, control testing) round out a program that can detect, resist, and rapidly recover from sophisticated attacks.

Building a Threat Intelligence Program

Staying a step ahead of attackers requires insight into who they are and what they intend to do. A sound threat intelligence program systematically gathers and analyzes information about current and emerging threats, turning raw data into actionable knowledge that enables the organization to design truly effective defenses.

Incident Response and Management

While threat intelligence tells you what is coming, an incident response (IR) program defines how you will act when it arrives.

A concise, rehearsed IR plan lays out the people, processes, and tooling required to detect, contain, eradicate, and recover from any event that threatens the confidentiality, integrity, or availability of your information systems. By linking IR playbooks to the same intelligence feeds that inform your defensive posture, you create a closed-loop cycle: intelligence drives preparation, and every handled incident feeds fresh insight back into the threat intel pipeline. The result is a coherent, end-to-end story – collect, analyze, prepare, respond, and improve – rather than a set of disconnected security activities.

Proactive Defense Measures

Security can't rely on alerts alone; it must anticipate attacks. Regular penetration tests, Red Team engagements, and independent security audits force your defenses to prove themselves before a real adversary does. These controlled "live-fire" exercises expose gaps in controls, processes, and staff readiness, letting you fix weaknesses while the stakes are low. The result is a security program that stays sharp and resilient ready for the next genuine assault instead of merely reacting after the fact.

Why These "Emerging Developments" Matter

Up to this point we looked at the core TTPs attackers rely on today and the baseline defenses used to stop them. The trends in the next section show how those very TTPs are evolving and, in turn, how our defenses must evolve as well. Each new development (AI-driven attacks, Zero-Trust adoption, quantum-safe crypto, etc.) either

- Gives adversaries fresh techniques for reconnaissance, exploitation, or persistence or

- Raises the bar for defenders, demanding new controls, tooling, and mindsets

Viewing these shifts through the TTP lens lets you anticipate which attacker behaviors will appear next and highlights the countermeasures your security program should start planning for now.

Emerging Developments in Cybersecurity

Let's explore the latest trends shaping the future of cybersecurity and what they mean for protecting our digital world.

- **AI-Powered Cybersecurity Threats Are on the Increase**

  - **Offensive AI**: We are using AI not just for good, but also for developing even more powerful cyber-attacks. Cybercriminals are using machine learning for automating the development of malware. The most advanced techniques for improving phishing and vulnerability scanning are automated and use AI.

  - **Defensive AI**: We can't just sit and let the offenders use AI for cyber-attacks. We have to use the same tools to build even more powerful defenses. And the best we can do with AI is use it for the same advanced anomaly detection, threat prediction, and incident response that we use our human brains for when working at top speed.

- **Zero-Trust Architecture Reaches Widespread Adoption**: "Trust no one, verify everyone." This mantra reflects the key working principles of the ZTA. The first principle comprises strong identity verification and truly fine-grained resource access for each and every user. The second principle entails micro-segmentation of the network and, to put it colloquially, keeping the bad guys from spreading inside the good (i.e., breached) network.

- **Widespread Connectivity**: The widespread connectivity of 5G and IoT means that there are more devices to control. That's more attack surfaces for hackers. If we don't secure those devices, they'll be part of the botnet "army" that hackers use to launch some of the largest online attacks we see today.

- **Cryptographic Vulnerabilities and Quantum-Safe Encryption**: Cryptographic vulnerabilities by utilizing quantum computing may expose the encryption we're using today, becoming at risk of being broken by quantum computers. To stay safe, we're adopting new algorithms that have been rigorously tested that will form the basis of what we call quantum-safe encryption.

- **Growing Demands for Regulation and Compliance**: Data protection regulations are maturing and divergence of industry-specific rules giving rise to more stringent requirements to be implemented in healthcare, finance, critical infrastructure, and similar industries.

- **Cross-Collaboration**: Collaboration between organizations can strengthen collective cybersecurity. Real-time intel, fed to proactive security tools, gives hackers one less opportunity to waltz in through the front door.

- **Cloud Security Mindset**: The level of maturity in cloud security is still a long way from where it needs to be. Enterprises are far too comfortable with the notion that their cloud service provider (CSP) has the security part covered. But that's not the case, as much responsibility still rests with the enterprise (shared responsibility model). We've seen far too many instances where an otherwise secure CSP was made to look bad because the enterprise either didn't configure its cloud resources properly or didn't secure its side of the shared cloud boundary.

Human Factor

The biggest vulnerabilities remain people, not just technology. Social engineering techniques especially phishing and its targeted form, spear phishing, are still the most common way attackers gain an initial foothold. Equally critical is the insider threat: employees or contractors who, whether careless or malicious, put data at risk. Continuous security awareness training, coupled with behavioral analytics to flag unusual user activity, is essential for detecting and mitigating these human-centered risks early.

Generative AI–Assisted Attacks

Attacks using generative AI will evolve. Cybercriminals will have access to generative models capable of producing vast amounts of content, including types of content that can be used to compromise a target. They might also have access to the kinds of models that can do it in a personalized way mimicking not only the kinds of content that a given individual might create but also using the kinds of traits that a given individual has in a manner that is much more convincing than what we've seen so far (e.g., by utilizing **FraudGPT, DarkBERT**, or **PoisonGPT**).

Counteracting AI-Driven Cyber Threats

Detection with AI: Security tools now use machine learning models to spot anomalies, deepfake artifacts, and other hard-to-see attack patterns. The art of continuous model validation (regularly testing and recalibrating ML models to catch drift, bias, and adversarial manipulation) is essential; without routine checks, a model can "learn" the wrong lessons and eventually let bad actors slip through your defenses.

What You Have Learned

In this chapter, we took an in-depth look at leading regulatory frameworks under NIST and OWASP, as well as other industry-aligned guidelines. We explored the concept of tactics, techniques, and procedures (TTPs) from a threat actor's point of view, underscoring why understanding these methods is critical for organizations.

From there, we examined how an attack unfolds at each stage from initial access to execution, persistence, and evasion and discussed how organizations can better protect themselves by mapping defenses to these typical attack pathways. Finally, we highlighted the crucial (and often vulnerable) human element in cybersecurity, alongside the emerging role of generative AI in shaping new frontiers of both offense and defense.

Summary

The battleground of cybersecurity is dynamic, where the latest tools and technologies are used by both attackers and defenders. As we move into an era defined by the cloud, IoT, and AI, advancements in these domains present new opportunities for threat actors to launch attacks. We must be ready to confront the core threats of tomorrow, threats that are already evolving in our present.

How These Take-Aways Reinforce the TTP Discussion:

1. People remain the easiest tactic to exploit, so make them part of your defense.

    In the attacker's playbook, social engineering techniques are still the fastest route to initial access. Building a "security-first" culture (continuous training, simulated phishing, strong MFA) directly counters those tactics and procedures by denying adversaries the human foothold they expect.

2. An incident response plan turns raw TTP knowledge into real-time action.

    Mapping attacker techniques to predefined playbooks means you're not improvising under fire: when your SOC sees credential-stuffing attempts, the next steps – contain, eradicate, recover – are

already scripted. That tight loop of detect ➤ respond ➤ adapt
keeps pace with adversaries who constantly refine their own
procedures.

3. Layered, AI-assisted detection closes the gap between observing
a TTP and stopping it. Zero-Trust segmentation, cloud-native log
analytics, and ML-driven anomaly detection give you coverage
for every stage of the kill chain whether it's lateral movement
techniques in Azure, cryptojacking in AWS, or command-and-
control traffic in GCP. By instrumenting each layer, you ensure that
when one tactic slips through, another control identifies the next
technique in the sequence and breaks the chain.

Taken together, these points show how good "**people, process, and technology**"
practices translate the abstract language of tactics, techniques, and procedures into
concrete defenses that frustrate attackers at every step.

CHAPTER 4

Implementing Zero Trust Security Frameworks: Cloud-First Approaches with AWS

The ongoing evolution of cyber threats requires a fresh approach to network security. They appear from any direction and don't respect borders, penetrating deep into the heart of your organization. As a result, traditional perimeter defenses, such as firewalls, have been rendered insufficient. When you consider that an increasing number of attackers now emerge from within your own fortress, it becomes clear that what is needed is a strategy that invariably presumes breach and assures trustworthiness at every layer from user to device to system regardless of where in your network the entity exists. That strategy is called Zero Trust.

We will start with a summation of **Zero-Trust frameworks, specifically NIST SP 800-207**, the **Forrester ZTX (Zero Trust eXtended) framework**, and the **Cloud Security Alliance (CSA) Zero-Trust architecture**. They offer the viewer a unique inroad to understand the way the architecture can be built. You might say they offer three different routes to the same destination, which is the "never trust, always verify" mindset. Once we've reviewed these frameworks, we'll move on to something we really care about – the **how-to** of building a Zero-Trust architecture.

A central concept is using micro-segmentation inside a virtual private cloud (VPC).

Instead of placing every workload in one large, flat network, you carve the VPC into many small, software-defined segments each with its own routing rules, security groups, and network ACLs. These fine-grained "mini-networks" isolate applications or even individual tiers (web, API, database) so that traffic must pass through explicit controls

115

© Syed Rehan 2025
S. Rehan, *Cybersecurity with AWS*, https://doi.org/10.1007/979-8-8688-1554-6_4

before crossing segment boundaries. Although public cloud platforms don't enable this isolation by default, you can enforce it with native VPC features (subnets, security group policies, network firewalls) to achieve the same outcome as traditional data center segmentation – only now it's entirely virtual and policy-driven.

You will leave this chapter with the foundational knowledge necessary to design and sustain an architecture that fits within a Zero-Trust ecosystem. Such an architecture may not be mission impossible, but it does require the kind of strong, adaptable design that can dynamically respond to would-be threats to an organization's most valuable resources, all while maintaining a resilient security posture that covers both on-premises and cloud-native infrastructures.

For practical hands-on implementation of Zero-Trust principles in AWS, it's important to have an AWS account set up with the necessary permissions to run AWS services.

Zero-Trust Frameworks and Standards

We have already touched on the Zero-Trust principle "trust no one, verify everyone" in a previous chapter. In this chapter we notch up a gear and look at how Zero Trust shifts away from the traditional perimeter-based security model and how notable frameworks inherently use Zero Trust and treat every user, device, and system as potentially hostile until proven otherwise. "Never trust, always verify" is the key principle of Zero Trust.

Remember the key principle: "Never *trust*, always *verify*."

Why Zero Trust?

We learned in the earlier chapter how attackers use their TTPs and how they move laterally once they compromise one endpoint and obfuscate their tracks once the environment is compromised. Micro-segmentation is one of the key techniques for Zero Trust, which means shrinking the blast radius of any breach, limiting to within its micro-segment zone. We will see with leading frameworks how "Zero-Trust" principles align well with governance requirements, emphasizing strict access controls and comprehensive logging.

This approach reduces implicit trust in the environment, enhancing overall security posture. "Zero Trust" is about continuous verification, least-privilege access, and assuming breach – all of which support, rather than conflict with, stringent governance and logging requirements.

Leading Frameworks and Standards

Many organizations and influential thinkers have offered frameworks to shape the adoption of Zero Trust. A single template will not suit every organization's risk, culture, and tech stack, so below three "reference" frameworks have emerged. They do not compete; instead, they address the same problem from complementary viewpoints that you can layer upon each other (Table 4-1).

Table 4-1. *Frameworks: Their Roles and Contributions to Your Zero-Trust Program*

Where It Helps	Framework	What It Adds to Your Zero-Trust Program
Baseline, vendor-neutral terminology	NIST SP 800-207 – Zero-Trust architecture	Defines the core concepts (policy decision point vs. policy enforcement point, continuous verification, least-privilege access) and a step-by-step migration path. Use it as your common language when you brief executives or compare vendor offerings.
People, process, and governance lens	Forrester ZTX model	Expands the idea beyond networking controls to six "pillars" (Networks, People, Devices, Workloads, Visibility and Analytics, Automation and Orchestration). Helpful for building a funding roadmap and assigning ownership across security, IT, and business units.
Cloud and shared responsibility specifics	Cloud Security Alliance (CSA) Zero-Trust guidance	Translates Zero-Trust principles to AWS, Azure, GCP, and hybrid estates: identity as the new perimeter, micro-segmentation in VPCs/VNets, cloud-native logging, IaC guardrails, etc. Ideal when your workloads already run in one or more public clouds.

NIST SP 800-207 (Zero-Trust Architecture)

Created by the National Institute of Standards and Technology (NIST). Provides a vendor-neutral guide to constructing and upholding a Zero-Trust system. Centers on the enforcement of policies, rulemaking, and the nudging of decision-makers toward risk-based, situational judgments.

Forrester ZTX (Zero-Trust eXtended) Model

Forrester brought the concept of "Zero Trust" to the forefront. The ZTX model sees Zero Trust as an "extended" system, dealing with not only technology but also people, processes, and governance. It proposes multiple theoretical "pillars":

- Networks
- People
- Devices
- Automation
- Visibility and Analytics
- Orchestration and Incident Response

Cloud Security Alliance (CSA): Zero-Trust Architecture

CSA offers best practices for how to build a ZTA in a cloud or hybrid environment. Emphasizes identity, micro-segmentation, and managing secure workloads in the cloud. Offers practical advice on how to align a ZTA with the "shared responsibility" security model that major cloud providers use (AWS, Azure, GCP, and Oracle Cloud).

How to Use Them Together

Here's a practical way to combine these frameworks for comprehensive and effective cloud security:

1. **Start with NIST** to create a baseline architecture and vocabulary.

2. **Overlay ZTX** to plug in the human and operational pillars (e.g., security culture, automation playbooks).

3. **Apply CSA guidance** when you implement controls in each cloud account/subscription.

By combining the strengths of all three, you get both strategic coverage and actionable, cloud-ready guidance without locking yourself into any single vendor's view.

Step-by-Step Zero-Trust Pilot on AWS: A Suggested Roadmap

Here's a practical roadmap to help you build and grow your Zero-Trust security on AWS, phase by phase:

1. **Phase 1: Hardening of Identity**

   - Either enable MFA for IAM users or move people to AWS SSO.

   - Replace outdated credentials with IAM roles.

2. **Phase 2: Network Segmentation**

   - Construct a fresh VPC with several subnets.

   - Apply the least-privilege SG (security group) rules to both outgoing and incoming traffic.

3. **Phase 3: Ongoing Observation**

   - Write a simple Lambda for automated quarantining, use Security Hub, and activate GuardDuty.

4. **Phase 4: Zero Trust at the Application Level**

   - Connect Cognito to your in-house or client-facing applications.

   - Install a private API Gateway endpoint with an internal microservice that is only reachable by VPC endpoints.

5. **Phase 5: Expand and Enhance**

   - Apply the same patterns for onboarding more applications.

   - Assess supplementary controls, such as PrivateLink, Shield Advanced, and WAF.

   - Update AWS Configuration rules and compliance checks frequently to make sure newly added resources follow the Zero-Trust guidelines.

6. **Phase 6: Iterate and Repeat – Continuous Zero-Trust Tune-Up**

   - **Review Telemetry and Tests**: Analyze GuardDuty findings, Config/ Security Hub drift alerts, or Red/Blue Team or pen test reports.

- **Remediate and Tighten:** Patch vulnerable services, refine IAM/security group rules, retire unused roles, and update baselines in IaC.

- **Update Controls**: Add new AWS best practice Config rules, and enable emerging services/features (e.g., IMDSv2-only, Verified Access).

- **Retrain and Drill**: Brief teams on lessons learned, refresh playbooks, and rerun incident response and access review exercises.

- **Schedule Next Cycle**: Set a cadence (e.g., quarterly) for repeating this loop so Zero-Trust maturity keeps pace with change.

Practical Steps to Implement Zero Trust on AWS

This part of the chapter will cover the practical implementation of Zero Trust in an AWS context. We will use AWS services and the principles of ZT to ensure our environment in AWS is secure.

First and foremost, we need to ensure that our identity and access management system is secure for all users of our AWS services. All of these suggestions are strongly recommended by AWS itself:

1. **Ensure That Everywhere Multi-factor Authentication (MFA) Is Active**

   a. For the root user and all IAM users, ensure hardware MFA tokens or virtual MFA apps are used.

2. **Embrace Role-Based Access**

   a. Replace any long-lived, hardcoded access keys (for EC2 instances, Lambda functions, ECS tasks, and similar workloads) with short-lived IAM roles that the service assumes at runtime.

   b. Ensure these roles have limited duration and necessary privileges and consider IAM permission policies for more granular control.

3. **Make Critical Access Just-in-Time (JIT_**

   a. Use AWS IAM Identity Center (AWS SSO) to allow administrative access only when necessary.

   b. Use it in combination with your corporate identity provider for even less access when it isn't needed.

Hands-On Exercise: IAM Hardening

Let's walk through a practical exercise to tighten IAM roles and secure your EC2 instances step by step:

1. Create an **Amazon EC2** instance's IAM role by logging into the **AWS Console**:

   a. Select **IAM ➤ Roles**:

      i. Then select **Create Role**.

      ii. Choose **AWS Service ➤ EC2 ➤ Next**. *Only attach the minimum necessary permissions.* (If the instance must read objects in one specific bucket, create (or attach) a custom policy that allows *ListBucket/ GetObject* **solely on that bucket** rather than applying a broad policy such as *AmazonS3ReadOnlyAccess*, which exposes all buckets in the account.)

      iii. Give the role name and you can use the default description.

      iv. Select **Create role**.

      v. For more detailed S3 bucket-level permissions, it is advisable to create a custom policy, which is finely grained (we will do this in a subsequent chapter).

2. **Choose EC2 service from the selection:**

   a. Start an **Amazon EC2** instance using any AMI.

   b. Select **Instances ➤ Launch Instances ➤ Give name**.

   c. Select any AMI (we will use ubuntu 24.04 LTS).

    d. Once the instance is launched

       i. Assign the instance the **IAM role** we created earlier.

      ii. Select the created instance:

1. Select **Actions ➤ Security ➤ Modify IAM role.**

2. Select the **IAM role**.

3. Select **Update IAM role.**

    e. Verify that the instance does not contain any static access keys:

       i. **Console/CLI Check**: From the EC2 console (or *aws ec2 describe-instances*), confirm that no IAM access key/secret key pairs are listed under "**User data**" or baked into AMI metadata.

      ii. **On the Instance**: SSH in and search for keys in common locations (*~/.aws/credentials*, environment variables, application config files). If you find any *aws_access_key_id/aws_secret_access_key*, remove them and rely on the IAM role you just attached.

    f. AWS recommends as best practice to use temporary security credentials (i.e., IAM role) rather than creating access keys.

3. Now on the IAM Console page

    a. Go to **Users**; select **user (root or IAM users) ➤ Security credentials**.

    b. Under **Multi-factor authentication**, select **Assign MFA device**. This can be used to enable MFA for both the root account and an IAM user account.

    c. Follow through the instructions to set up any of the following:

       i. Passkey or security key

      ii. Authenticator app

     iii. Hardware time-based one-time password (TOTP) token

What You've Accomplished (and Why It Matters)

By walking through those steps, you have

1. Bound an MFA device to the most powerful identities in the account (root and selected IAM users):

    a. This adds a second, independent factor, something you have on top of the password or access key the user knows.

2. Raised the bar for attackers:

    a. Even if a password or access key leaks, an adversary still can't log in or create new keys without the one-time code generated by the device or authenticator app.

3. Aligned your account with AWS security best practice:

    a. AWS explicitly recommends MFA for every root user and any IAM principal with console access or powerful API permissions.

Next Quick Checks

Before you wrap up, make sure everything works smoothly and securely with these quick checks:

-   Test the new login flow. Sign out and make sure the MFA prompt appears for that user/root account.

-   Secure your backup codes (if provided by the authenticator). Store them in a password manager or another offline vault so you're not locked out if the device is lost.

-   Repeat for other privileged users and any break-glass accounts to ensure consistent protection across the environment.

In short, you've just closed one of the most common initial access gaps – single-factor logins – and taken a foundational step toward a Zero-Trust, least-privilege AWS environment.

Micro-segmentation with AWS VPC

Let's adhere to some guidelines based on AWS recommendations while we carry out micro-segmentation in the AWS environment to ensure we are following the Zero-Trust framework:

1. **VPC and Subnet Isolation**

   a. Make unique subnets for each application (applying an application-centric approach), such as web, app, and database.

   b. For critical services that don't require public internet access, use private subnets.

2. **Security Groups (SGs)**

   a. Consider every SG to be a micro-perimeter.

   b. Adjust inbound rules so that only required ports from particular SGs or IP ranges are permitted (e.g., only TCP:443 from a load balancer SG to a web server SG).

   c. Outbound rules by default are set to all permitted; to lower the risk, think about limiting outgoing traffic.

3. **Network Access Control Lists (NACLs)**

   a. Network ACLs serve as stateless firewalls at the subnet boundary and are frequently employed to prohibit known malicious IP addresses or as an extra security measure layer.

Hands-On Exercise: VPC Micro-segmentation

By creating micro-segmentation inside your VPC, you fence each tier (web, app, database) into its own subnet, restrict traffic to only what's required, shrink any breach to a single segment, and satisfy least-privilege and compliance mandates such as PCI DSS or HIPAA.

1. **New VPC Creation**

   a. To begin, access the VPC service from the AWS Console and select the option to create a VPC.

   b. You will need to select an IPv4 CIDR block. A suitable choice for this might be 10.0.0.0/16.

2. **Subnet Creation**

   a. The next step is to create several subnets within the VPC.

   b. Start with a public subnet at 10.0.1.0/24, which will be used for load balancers and NAT gateways.

   c. Then, create a private subnet on 10.0.2.0/24. This subnet will be used for EC2 instances that do not need public IPs but must still function as servers.

3. **EC2 Instances in the Private Subnet**

   a. Launch a pair of EC2 instances in the private subnet.

   b. The first instance will serve as a web server, and the second will act as a database server.

   c. For these to work together, you need to set up the appropriate security groups on each instance.

4. **Test Connectivity**

   a. Verify from the web instance that you can connect to the DB instance using port 3306.

   b. Try to SSH directly to the DB instance (it should not work if the security group has been set up right to block it).

With this we have successfully created VPC micro-segmentation.

Continuous Monitoring and Dynamic Policy Adjustments

Stay ahead by constantly watching your environment and automatically adjusting policies to keep your systems secure and compliant.

1. **Amazon GuardDuty**

   a. Identifies hacked instances, harmful network activities, or unusual API calls.

   b. To initiate automated remediation (such as quarantining an EC2 instance), it integrates with Amazon EventBridge.

2. **AWS Config**

   a. Tracks modifications to the configuration (for instance, when an S3 bucket is inadvertently opened).

   b. Implement Zero-Trust best practices by using Config rules (e.g., make sure all new security groups block inbound 0.0.0.0/0 on essential ports).

3. **AWS CloudTrail**

   a. Records each API request, which is essential for forensic examination.

   b. Continuous verification, which is what Zero Trust entails, is aided by CloudTrail logs.

Hands-On Exercise: Automated Remediation with Amazon GuardDuty

Detection without action leaves gaps. By wiring Amazon GuardDuty findings into Amazon EventBridge and an isolation Lambda, you turn a passive alert into an automatic containment play: the moment GuardDuty flags a compromised EC2 instance, the instance is instantly fenced off by a quarantine security group, stopping attacker movement while giving you safe SSH/RDP access for forensics. The steps below walk you through building that closed-loop response:

1. **Turn on GuardDuty in Your Region**

   • To activate GuardDuty, navigate to GuardDuty ➤ Get started ➤ Turn it on.

2. **(Optional) Simulate a Finding**

   • Make use of the console's GuardDuty sample results.

3. **Configure the EventBridge Rule**

   • Go to Rules ➤ Create rules in EventBridge.

   • Set a rule to activate on a certain finding type (e.g., *UnauthorizedAccess:EC2/MaliciousIPCaller.Custom*) and select GuardDuty as the event source.

   • Select the AWS Lambda function as the target.

4. **Quarantine Lambda Function**

- Create a small Lambda function that, when triggered, swaps the EC2 instance's current security group for a **"quarantine" security group**: a group whose only rule is **ALLOW inbound SSH/RDP *from your trusted IP* and DENY all other inbound and all outbound traffic**. This effectively isolates the instance while still letting you investigate it.

- Test by creating a GuardDuty finding sample and verifying that your instance is locked down automatically.

Identity Federation and Application-Level Controls: Where to Start?

If we translate Zero-Trust design into the identity realm, it would say something along the lines of "no long-lived keys, one source of truth for identities, least privilege all the way down."

The three options below are typical building blocks you can mix and match – pick what fits your stack rather than turning every knob at once:

1. **AWS Cognito**

- Oversee user groups for web/mobile or SaaS apps.

- Use Amazon API Gateway in conjunction with JSON Web Tokens (JWTs) to implement fine-grained access rules to APIs.

- **Typical When:** You're shipping a consumer or multitenant SaaS product.

2. **AWS SSO, or AWS Single Sign-On**

- To standardize credentials, integrate with Azure AD, Okta, or corporate Active Directory.

- Assign roles in AWS applications or organizations while making sure user sessions are brief.

- **Typical When:** You already have an IdP and want federated unified employee sign-on to AWS accounts or SaaS you build.

3. **Temporary Credentials and Signed Requests**

- Ephemeral credentials can be issued via Security Token Service (STS).

- Aids in lowering the possibility of long-lived access keys leaking.

- **Typical When:** Workloads (EC2, containers, CI/CD) need temporary programmatic access.

Start with the service or section that matches your current pain point (e.g., federating unified employee sign-on using existing IdP), and then layer in the others as your architecture matures.

Hands-On Exercise: Cognito + API Gateway

Zero Trust isn't just "**no network trust**" – it's strong identity at every hop. In AWS that often means the following:

- **Cognito:** Issues short-lived JSON Web Tokens after a user has proved who they are

- **API Gateway:** Checks that token before any backend code runs

By wiring the two together, you'll see, end to end, how user login turns into a signed request that Lambda will only accept when identity, token validity, and scope all line up.

1. **Create a Cognito User Pool**

- Select Cognito ➤ Manage User Pools ➤ Create a User Pool.

- Set up email-based sign-up, and add an MFA requirement if you want.

2. **Set Up API Gateway**

- Create a REST API or HTTP API in Amazon API Gateway.

- Configure Cognito Authorizer to require an ID token from your user pool:

   1. In API Gateway select the API ➤ Authorizers ➤ Create Authorizer.

   2. **Authorizer Type:** Select Cognito (JWT).

3. **User Pool**: Create a new user pool.

4. **Token Source**: **Default** *Authorization* will be fine.

5. Select Audience & Issuer override.

6. **Time to Live (TTL)**: TTL (cache time) to something tangible, i.e., 300 seconds.

7. **Create an API Route**: Now attach the Cognito Authorizer to our lambda method.

3. **Deploy a Test Lambda Behind This API**

- The Lambda function returns a simple "Hello from Zero Trust!" message.

- Ensure only valid Cognito tokens can invoke the Lambda via the API.

4. **Test**

- Sign up a new user in the Cognito user pool, and get a valid JWT from the hosted UI or via your application.

- Use the JWT to make an API call, and ensure you receive a success response.

- Attempt to call without the JWT or with an invalid token and ensure you get an unauthorized error:

  1. **Test Using AWS CLI (Command Line Interface) (Quick Test Method):**

- Make sure the app client has *USER_PASSWORD_AUTH* flow enabled.

- Run the following sample in the terminal screen using AWS CLI:

  1. Command (fill details per your setup).

  2. Copy *AuthenticationResult.IdToken* from the JSON output and use it in the *Authorization* header:

     - `aws cognito-idp initiate-auth \`

     - `--region <region> \`

- `--client-id <appClientId> \`

- `--auth-flow USER_PASSWORD_AUTH \`

- `--auth-parameters USERNAME=<user>,PASSWORD=`
  `<password>`

By using the AWS CLI terminal test command, we can obtain and test short-lived, signed JWTs that API Gateway's Cognito Authorizer will accept, after which it will validate your test flow.

Extending Zero Trust to the Cloud Edge

Discover how AWS services help bring Zero-Trust security closer to your users and devices at the network edge.

1. **AWS WAF (Web Application Firewall)**

   a. Guard against common exploits (XSS, SQL injection) for web applications.

   b. Serves as a Layer 7 policy enforcement tool to supplement Zero Trust for your endpoints that are visible to the public.

2. **AWS Shield**

   a. DDoS defense for ALBs, CloudFront, and Route 53 resources

   b. Assists in guaranteeing availability, which is essential in a Zero-Trust setting (where online continuous verification is required)

3. **AWS PrivateLink**

   a. Use AWS PrivateLink to discreetly expose services as VPC endpoints.

   b. Stop information from traveling over the open internet when using AWS services (S3, DynamoDB, etc.).

Governance, Risk, and Compliance (GRC) in Zero Trust on AWS

Learn how AWS tools help you map, audit, and report on compliance to keep your Zero-Trust strategy aligned and effective.

1. **Map Controls to Compliance**

   a. You can consult compliance reports (such as SOC 2 and ISO 27001) from AWS Artifact.

   b. AWS Config rules and AWS Security Hub compliance checks can be used to assess your environment. Many Zero-Trust policies also correspond with frameworks such as CIS Benchmarks, PCI DSS, or HIPAA.

2. **Auditing and Reporting**

   a. To combine results (Amazon GuardDuty, Amazon Inspector, Amazon Macie, AWS IoT Device Defender, etc.) into a single pane of glass, use AWS Security Hub.

   Keep track of all cross-service activity logs in AWS CloudTrail, and configure log archiving to an S3 bucket with stringent bucket policies.

What You Have Learned

In this chapter, we touched upon various core AWS services and assessed how those services map onto the principles of Zero Trust. We discussed how to practically implement VPC micro-segmentation, implement automated remediation via GuardDuty, and perform identity federation and application controls using Cognito and API Gateway. These are all basic recommendations to set up a good starting point for an organization in its Zero-Trust journey.

It is worth noting, however, that Zero Trust is a trust model and is not about setting things up and forgetting them. It requires iteration – changes and adjustments – to move toward or maintain a robust state of Zero Trust. The threats will evolve, the organizational needs will change, and the continuous adaptation will be needed to maintain and enhance your overall Zero-Trust posture.

Summary

Zero Trust in AWS is never "one-and-done." It is a cycle that tightens with each pass:

- Start with strong identity. Enforce MFA, move human users to IAM Identity Center (AWS SSO), and replace long-lived keys with short-lived STS tokens and role assumptions.

- Divide up the network. Design VPCs, subnets, security group rules, and private endpoints so that workloads only see and can only talk to the resources they truly require.

- Watch everything, all the time. Feed CloudTrail, GuardDuty, Config, and Security Hub into automated playbooks so that suspicious activity is quarantined in seconds, not hours.

The hands-on exercises we just finished map directly to the guiding principles in NIST SP 800-207, Forrester's ZTX framework, and the CSA Zero-Trust architecture document: authenticate first, minimize implicit trust in the network, and continuously verify compliance. Each step in the project leverages the last hardening of identity enables more secure segmentation, which enables cleaner telemetry for automated response – so every user, device, or microservice must prove itself before it gets access.

In short, Zero Trust on AWS isn't marketing jargon; it's a practical blueprint for shrinking your attack surface and limiting blast radius if a breach happens. Bake these patterns into day-to-day operations, extend them across accounts and regions, and you'll keep raising the security bar as the threat landscape evolves.

CHAPTER 5

Implementing Identity-Centric Zero Trust with IAM Policies and Roles

Access control management is fundamental to any secure system, including those built on AWS. In this chapter, we will discuss the high-level principles of access control in relation to AWS services and then dive into the practical aspects of managing access control in AWS. This starts with the AWS Identity and Access Management (IAM) service, which is used to manage access to AWS resources and services. IAM is the enabling service for both access management policies and secure access to AWS resources. Following IAM, we move on to AWS Cognito, a service designed to manage access to applications securely, allowing you to set up diverse and robust access schemes for the users of your applications.

We have divided the chapter into three sections:

A. **IAM Policies and Roles**: Learn to define fine-grained access controls and apply them through reusable IAM roles.

B. **Implementing Zero Trust**: Focus on enforcing strict access principles, such as least privilege, MFA, and logging unauthorized activity.

C. **Continuous Authorization and Adaptive Access Controls**: Explore how to dynamically adjust access permissions based on user behavior and risk profiles.

© Syed Rehan 2025
S. Rehan, *Cybersecurity with AWS*, https://doi.org/10.1007/979-8-8688-1554-6_5

In this chapter we will look at how we can secure **Amazon S3**, but what we talk about with regard to IAM policies, Zero-Trust principles, and security best practices is just as relevant to other AWS services like EC2, RDS, and Lambda. Those S3-specific IAM policies you'll find later can be applied as generic policies to a great many services especially where access is being directly granted to users or groups. For things like EC2 and Lambda, which rely on IAM roles that the service automatically assumes (which we call "*service-based trust*"), you will create additional trust policies. Once you pass the general layer, that's when you'll be entering more customized, S3-specific configurations.

In this chapter we will leave you with a comprehensive understanding of the methods and strategies necessary to construct an identity security system for AWS that is not only scalable but also modern and secure. This chapter assumes you have an active AWS account and a basic knowledge of IAM and AWS Command Line Interface. If your AWS account is set up with AWS administrator permissions, you are good to go! If not, you might encounter some access issues that are best resolved with the help of your system administrator.

Finally, if you don't have AWS Command Line Interface installed, please do that first before proceeding with the next part of this chapter.

We are concentrating on these themes:

- Understanding the creation and management of IAM policies and roles that enable fine-grained access control across AWS services

- Implementing principles of Zero Trust that result in very reliable access control, such as using "least privilege" (only those permissions necessary for a person to do their job) and multi-factor authentication (MFA)

- Setting up continuous authentication and access control systems that adapt to the situation while allowing the right people into the right places at the right times

This work is fundamental to establishing a reliable security framework for AWS implementations that aligns with good, modern security practices.

Section A: IAM Policies and Roles – Building Foundational Access Control

In this Section A, you will observe how to define an IAM read-only policy for an Amazon S3 bucket and assign it to a role. This step-by-step hands-on tutorial is intended to teach you the fundamentals of IAM permissions, role assumption, and safe delegation of access via temporary credentials. This is a generic and adaptable pattern that can be applied to many AWS services, but we are employing S3 + Lambda within this instance since it is simple to deploy and test.

You'll walk away understanding

- How to build fine-grained, centralized IAM policies

- Why custom IAM beats basic S3 bucket policies in many production cases

- How to verify policies using AWS CLI with temporary credentials

Step 1: Create a Custom IAM Policy

Let's Walk through a hands-on example to build a secure, read-only IAM policy for an S3 bucket step by step.

What are we going to build?
We will create a focused permission policy. With this policy it will only permit read-only access to an S3 bucket. It will allow only one action: reading files in the bucket and its folders. It would not allow any other operations, such as writing to the bucket, deleting objects from the bucket, or performing any other sensitive actions that would compromise the security of the bucket and its contents.

Why are we doing this?
AWS Identity and Access Management policies define what users and roles can do and access in AWS. By creating a tailored policy, you ensure fine-grained control over what users or services can do and access, which minimizes security risks and aligns with the principle of "*least privilege*."

Why not just use S3's built-in read-only access?
Amazon S3 does offer native ways to grant read-only access through bucket policies or access control lists (ACLs), which are useful for simple, public, or scoped-down

135

access needs. However, using **custom IAM policies** instead brings a few key advantages especially when you're aiming for tighter security and more control:

- **Centralized Permission Management**: IAM lets you manage all user, group, and service permissions across AWS from a single place. This avoids the scattered permission sprawl that can occur if you manage access through individual S3 bucket policies or ACLs alone. I would say this is by far the most tempting factor why you use custom IAM policies.

- **Precision and Flexibility (Fine-Grained Control)**: IAM policies support conditional logic letting you define *when, how,* and *under what context* a user or service can access data. For example, you could allow access only from a certain IP address, at specific times, or for certain object prefixes – something S3 bucket policies can't easily do right now.

- **Better Alignment with Zero-Trust Principles**: IAM is foundational to AWS's Zero-Trust model. It ensures that every access request is explicitly verified and allowed based on identity and context making it a more secure and modern approach than legacy-style ACLs.

While S3's native controls are convenient for quick or limited setups, custom IAM policies give you the **security, scalability, and governance** needed for serious production environments. The same method of generating tailored IAM policies can be employed with other AWS services to uphold consistently high cybersecurity standards. For instance, when using

- **Amazon EC2**: You can restrict access to certain instances or particular actions (like starting or stopping an instance) using IAM policies.

- **Amazon RDS**: You can use IAM policies to control access at a very granular level, restricting who can perform what kind of operation on your databases.

- **AWS Lambda**: You can define roles for your Lambda functions that restrict those functions to only accessing the resources necessary for their job.

- **Amazon SQS/SNS**: IAM can be used to restrict access to your SQS message queues and SNS topics.

Log in to your **AWS Management Console** and navigate to **IAM** (Figure 5-1).

Figure 5-1. *Navigate to AWS IAM*

Navigate to **Policies** under Access management (Figure 5-2).

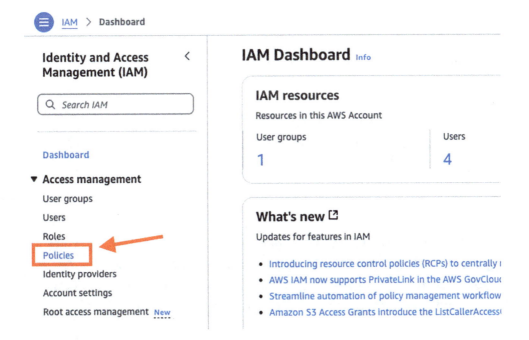

Figure 5-2. *Navigate to Policies*

Click **Create policy** and select the **JSON** tab (Figure 5-3).

Figure 5-3. *Select Create policy*

Paste the following JSON snippet into the editor (delete the default policy already in the editor; change ***example-my-secure-bucket*** to the bucket name you intend to use or have already created):

Note   S3 bucket names are globally unique, so pick a unique name ideally timestamped or with random characters.

```
{
    "Version": "2012-10-17",
    "Statement": [
        {
            "Effect": "Allow",
            "Action": ["s3:GetObject"],
            "Resource": ["arn:aws:s3::: example-my-secure-bucket/*"]
        }
    ]
}
```

This policy allows read-only access to a specific S3 bucket – one that you should create beforehand (e.g., a bucket named *example-my-secure-bucket*).

As you'll see in the policy's *GetObject* action, it only permits reading objects within that bucket and does not allow any write, delete, or administrative actions.

- **Next, review**.

- Give the policy a name, like *ReadOnlyS3Policy*.

- Give a description, i.e., S3 read-only policy.

- Click **Create policy** (Figure 5-4).

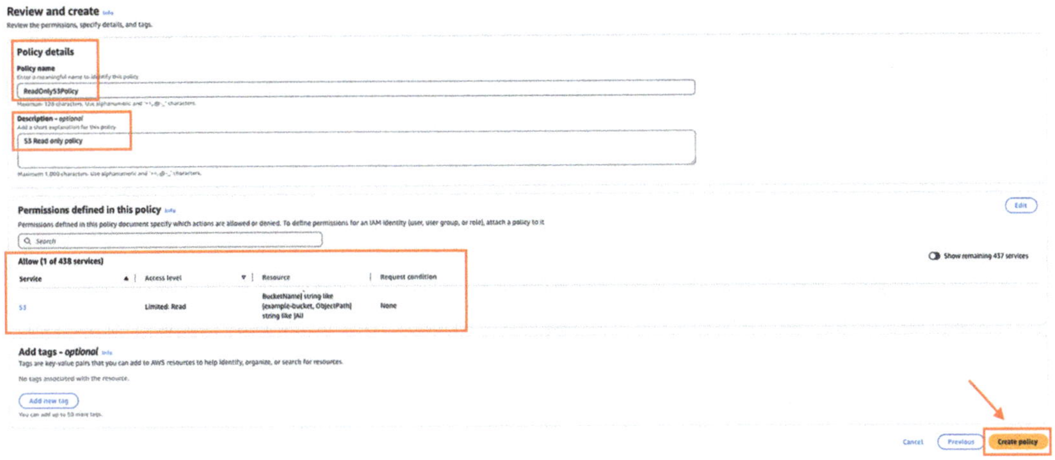

Figure 5-4. Create policy

Step 2: Create an IAM Role and Attach the Policy

Let's set up a role to securely delegate access without sharing any credentials, perfect for services like Lambda to interact with S3.

Why are we doing this?

Roles serve the purpose of bestowing temporary access to AWS resources. You can attach the policy to a role, thus allowing you to designate specific AWS services or users to assume the role without the need to hardcode any kind of sensitive credentials.

What is happening here?

We'll create an IAM role that uses the read-only policy we've just defined. Any AWS service or custom application that needs managed access to the S3 bucket can assume this role. For our use case, we'll have AWS Lambda assume the role primarily because it's quick to set up and run and makes testing and ensuring the policy works as expected a snap. But you can also attach the same role to an EC2 instance, ECS task, or any other compute resource that requires secure S3 access.

- In the **IAM Console**, go to **Roles** and click **Create Role**.

- Choose the type of trusted entity. For example:

  - Select **AWS service** and then choose **Lambda** if you're creating a role for a Lambda function (Figure 5-5).

139

Figure 5-5. *Select AWS Lambda*

Click **Next** and attach the *ReadOnlyS3Policy* created earlier (you can filter by name) (Figure 5-6).

Figure 5-6. *Policy selection*

Name your role (e.g., *S3ReadOnlyRole*) and click **Create Role** (Figure 5-7).

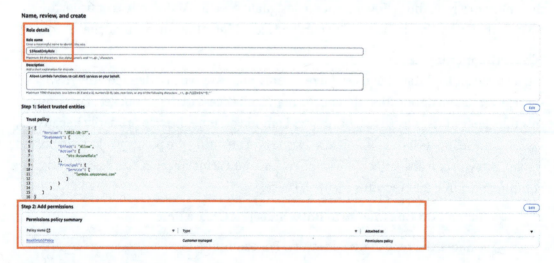

Figure 5-7. *Create Role*

Step 3: Test the Policy and Role

Now that your policy and role are in place, it's time to validate that they behave exactly as intended.

Why are we doing this?

The "why" of testing seems apparent; not everyone programmed to a policy can be trusted to have access to everything. Yet, we can't always know the "what" of our programmed security till it is tested and we "see" with our own eyes (or through the evidence of logs) that it functions as expected.

What is happening here?

You are playing the role and using impermanent credentials to assess the permissions that the policy defines. This mirrors the actual use case and verifies that the security arrangement is in good working order.

Use AWS CLI to assume the role and verify access:

```
aws sts assume-role --role-arn "arn:aws:iam::ACCOUNT_ID:role/
S3ReadOnlyRole" --role-session-name "VerifyPolicySession"
```

The command will output a JSON response containing *AccessKeyId*, *SecretAccessKey*, and *SessionToken*.

It will look something like this:

```
{
    "Credentials": {
        "AccessKeyId": "ABC123XYZ456",
        "SecretAccessKey": "abc123xyz456",
        "SessionToken": "abc123/sessiontoken456xyz",
        "Expiration": "2024-12-31T12:00:00Z"
    }
}
```

If you had error due to permissions or were unable to run the STS assume role, it may well be your AWS CLI configurations are not correctly configured; please follow AWS setup guidelines on CLI and try again. Once we have the temporary credentials, we can export them in the terminal and set up per below.

Run the following commands to export the temporary credentials received.

For Linux/MacOS Users:

```
export AWS_ACCESS_KEY_ID=<replace with your ACCESS_KEY>
export AWS_SECRET_ACCESS_KEY=<replace with your SECRET_KEY>
export AWS_SESSION_TOKEN=<Replace with your SESSION_TOKEN>
```

For Windows Users:

```
set AWS_ACCESS_KEY_ID=<replace with your ACCESS_KEY>
set AWS_SECRET_ACCESS_KEY=<replace with your SECRET_KEY>
set AWS_SESSION_TOKEN=<replace with your SESSION_TOKEN>
```

Test access to the S3 bucket by running the following command (you can use CloudShell if your role permissions are set correctly and safely without compromising the organization security policies to assume role):

```
aws s3 ls s3://example-my-secure-bucket
```

By doing this test, we can ensure that only the permissions defined in the policy are effective. Once you have run the test, you will see all the content of the directory. For my bucket I have a sample file (*Readme.txt*) that shows through (Figure 5-8).

```
[cloudshell-user@ip-10-130-94-219 ~]$ aws s3 ls s3://example-bucket
2024-12-19 19:39:26          30 Readme.txt
```

Figure 5-8. *S3 bucket output*

Section B: Implementing Zero Trust – Enforcing Least Privilege

While Section A showed us how to grant access, Section B is where we see how to restrict it even further. You will see how to apply Zero-Trust principles to your IAM policy by restricting access all the way down to a specific folder within the S3 bucket, instead of the entire bucket. This exercise demonstrates least privilege in practice, one of the original principles of Zero Trust.

You'll walk away understanding the following:

- Strategies for limiting IAM policies to particular resources, e.g., folder-level permission on S3.

- How these restrictions reduce your attack surface.

- One can apply the same strategy to other AWS resources, such as EC2, RDS, and DynamoDB.

Step 1: Enforce Least Privilege

Start by narrowing access down to only what's absolutely needed – no more, no less – to protect your resources with precision.

Why are we doing this?

The principle of least privilege means that users and roles are granted only those permissions absolutely necessary to accomplish their tasks to a granular level. This reduces the breach surface and limits the impact of possible security incidents.

What is happening here?

You're tightening the policy even more, allowing access only to particular folders in the S3 bucket –things can be done to and with files within those folders – while denying access to the bucket itself and anything else inside it (granular fine level or on an "as needed" basis – "least privilege").

Why not use S3's built-in features for this?

You can use S3 bucket policies and ACLs (access control lists) to control access to your S3 buckets and objects. But IAM policies are a better way to manage permissions and roles across your AWS resources. IAM policies allow you to enforce consistent permissions and security across your AWS environment, including S3, at a much broader and more flexible level. You can use IAM policies to define the S3 permissions for any user, group, or role across AWS. And because IAM policies are not S3-specific, you can also use them to manage the permissions for all your other AWS resources.

Just as with S3, IAM policies enforcing least privilege can be applied to other AWS services:

- **Amazon EC2**: Allow specific actions like starting/stopping instances for designated users.

- **Amazon RDS**: Grant permissions only for backups or monitoring.

- **Amazon DynamoDB**: Control access to tables and specific operations like reads or writes.

Update your IAM policy to apply more *fine-grained access controls*. For example, limit access to a specific folder in the bucket:

```
{
    "Version": "2012-10-17",
    "Statement": [
        {
            "Effect": "Allow",
            "Action": ["s3:GetObject"],
            "Resource": ["arn:aws:s3::: example-my-secure-bucket/
            sample-folder/*"]
        }
    ]
}
```

Save and attach this updated policy to the IAM role (in our case we used "*S3ReadOnlyRole*").

Section C: Continuous Authorization and Adaptive Access Controls

In a legacy model, access is set up once at login and relied upon throughout a session. But in a Zero-Trust environment, authorization must be dynamic; it must react to changing context such as user behavior, device risk, and location. This is the underpinning principle behind continuous authorization: not just authenticating identity once, but continuously determining if access should still be granted.

In this section, we will discuss about the deployment of risk-based adaptive access with AWS-native tools:

- Amazon Cognito for continuous monitoring of the user context and adaptive authentication via threat detection and MFA.

- AWS WAF (Web Application Firewall) offers dynamic access controls that are conditional on geographic location, anonymous traffic, or behavior.

- Web ACLs to deploy rules like country blocking or OWASP (Open Web Application Security Project) rule sets for emerging web threats.

By combining these tools, one will build an access control framework that is context-aware, adaptive to changing threats, and aligned with Zero-Trust paradigms. Whether one is running a mobile app or a web backend, these settings will help guarantee that the users are not just authenticated but continually authorized to access sensitive resources.

Step 1: Set Up Continuous Authentication with Amazon Cognito

Start by enabling real-time identity checks so your setup can spot unusual user behavior and react instantly.

Why are we doing this?

Amazon Cognito enables us to perform continuous authentication. Why perform continuous authentication? It helps us secure systems by monitoring user behavior in real time and enforcing additional security measures when something appears amiss.

Log in to the **Amazon Cognito Console** and create a new **user pool** (Figure 5-9).

Figure 5-9. *Create user pool*

Let's use a mobile app as an example; such apps often have region- or time-based restrictions (e.g., taxi or grocery services). Continuous authentication helps enforce these by verifying user logins against expected patterns (Figure 5-10).

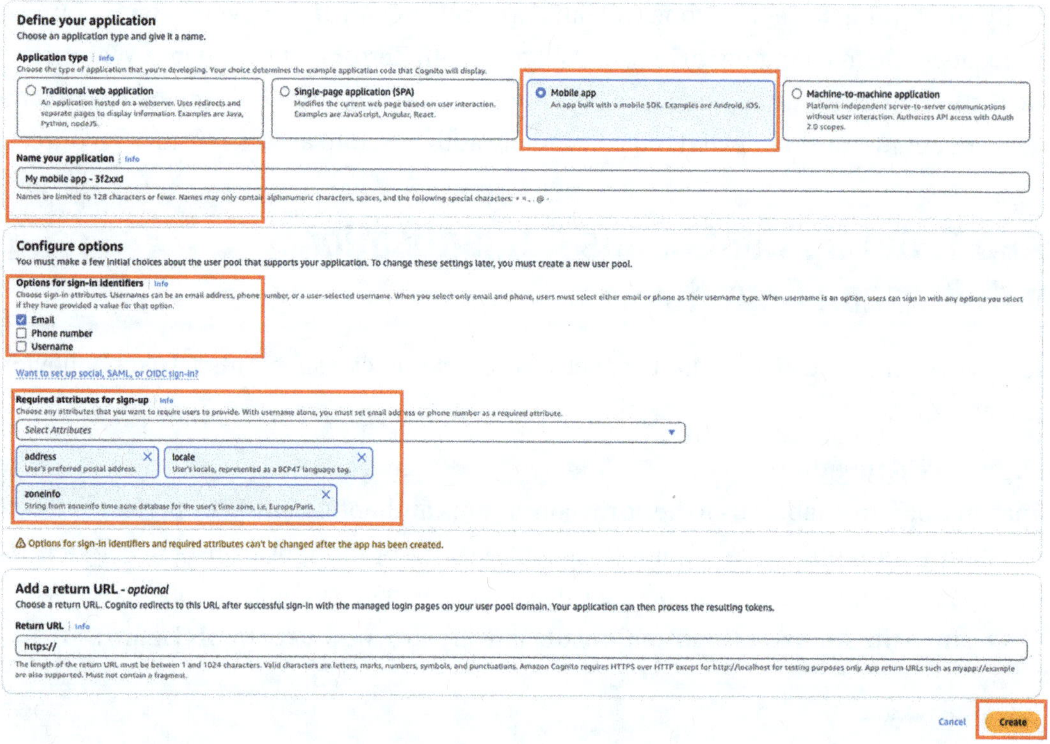

Figure 5-10. *Define a user pool for a mobile app*

Adaptive authentication can be put into action within Amazon Cognito by configuring the user pool to utilize threat protection and setting up risk-based authentication. Follow these steps to get everything just right:

Activate threat protection. To set up an adaptive authentication flow in an Amazon Cognito user pool, begin by navigating to the Amazon Cognito Console. Choose the user pool for which you want to create an adaptive authentication flow. On the left sidebar, locate "Threat protection" under the Security section and select it. Finally, enable threat protection by moving the user pool to the Plus plan.

Next, configure the three risk levels (Low, Medium, and High). For each risk level, you can specify the action that is to be taken when sign-in attempts are assessed to be at that risk level (Figure 5-11).

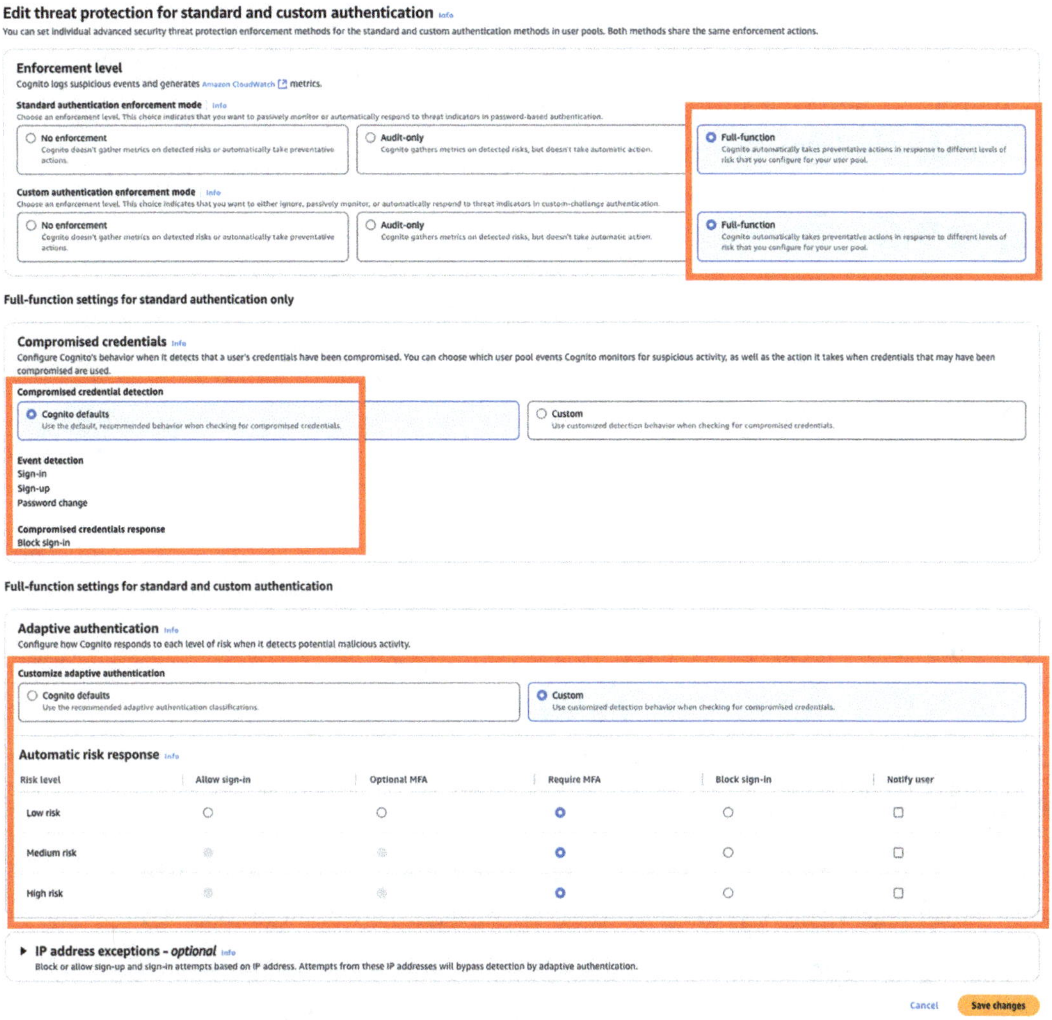

Figure 5-11. *Enable Advanced Threat Protection (ATP) enforcement*

The options are as follows:

1. Allow the sign-in to succeed.

2. Require additional authentication.

3. Block access.

To make the authentication flow more secure yet user-friendly, set up multi-factor authentication (MFA), should your use case demand it. Next, move on to the "Applications" section of the Cognito Console and select "*App clients.*"

Ensure the app is able to send "additional user context data." This next step may be performed on your server, in your app, or in a combination of both. Use the Amazon Cognito SDK within your application to collect user context data.

Enable **multi-factor authentication (MFA)** in the user pool settings under Authentication and Sign-in (Figure 5-12).

Figure 5-12. *Set up MFA*

Step 2: Implement Adaptive Access Controls with AWS WAF

Let's set up smart, context-aware protections that automatically respond when something looks suspicious like a login from a new country or an unusual IP.

Why are we doing this?

Adaptive access means that if you are accessing a resource and something about you seems off (like you're logging in from another country), access is restricted until the system can figure out what is going on. The access control is somewhat like a high-tech bouncer who doesn't let you into a club if there's anything suspicious about you.

To make this work, you will need to do some configuration by following the steps below:

- Go to AWS WAF (Figure 5-13) and create a Web ACL (access control list).

Figure 5-13. *Access the AWS WAF Console*

Set rules in the Web ACL (Figure 5-14) using geo-restriction (which may work differently than it sounds) to block access from specific regions. During setup, make sure to add your user pool under the "Add AWS resources" section (Figure 5-15).

Figure 5-14. *Set up Web ACLs*

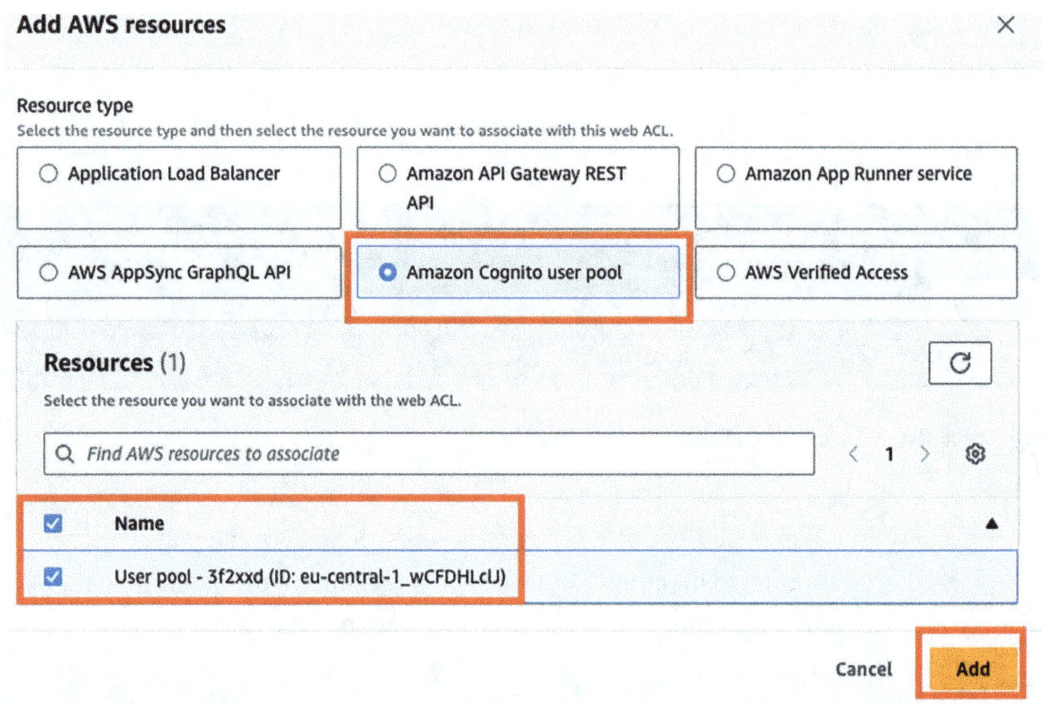

Add AWS resources   ✕

Resource type
Select the resource type and then select the resource you want to associate with this web ACL.

○ Application Load Balancer   ○ Amazon API Gateway REST   ○ Amazon App Runner service
                                   API

○ AWS AppSync GraphQL API   ● Amazon Cognito user pool   ○ AWS Verified Access

Resources (1)   ⟳

Select the resource you want to associate with the web ACL.

🔍 *Find AWS resources to associate*   ‹ 1 ›   ⚙

☑   **Name**   ▲

☑   User pool - 3f2xxd (ID: eu-central-1_wCFDHLcU)

                                                         Cancel   **Add**

Figure 5-15. *Add the user pool resource during Web ACL creation*

It is also possible to assign managed rule groups while configuring AWS WAF; these rule groups are preconfigured by AWS and its partners to simplify the work of the user.

These rule sets are accessible when configuring or modifying a Web ACL and provide protections such as bot mitigation, filtering of anonymous IPs, and enforcement of OWASP Top 10 security best practices (e.g., protection against injection, XSS, and broken authentication).

These are accessible in the "Add rules and rule groups" step when you set up your Web ACL in the AWS WAF Console. Here, you can select the managed rule groups to add and configure priorities that will establish the enforcement order. This filters traffic based on several layers of context (e.g., geo-location, user agent, source IP) before it reaches your protected resource.

What You Have Learned

After finishing this chapter, you understand how to manage access control effectively in AWS using IAM policies and roles and Zero-Trust principles. You are now familiar with the least-privilege principle, which states that users should have only those permissions that are necessary to perform their tasks. You also understand that achieving least privilege in AWS requires thoughtful design and continuous effort over time.

You have learned that multi-factor authentication (MFA) and continuous monitoring of user accounts can and should be used to enhance the security of the access control system. Moreover, you have gained experience setting up adaptive access controls (those that adjust to the current risk level of the user and the environment) and continuous authorization (ensuring that the user is still the user throughout the session).

Summary

This chapter covered three primary components:

- How to set up IAM policies and roles to allow specific, necessary access to your AWS resources

- How to enforce the Zero-Trust principle of least privilege, using IAM policies, with the additional safety net of multi-factor authentication

- How to configure continuous authentication and adaptive access controls for your AWS environment, using Amazon Cognito and other AWS services, that allows you to make smart decisions about how your access controls work

CHAPTER 6

Strategic Data Protection: Implementing Encryption and Data-Centric Zero Trust Security

Ensuring the protection of data has transitioned from being a mere best practice to an absolute imperative in today's digital era, where everything is interconnected and depends on a steady flow of data. For an organization, a reliable data protection framework underpins everything it does. Organizations amass enormous volumes of data; they use it to drive not just their daily operations but also their long-term strategic planning and now use it for AI, too. And in this privileged digital world, data is their only lifeline to maintain competitive differentiation. But it is also their Achilles' heel. Because they use so much of it, they are so overly exposed to risks associated with data loss, whether that loss occurs inside the company or outside it at the hands of bad actors.

To address these problems efficiently, businesses must carry out data safeguard strategies that are more sophisticated than classic "fortress" security. Encryption and a security model such as Zero Trust are two critical components of any seriously undertaken data safety strategy. Although these methods are superior to others in providing safe access to information, they also function well in providing access to safe information. Encryption and Zero Trust are both essential: the first **protects the data itself ("access to safe information")**, while the second **protects the pathway to that data ("safe access to information")**. Together they ensure that what users reach is encrypted and that only the right users can reach it.

© Syed Rehan 2025
S. Rehan, *Cybersecurity with AWS*, https://doi.org/10.1007/979-8-8688-1554-6_6

Transforming data into an unreadable format (encryption) ensures that even if it is intercepted or compromised, it remains inaccessible to unauthorized parties. This is crucial for protecting sensitive information such as

- Customer data

- Financial records

- Intellectual property

The Zero-Trust model, by not assuming any implicit trust within or outside the organization's network, forces a virtually continuous evaluation of every access request to the data, which remains elementary in the reduction of the organization's attack surface.

The procedure always starts with familiarizing yourself with your data – what you possess, where it resides, how it serves the company, and how dangerous it would be in the wrong hands. Once you've mapped out that landscape, you can **encrypt everything by default** and then **classify**, subjecting the crown jewels to more severe controls and low-value or public data to fewer controls and not bothering with protecting large quantities of logs or telemetry whose business value isn't worth full-fledged encryption. This alignment of resources, rewards, and risks enables you to allocate security spend where it's most important and keeps your organization's mission and its most important information safe.

Data security is improved through the process of tokenization, which replaces sensitive data elements with unique identifiers. This limits the chances of exposure during a breach because the original data is kept hidden. A comprehensive data protection strategy includes tokenization and establishes a robust line of defense that effectively protects an organization's key data assets. That line of defense also ensures that any breach that might occur has a diminished impact. The recommended steps are **data encryption**, **data classification**, and finally **data tokenization**; with these steps we can achieve compliance with all relevant industry regulations. Organizations that use this kind of setup maintain the trust of their stakeholders and the confidence of their customers.

These challenges require enterprises to adopt a security model that pivots on data. That means the basis of their model is no longer on the perimeter or on the endpoints; it is on the data. A data-centric security model requires enterprise architects to rethink their strategies for not only how to protect the data but also how to make it accessible to users, users in the enterprise as well as users outside the enterprise. This chapter tells you how to do that.

Encryption and Zero-Trust Data-Centric Security

Let's explore how encryption protects your sensitive data at every stage, fitting perfectly with Zero-Trust principles.

Understanding Encryption Methods

The process of converting data to an unreadable format (ciphertext) can happen to any type of data, but most often it happens to plaintext data. People who are authorized to do so have the appropriate decryption key that allows them to convert the encrypted unreadable format (ciphertext) back to plaintext readable data. This is a basic, yet very important, security mechanism that works to keep valuable sensitive data safe when it is stored or being transferred or in some cases even when it is being actively used.

Types of Encryptions and Data Integrity Technique:
We'll break down the main encryption types and how hashing ensures your data hasn't been tampered with.

1. **Symmetric Encryption**

   - Employs a solitary key for both enciphering and deciphering

   - **Examples**: AES (Advanced Encryption Standard), DES
     (less secure)

   - Most appropriate for the encryption of large amounts of data
     because of its quickness

2. **Asymmetric Encryption**

   - Employs a key pair: a public key for encryption and a private key
     for decryption

   - **Examples**: RSA, Elliptic Curve Cryptography (ECC)

   - Frequently employed for protecting communications (e.g.,
     HTTPS) and for key exchange

3. **Hashing (Data Integrity)**

   - Data is transformed into a hash value of a set size, and this is
     done in such a way that the original data cannot be obtained from
     the hash value.

155

- **Examples**: SHA-256 and MD5 (not recommended due to vulnerabilities).

- Mainly utilized for the purpose of authenticating data integrity.

Putting Encryption into Action Within the Enterprise:

Let's explore practical ways to protect your data using encryption throughout your organization.

- **Data at Rest**: Use AES-256 encryption to secure your files, databases, and backups, so that even if your storage devices are compromised, the data within them remains safe.

- **Data in Transit**: Employ protocols such as TLS (Transport Layer Security) to protect the information being sent secure over the network.

- **End-to-End Encryption (E2EE)**: Make certain that information stays encoded all the time it takes to travel, readable only by those it was meant for.

- **Key Management**: Put into practice strong key management techniques such as key rotation, as well as secure storage and limited access to these very keys.

Encryption-Centric Compliance Snapshot

As you design an encryption product, you have to meet or beat the crypto-specific criteria inherent in today's big data protection regulations:

- **GDPR (EU)**: Requires "state-of-the-art" technical safeguards. Article 32 directly calls out encryption (at rest and in transit) as a major control for any EU citizen's personal information.

- **HIPAA (United States)**: Generally, views encryption of ePHI as an "addressable" implementation specification; in practice, regulators expect AES-level strength for data at rest and TLS for data in transit, along with rigorous key management controls.

- **CCPA/CPRA (California)**: Does not require algorithms, but inauspiciously raises liability if a breach involves unencrypted personal information putting disk-, database-, and field-level encryption solidly into the de facto safe harbor.

- **EU Cyber Resilience Act (CRA)**: Compels producers to integrate robust cryptography throughout the lifecycle of a product, from secure boot and firmware signing (asymmetric keys) to encrypted data storage and secure update channels.

Standardizing your key sizes, algorithms, rotation schedules, and HSM/KMS use against these standards means your encryption posture isn't merely technically sound; it's also regulator-ready.

Data-Centric Zero-Trust Security

We have already seen that Zero Trust is a security model based on the principle of "never trust, always verify." In a Zero-Trust framework for data-centric security, protection of the data is prioritized, and access is granted based on the continuous verification of user identity (authentication), user rights (authorization), device security, and data context.

Key Principles of Data-Focused Zero Trust:
Understanding the core ideas that keep your data secure by limiting access, segmenting networks, and continuously verifying users is essential.

- **Access on a Need-to-Know Basis:** Data and system access must be limited according to the specific user roles and responsibilities of the individuals requesting access. That way, only those who must see the information in question can see it, allowing us to audit and track and trace any malice, be it an internal or external threat actor utilizing these credentials.

- **Micro-segmentation:** Segment the network into heavily restricted regions to restrict lateral attacker movement. In conjunction, use data-driven segmentation tags and group workloads by the sensitivity level of data they process (PCI DSS data, Payment Card Industry data; PII, personally identifiable information; publicly visible data set; etc.) so every region inherits the same access controls, encryption, and monitoring levels that data set demands.

- **Ongoing Authentication and Supervision**: Regularly check the identities of users and keep an eye on what they do to spot anything suspicious. Carrying out proactive audit is critical in cybersecurity and specifically for data security.

- **Data Protection by Design**: Make sure security measures are built into data management processes and systems and that protection is in place all through the data lifecycle and along the phases of CRUD (Create, Read, Update, Delete).

Implementing Data-Centric Zero Trust in the Enterprise:

Learn how to secure your data by focusing on strong identity controls, clear data classification, comprehensive encryption, and smart remote access management.

- **Identity and Access Management (IAM):**

  - Enhance identity verification by using multi-factor authentication (MFA) and Single Sign-On (SSO).

  - Put into practice role-based access control (RBAC) and attribute-based access control (ABAC).

- **Data Classification:**

  - Organize the data according to its importance and delicacy to the organization.

  - Employ designations like "Confidential," "Internal Use," and "Public."

  - Safeguard sensitive data such as personally identifiable information (PII) and intellectual property.

- **Encryption Everywhere:**

  - Encrypt data in all states: at rest, in transit, and in use.

- **Zero-Trust Network Access (ZTNA):**

  - Ensure secure remote access by replacing traditional VPNs with ZTNA solutions.

  - Ensure the context in which access is granted is based on user location, device health, and data sensitivity.

Steps to Implement Encryption and Zero Trust

Let's walk through a clear, step-by-step process to assess your security, identify gaps, and set up strong encryption and Zero-Trust controls.

Step 1: Assess Your Current Security Posture

- Undertake a comprehensive assessment of your data resources, pinpointing delicate details and their sites.

- Assess current cryptographic techniques and methods for regulating access to data.

- Spot deficiencies in adhering to regulations and industry standards.

  - **Discover Where Data Lives**

    1. Run AWS Macie/Azure Information Protection/Google DLP to list S3 buckets, blobs, DBs, and shares.

    2. Tag everyone with purpose and every owner; export the report to CSV.

  - **Label Data Sensitivity**

    1. Use the scanner's out-of-the-box PII/PCI rules for a first cut.

    2. Go through each data owner and ask

       1. If this leaked, how bad would it be?

       2. Label them as *Public/Internal/Confidential/ Restricted.*

- **Catalog Crypto and Key Hygiene**

  1. *aws kms list-keys*, **Azure Key Vault, or GCP KMS**: Note algorithms, rotation status, and where keys are stored (KMS, HSM, file).

  2. Review database/server TLS configurations for weak ciphers.

- **Map Who Has the Potential to Touch the Data**

  1. Run IAM Access Analyzer/Azure IAM graph/GCP Policy Analyzer.

  2. Highlight any user, role, or workload with permissive "*" permissions or long-lived keys.

- **Check Compliance Gaps**

  1. Compare each store against mandates that apply to you (e.g., PCI DSS encryption at rest, HIPAA audit logging, GDPR residency).

  2. Record all instances of "non-compliance," specifically where security controls are missing or insufficient or fall short of required compliance standards.

- **Generate a Single Matrix**

  1. Rows = data stores, Columns = location • sensitivity • encryption state • key details • authorized principals.

  2. The red cells (no encryption, weak keys, over-privileged access) are now your Zero-Trust and encryption backlog.

Step 2: Define a Data-Centric Security Strategy

- Develop a framework for classifying data that allows a prioritization of protective efforts.

- Develop a plan for putting encryption into action, along with managing the keys.

- Zero-Trust principles should be applied throughout the company.

- **These are as follows:**

1. Trust no one, and verify everyone who accesses resources.

2. Don't trust any device either, and enforce strict authentication.

3. Always enforce segmentation (network and data) and least-privilege access.

4. Always inspect and log all access and use of resources.

5. Always assume an adversary is present and has already compromised some resources.

Step 3: Deploy Encryption Technologies

- Implement tools for the encryption of databases, file systems, and communications.

- Make use of hardware security modules (HSMs) or cloud-based key management services to manage encryption keys securely.

- Educate staff about the significance of encryption and the correct usage of encryption tools.

Step 4: Adopt a Zero-Trust Framework

- Implement IAM solutions that provide MFA and SSO capabilities.

- Employ ZTNA to ensure that remote access is secure.

- Watch over user actions and data access patterns with sophisticated analytical tools and threat detection systems.

Step 5: Continuously Improve and Monitor

- Consistently examine and refresh encryption directives and Zero-Trust protocols.

- Carry out penetration testing to find weaknesses.

- Remain in the know about new dangers and technologies, and adjust your strategy as needed.

Challenges and Best Practices

Let's explore the common hurdles you might face and practical tips to overcome them
smoothly.

Challenges

- **Complicated Implementations**: Implementing encryption and Zero
  Trust can be a big technical and operational job.

- **Price**: Robust encryption and Zero-Trust solutions might need a
  hefty investment.

- **Change Resistance**: Employees and stakeholders may resist the
  adoption of new security practices.

Best Practices

- Begin by concentrating on key systems and essential data;
  then expand.

- Utilize security services that are based in the cloud to lower the
  complexity of operations.

- Encourage a culture of security awareness by conducting training
  and communications on a regular basis.

- Work with reliable suppliers and associates to effectuate top-notch
  solutions.

Modern enterprises must ensure that even the most sophisticated threats can't touch
their data. To do that, they need to safeguard their sensitive information with a cadre
of protection methods. Implementing those protection methods requires some effort
on the part of medium and large organizations; those measures are often layered, and
they're quite extensive. Data is encrypted at every stage – at rest, in transit, and in use.
And when those encrypted boxes are opened, the contents inside are good to go.

Because there is an encrypted egress (i.e., the point at which data exits the system or
network), trust is never compromised, which is to say that data is secure against prying
eyes and hands at every possible point.

Data Classification and Tokenization in a Zero-Trust Framework

A Zero-Trust architecture is based on the assumption that all access requests must be authenticated and authorized regardless of where they originate. To realize it successfully, there are **two foundational elements** that are essential: ***data classification and tokenization***. Data classification is the act of categorizing data into groups based on its sensitivity and value so that organizations can apply tailored security controls on each group. It's the "divide and rule" strategy that ensures risk-based protection. Tokenization, however, protects highly sensitive data by replacing it with non-sensitive equivalents (tokens). That way, even if data is accessed through unauthorized channels, the real information remains concealed, minimizing the impact of potential breaches.

Understanding Data Classification

The organizing of data into categories hinges on the process of data classification for an age when data seems to be in unlimited supply. You would classify data based on three principal determinants: its sensitivity, its value, and the regulations it requires your organization to follow. Classifying data enables an organization to define and implement an effective data protection strategy.

Importance of Data Classification

Sorting and labeling your data properly is key to security, compliance, and operational efficiency.

- **Increased Protection**: Guarantees that confidential information is sufficiently safeguarded from unapproved entry.

- **Meeting legal and industry-specific requirements** such as GDPR, HIPAA, and CCPA is what helps organizations conform to regulations through the complex, many-layered system of oversight that comprises regulatory compliance.

- **Efficiency in Operations**: Enhances the running of the organization by organizing data according to its application and value.

- **Cost Optimization**: Focuses resources on protecting critical data to minimize storage and security expenses.

Steps to Implement Data Classification

Here's a straightforward process to help you organize and protect your data effectively:

1. **Identify and Inventory Data Assets**

   - A complete audit must be done to find all types of sources of data. This includes structured data, as well as unstructured data.

   - Use automated tools to pinpoint delicate materials like PII and intellectual property.

2. **Define Classification Levels**

   - Establish categories for classification, such as

     - **Public**: Information that can be safely distributed and has no potential for harm

     - **Internal Use**: Data used internally that does not need to be public

     - **Confidential**: Sensitive data that, if disclosed, could cause harm

     - **Highly Confidential**: Data with the highest sensitivity and confidentiality, like PII and financial information

3. **Label Data**

   - Employ metadata or tagging systems to mark data in accordance with its classification.

   - Maintain uniform labeling throughout all systems and platforms.

4. **Develop Access Controls**

   - As mentioned earlier install role-based access control (RBAC) and attribute-based access control (ABAC) to limit data access according to the classification of that data.

5. **Monitor and Update**

   - Consistently assess and refresh classification guidelines to keep pace with the evolving business landscape and shift in regulatory requirements.

Understanding Tokenization

Tokenization is a technique for protecting sensitive data. The data is replaced with a non-sensitive substitute called a token that retains the essential information for business processes. There is no exploitable value in a token if a tokenized data set is breached.

Here's how it works:
Let's break down the key steps involved in keeping your sensitive data safe through tokenization.

1. **Data Substitution**

   Data of a sensitive nature (e.g., credit card numbers) is substituted with a distinctive token that is generated via the use of algorithms or lookup tables.

2. **Token Vault**

   The centralized token vault securely stores all of the original sensitive data.

3. **De-tokenization**

   When needed, the original data can be reconstructed from the tokens, using secure methods and access controls.

Benefits of Tokenization:
Discover how tokenization helps protect sensitive data while making compliance and secure sharing easier.

- **Ensuring** sensitive information is never directly exposed mitigates the risk of data breaches and boosts data security.

- **Following Rules and Regulations**: Makes it easier to follow rules and regulations like PCI DSS (Payment Card Industry Data Security Standard - set of security standards for entities that handle payment card data to protect cardholder information) and makes sure the organization is in compliance with such rules.

- **Operational Flexibility**: Allows for safe data sharing across apps and services without putting security at risk.

Implementing Data Classification and Tokenization in a Zero-Trust Framework

Let's break down how to protect your data step by step within a Zero-Trust security model.

Step 1: Establish a Zero-Trust Foundation

- **Assume All Users, Devices, and Systems Are Untrusted Until Proven Otherwise**: Take a "never trust, always verify" attitude.

- **Establish Identity and Access Management (IAM)**: Verify identities using multi-factor authentication (MFA) and continuous monitoring.

Step 2: Integrate Data Classification

- **Across Systems, Apply Data Classification Rules**: Classify data consistently within databases, file systems, and cloud environments.

- **Utilize Automation**: Implement tools that automatically scan and classify data using predefined rules.

Step 3: Deploy Tokenization Solutions

- **Pick a Tokenization Platform**: Choose a solution that integrates perfectly with your current structure.

- **Ensure That the Token Vault Is Protected**: Use encryption and access controls to prevent unauthorized access to the token vault.

- **Test and Validate**: Carry out thorough testing to confirm that the tokenization process does not interfere with business operations.

Step 4: Align with Compliance Requirements

- Align your data classification and tokenization strategies with the pertinent regulations.

- Keep precise and comprehensive records of tokenization tasks for audit reasons.

Step 5: Monitor and Evolve

- Review the effectiveness of your classification and tokenization strategies on a regular basis.

- Adjust to new and developing threats and regulatory shifts.

Challenges and Best Practices

Let's explore the common hurdles and proven strategies to handle data classification and tokenization effectively.

Challenges

- **Classification and tokenization** across large data sets can be a daunting task.

- **Expense**: Platforms and tools of high quality for tokenization can necessitate a considerable investment.

- **Change Resistance**: Employees might resist new tools and processes.

Best Practices

- **Commence on a Small Scale**: Start with a high-stakes data pilot, and then expand.

- **Make the Most of Automation**: Employ AI and machine learning tools to make data classification and tokenization easier.

- **Employee Training**: Conduct regular training sessions to increase awareness and proficiency among employees.

- **Collaborate with** vendors and consultants to ensure best practices are followed.

Zero-Trust security can be implemented only when there is a robust understanding of data. This is fundamental because the Zero-Trust model revolves around protecting the most critical assets and data regardless of where they reside. To protect an organization's data, it is first crucial to know what data exists, where it is located, and how to segregate it based on its value to the organization (intelligence). This includes not just the obviously critical data, such as trade secrets or proprietary algorithms, but

167

also any number of ordinary data sets that could be mined for intelligence by a malicious actor. Once you have a handle on what data there is and what its potential is, you have to use that knowledge to start building a security model around it.

What You Have Learned

This chapter has led us to encryption and data-centered Zero-Trust security, explaining their principles and practical applications. We covered some of the methods of encryption and how they facilitate enterprise-level security. We then went step by step through the foundation of Zero Trust through data classification and tokenization explaining why both are necessary, how they complement each other, and practical steps for implementation.

Summary

We covered how information is secured with encryption at all levels and data classification, or determining what you wish to protect. Tokenization was presented as an extremely solid solution to lock down sensitive information, especially when combined with classification. Combining the methods gives a valuable layer for a Zero-Trust strategy. As a finishing touch, we outlined common implementation challenges and best practices so that businesses could feel prepared to go ahead on creating secure data-centric environments.

CHAPTER 7

Continuous Monitoring, Anomaly Detection, Compliance, and Incident Response in AWS: Strategies and Automation

Organizations today depend heavily on cyber infrastructure so much so that they are all the more susceptible to cyber-attack. With more frequency and greater level of sophistication of attacks, a strong security position should be based on **three** pillars: persistent monitoring and anomaly detection, regulatory compliance and audit preparedness, and an incident response plan specifically tailored to cloud-based, Zero-Trust environments now.

We begin with monitoring. In today's threat landscape, visibility is paramount. Threats reside both inside and outside the organization; thus, constant monitoring of all systems, networks, and activities is imperative. This requires not just tools, but also a mature process that can identify "normal" vs. "abnormal" activity to facilitate early threat detection before matters spiral out of control.

Next is compliance, which ensures your security controls align with internal needs and external regulations. Compliance is not checkboxes; it's ensuring your security policies line up with guidelines like GDPR, HIPAA, and ISO 27001 and that they are consistently enforced within your environment. We'll cover how automation and compliance auditing tools enable security hygiene.

© Syed Rehan 2025
S. Rehan, *Cybersecurity with AWS*, https://doi.org/10.1007/979-8-8688-1554-6_7

Finally, we turn to incident response. In addition to the Zero-Trust essentials from earlier chapters where neither user nor device is trusted by default, we'll see how incident response is assisted by breach assumption and minimizing lateral movement. We'll also explore cloud-specific response strategies through the lens of AWS as a use case, including how playbooks, automation, and cloud forensics allow teams to respond quicker and smarter.

By the end of this chapter, you'll understand how these three pillars – monitoring, compliance, and response – work together to reduce risk and enable rapid action in the face of threats.

Continuous Monitoring and Anomaly Detection Using AWS Cloud

Proactively monitoring systems and spotting anomalies is vital to operational efficiency, security, and business continuity. Continuous monitoring and continuous anomaly detection let organizations spot the unusual, assess the situation, and take action before the situation necessitates calling the fire department.

The robust tools and services offered by AWS Cloud let businesses implement as much or as little monitoring and anomaly detection as they want or need.

Understanding Continuous Monitoring and Anomaly Detection

Learn how continuous monitoring keeps systems healthy and secure, while anomaly detection spots unusual activities before they become problems.

Continuous monitoring involves the real-time collection, analysis, and reporting of system metrics, logs, and events to ensure systems are performing optimally and securely.

It provides insight into system performance, security, and satisfaction of compliance requirements.

Anomaly detection focuses on identifying deviations from expected behavior within a system. Deviations can signal possible security threats, operational problems, or system malfunctions. These anomalies are detected by discerning patterns in data and identifying unusual behaviors.

Benefits of Continuous Monitoring and Anomaly Detection:

Discover how ongoing vigilance helps you catch threats early, improve operations, and stay compliant, all with less manual effort.

- **Proactive Threat Detection**: Entails recognizing prospective dangers and security breaches before they inflict serious damage.

- **Operational Efficiency**: Obtain knowledge about system performance, allowing for more rapid troubleshooting and optimization.

- **Compliance Assurance**: Ensure adherence to regulatory requirements and standards by supervising key controls.

- **Scalability and Automation**: AWS services can be used to automate the monitoring and detection processes. This reduces the manual overhead and makes it easier to achieve 24/7 monitoring.

AWS Services for Continuous Monitoring and Anomaly Detection

A suite of services from AWS is designed to provide continuous monitoring and anomaly detection.

Amazon CloudWatch:

- Gathers and oversees metrics, logs, and event occurrences from AWS resources

- Presents dashboards that can be customized and automated alarms that can be used to gain actionable insights

AWS CloudTrail:

- Tracks who did what and when in your AWS environment

- Records all API calls, CLI commands, and console activity across AWS services

- Best used for auditing, compliance tracking, and forensic investigations

- Acts as your "security camera logs" – providing a record of events

Amazon GuardDuty:

- Continuously analyzes the events that CloudTrail (and other services like VPC Flow Logs and DNS logs) collects.

- Uses machine learning and threat intelligence to detect suspicious activity, like unexpected API calls or connections to known malicious IPs.

- Best used for real-time threat detection and automated alerting.

- Think of it as your "security analyst" – interpreting activity and flagging threats.

AWS Config:

- Assesses and monitors setups of AWS resources to gauge adherence to rules and regulations

- Identifies modifications that might create vulnerabilities

AWS Security Hub:

- Security alerts and compliance checks from various AWS services are combined in one place.

- Offers a consolidated perspective on security findings.

Amazon Macie:

- Employs machine learning to keep an eye on and safeguard delicate information kept in Amazon S3

- Identifies anomalies in data access patterns

Amazon Lookout for Metrics:

- Anomalies in business and operational metrics are automatically detected.

- Assists with root cause analysis and offers insights that help define the corrective action.

Steps to Implement Continuous Monitoring and Anomaly Detection

Follow these clear steps to set up ongoing monitoring and spot unusual activity before it becomes a problem.

1. **Define Monitoring Objectives:**

   - Identify the vital systems, metrics, and logs to keep an eye on.

   - Establish goals for spotting anomalies, like security problems, performance snags, or compliance violations.

2. **Architect the Monitoring Framework:**

   - Leverage AWS CloudWatch to gather metrics and logs from your applications and infrastructure.

   - Capture and log API activities by enabling AWS CloudTrail.

3. **Leverage Machine Learning for Anomaly Detection:**

   - Amazon Lookout for Metrics and Amazon GuardDuty use machine learning to power their respective anomaly detection solutions. You can use either to implement anomaly detection in your applications.

   - Build models using past data to make better determinations.

4. **Automate Alerts and Responses:**

   - Set up CloudWatch alarms to send notifications or to trigger AWS Lambda functions when they detect anomalies.

   - For automated incident response workflows, use AWS Systems Manager.

5. **Integrate Security Monitoring:**

   - Consolidate security findings from GuardDuty, Macie, and other services by enabling AWS Security Hub.

   - Security alerts and compliance findings need to be reviewed and addressed on a regular basis.

6. **Implement Visualization and Reporting:**

   - In Amazon CloudWatch, create dashboards for real-time monitoring.

   - Using AWS QuickSight, schedule reports for essential stakeholders.

7. **Test and Refine:**

   - The monitoring system must be tested regularly to ensure its effective operation.

   - Revise thresholds, models, and configurations according to shifting demands of the business.

In general, the steps offer a strong basis for putting in place ongoing monitoring and abnormality spotting in an AWS setup, enabling you to find security threats and discern your system's working state before they become major problems.

Challenges and Best Practices

Let's explore the common hurdles in monitoring and detection and the proven strategies to overcome them effectively.

Challenges

The monitoring and threat detection systems of today are faced with several challenges from the real world. Arguably the most evident is the sheer volume of data being generated; organizations have to make sense out of huge quantities of logs, events, and telemetry. All this information can overwhelm even high-end monitoring systems. At the same time, reducing false positives (false alarms on benign activity) is important as well, but much more so is reducing false negatives – missed detection of true threats – since they pose much greater risk. Automation of detection and response reduces labor, but optimal balance between automation and human oversight is the ticket to prevention of mistake or overreaching. Finally, companies should ensure monitoring activities support evolving compliance and regulatory obligations, which makes already daunting tasks even more demanding.

Best Practices

Here are practical steps and proven methods to help you build a strong, scalable, and effective security monitoring strategy.

- **Start Small**: Start by monitoring the most important systems and then steadily extend that coverage to the entire infrastructure.

- **Use Automated Tools**: Use AWS's managed services to decrease the amount of manual human effort you perform and to make your systems scale more easily.

- **Establish Baselines**: Establish typical conduct to enhance the precision of identifying aberrations.

- **Implement Multi-layered Monitoring**: For a complete understanding, combine not only the metrics and logs but also the security findings.

- **Regularly Audit and Optimize**: Examine the monitoring conditions and improve the models using the returned feedback.

Modern enterprises require continuous monitoring and an immediate response to any penetration or cybersecurity attack on their components. AWS offers a much larger suite of services to be part of a single modern framework, which can be stitched together to achieve complete cybersecurity shield against bad actors, which is highly observant and immediately responsive, in which all services see and hear one another and know immediately when something unforeseen happens.

Incident Response Strategies Within a Zero-Trust Architecture in the AWS Ecosystem

Implementing a Zero-Trust architecture in the AWS ecosystem allows companies to significantly increase their security posture, because this model makes it clear that no entity can be trusted by default whether it's inside the network or outside of it. Couple this with readily available incident response strategies, and companies can considerably mitigate risk, substantially minimize damage, and quickly recover when bad things happen. Let's explore how to align incident response strategies with a Zero-Trust architecture for your organization, as well as for any stakeholders or systems operating within the AWS ecosystem.

Understanding Zero-Trust Architecture

As we learned in earlier chapters, the Zero-Trust security model is based on the principle of
"never trust, always verify" – ensuring that access to resources is granted based on identity,
context, and real-time risk assessment rather than a user's location or network boundary.

Incident Response in the AWS Ecosystem

Incident response is a structured process for detecting, analyzing, containing,
eradicating, and recovering from security incidents. When integrated with **Zero-Trust
principles**, which assume nothing inside or outside your network is trusted without
verification, you create a defense-in-depth strategy that's proactive, not reactive.

Zero Trust doesn't replace your incident response; it enhances it. It's about being
more intentional with **access controls**, **visibility**, and **automation** at every step.

Key Stages of a Zero-Trust–Aligned Incident Response:

Here's a clear step-by-step approach to prepare for, detect, respond to, and learn from
security incidents using AWS tools and best practices.

1. **Preparation**

   Form a cross-functional incident response team – security, IT,
   compliance, legal. Use AWS-native tools like IAM, CloudTrail, and
   Security Hub. Draft actionable playbooks and conduct regular
   tabletop exercises.

2. **Detection and Analysis**

   Continuously monitor API activity using **CloudTrail** and detect
   anomalies with **GuardDuty**. Investigate deeper using **Amazon
   Detective** when suspicious behavior is found.

3. **Containment, Eradication, and Recovery**

   Minimize blast radius using IAM controls and fine-grained
   policies. Use **AWS Lambda** to automate containment (e.g., isolate
   EC2). Restore services via **Systems Manager**, and protect backups
   using S3 versioning and replication.

4. **Post-incident Review**

   Use Security Hub findings and CloudTrail logs to analyze root
   causes. Feed these lessons back into your IRP and tooling.
   Incident response is iterative – tune and test regularly.

Practical Example – Suspicious EC2 Activity:

Say you detect **unusual outbound traffic** from an EC2 instance, possibly a sign of data
exfiltration.

Here's how AWS services support Zero-Trust incident response:

- **GuardDuty** detects the anomaly (e.g., contact with a known
  malicious IP).

- **CloudTrail** reveals what API calls were made and by whom.

- **IAM** enforces least privilege, reducing access impact.

- **Amazon Detective** traces the source – was it an insider or
  compromised workload?

- **Lambda** kicks off an auto-remediation, updating the EC2's security
  group to isolate it.

- **AWS Config** shows if the instance was misconfigured before
  the event.

- **Security Hub** correlates these signals and initiates workflow via
  EventBridge.

- **WAF and Shield** (for web apps) help mitigate incoming threats.

- **Amazon Macie** detects if any sensitive data was accessed or leaked.

- **Systems Manager** executes remediation scripts or shuts down the
  instance.

Steps to Implement an Incident Response Plan (IRP) in a Zero-Trust AWS Environment

Follow these practical steps to build a strong, automated, and adaptive incident response
plan that fits perfectly within a Zero-Trust AWS setup.

1. **Build an Incident Response Plan (IRP)**

    - Define team roles and escalation paths.

    - Write clear playbooks for common threats.

    - Align everything with Zero Trust and AWS security standards.

2. **Deploy Monitoring and Alerting**

    - Use CloudTrail + GuardDuty for logging and detection.

    - Create CloudWatch alarms for anomalous behavior.

3. **Enforce Access Controls**

    - Apply MFA everywhere.

    - Use IAM roles and policies for least privilege.

    - Regularly audit access with Access Analyzer.

4. **Automate Your Response**

    - Use Lambda and EventBridge for automatic action.

    - Kick off remediation with Systems Manager.

    - Aggregate findings using Security Hub.

5. **Segment and Protect Resources**

    - Enforce network boundaries with VPC segmentation.

    - Use WAF for web filtering and Shield for DDoS protection.

6. **Run Simulations and Train Regularly**

    - Perform drills with real-world AWS scenarios.

    - Train staff in Zero-Trust operations and tooling.

7. **Learn and Adapt**

    - Use Amazon Detective for post-incident forensics.

    - Update your IRP with every incident or close call.

    - Use insights to tighten controls and improve detection.

Challenges and Best Practices

Let's explore the common hurdles you might face and the best strategies to overcome them effectively.

Challenges

Address real-world obstacles when securing complex and evolving cloud environments:

- Incorporating Zero-Trust principles into older, established systems

- Dealing with the intricacy of several AWS accounts and regions

- Responding to high-level advanced threats in real time

Best Practices

Here are simple, effective steps to strengthen your security posture:

Adopt a Multi-layered Approach:

- Enforce controls at identity, network, and application layers to offer defense in depth.

- Every layer acts as a defense mechanism, reducing risk and exposure even if one other layer is breached.

- **Example:**

  1. **Identity**: Enforce least privilege, MFA, and continuous authentication.

  2. **Network**: Enforce VPC segmentation, private endpoints, and firewalls.

  3. **Application**: Enforce encryption, tokenization, input validation, and WAFs.

- **Leverage Automation:**

  - Employ Amazon Web Services (AWS) to automate the detection and response workflows.

Regularly Audit and Optimize:

- Examine IAM policies, security groups, and configurations to check for conformity with Zero-Trust principles.

Foster a Culture of Security:

- Educate workers on how to identify and react to possible dangers.

Leveraging incident response in the Zero-Trust architecture applied to the AWS ecosystem is an opportunity for organizations to improve their overall security posture, allowing them to effectively safeguard not just their resources but also their identities and, with a well-thought-out and well-practiced strategy, respond to a multitude of potential threats in an efficient and effective manner, thus reducing overall impact and downtime.

AWS's extensive array of security services allows companies to construct robust systems that maintain Zero-Trust principles, allowing your organization to bolster its security standing and adeptly steer through the intricacies of today's world of threats if you plan, automate, and keep on improving (remember what it's always about: respond, mitigate, recover, and iterate your IRP).

Advanced AWS Incident Response: Automation, Forensics, and Playbooks

Successful response to cloud security incidents requires quick detection, response, and forensic investigation. The goal is to reduce harm such as downtime for services, data loss, damaged reputation, or unexpected costs. AWS provides a suite of tools and services that enable organizations to build a structured and strong incident response capability, tightly coupled with Zero-Trust principles.

The incident response process is examined in this section in three primary areas:

1. AWS security incident response playbooks

2. Incident response automation

3. AWS forensics and evidence collection

1. AWS Security Incident Response Playbooks

Playbooks are predefined workflows that outline how to handle various security incidents. AWS helps you build these playbooks using automation, monitoring, and logging tools.

Key Playbook Components:

Here's a clear, step-by-step approach to prepare for, detect, contain, and recover from security incidents effectively.

- **Preparation**

    - Define roles and responsibilities for your response team (security, ops, compliance, legal).

    - Identify key AWS resources and classify likely incidents (e.g., data breaches, IAM misconfigurations).

    - Use **AWS Systems Manager documents (SSM documents)** – scripts or runbooks stored in Systems Manager to automate tasks like isolating an instance or collecting logs.

- **Detection and Analysis**

    - Use **CloudTrail** for API activity monitoring and **GuardDuty** for threat detection based on machine learning.

    - **AWS Config** tracks resource configurations and alerts you when they deviate from compliance baselines.

- **Containment**

    - Isolate impacted resources with VPC security groups.

    - Revoke permissions or rotate credentials for affected users/roles.

    - Block further attack traffic using **AWS WAF**.

- **Eradication and Recovery**

    - Remove malicious entities and restore services using **Amazon S3 backups** or **AWS Backup**.

    - Scan your environment with **Amazon Inspector** to identify and patch vulnerabilities.

181

- **Post-incident Review**

  - Use **Amazon Detective** to analyze root cause and user behavior.

  - Update your playbooks and training based on lessons learned.

2. Incident Response Automation

Automation minimizes human error, speeds up response, and ensures consistency.

Key AWS Services:
Explore the essential AWS tools that help you automatically detect and respond to
security events effortlessly.

- **AWS Lambda**

  Triggers predefined scripts when threats are detected

  Example: Automatically isolate a compromised EC2 instance by
  modifying its security group.

- **Amazon EventBridge**

  Routes security events to automated workflows

  Clarification: "Protection of routes" refers to routing events like a
  GuardDuty finding to the right remediation service, such as Lambda
  or Systems Manager.

- **AWS Security Hub**

  Centralizes findings from AWS and third-party tools

  Integrates with **AWS Systems Manager** and **AWS Step Functions** to
  automate workflows

  Note: Step Functions let you coordinate multiple AWS services
  into serverless workflows (e.g., isolate an instance, notify Slack, log
  action).

- **AWS Systems Manager Automation**

  Executes operational tasks through playbooks (SSM documents)

  Example: Shut down a suspicious EC2 instance with one click.

- **Amazon CloudWatch**

  Creates alerts and thresholds for real-time anomaly detection

  Example: If an IAM policy is unexpectedly changed, trigger a
  Lambda function to roll it back.

3. AWS Forensics and Evidence Collection

Forensics involves gathering, preserving, and analyzing digital evidence.
Here are stages to follow through:

- **Preparation**

  - Enable logging across services (e.g., CloudTrail, VPC Flow Logs,
    S3 Access Logs).

  - Store forensic artifacts in version-controlled, access-restricted S3 buckets.

- **Isolation and Preservation**

  - Quarantine compromised resources by removing from the
    network or placing in a secure VPC.

  - Create EC2 snapshots to preserve the system state.

- **Collection of Logs and Artifacts**

  - Analyze API activity using CloudTrail and **Amazon Athena**.

  - Run memory/network dumps via **Systems Manager Run Command**.

- **Analysis**

  - Correlate activity with **Amazon Detective**.

  - Use tools like **Amazon SageMaker** for anomaly detection with ML.

- **Chain of Custody**

  - Document every step taken during analysis.

  - Restrict access using IAM roles to preserve evidence integrity.

- **Reporting**

  - Build a detailed incident report.

  - Update response plans and train staff accordingly.

AWS Forensics and Evidence Collection

The field of forensics requires individuals or organizations to collect, preserve, and analyze data pertinent to security incidents to ascertain their breadth and depth and the fundamental reasons for their occurrence. Amazon Web Services (AWS) offers a variety of services along with best practices to carry out effective forensics while preserving all necessary legal and regulatory obligations.

Steps for Conducting Forensics in AWS

Here's a clear, step-by-step approach to gathering and analyzing evidence when investigating security incidents in AWS.

1. **Prepare for Evidence Collection:**

    - Make sure that all services have logging activated (e.g., AWS CloudTrail, VPC Flow Logs, and Amazon S3 Access Logs).

    - Utilize Amazon S3 buckets that have versioning and access controls for the secure storage of forensic information.

2. **Isolate and Preserve:**

    - Remove the compromised instances or IoT devices from the network or place them in a quarantined VPC or quarantine an IoT device in quarantine group to isolate them.

    - For EC2 instances, create snapshots of both the instance and its attached volumes to preserve the state of the affected systems.

3. **Collect Logs and Artifacts:**

    - Use CloudTrail logs to analyze API calls made by users or applications.

    - Utilize Amazon Athena to run detailed analyses on logs stored in S3.

    - Obtain memory dumps and network traffic data from EC2 instances by using tools such as AWS Systems Manager Run Command.

4. **Analyze Evidence:**

   - Using Amazon Detective, correlate logs and visualize the timeline
     of suspicious activities.

   - Utilize machine learning tools such as Amazon SageMaker to
     identify patterns or anomalies within the amassed data.

5. **Maintain Chain of Custody:**

   - Document all steps taken during the probe to maintain the
     integrity and admissibility of evidence.

   - Control access to forensic data by using AWS Identity and Access
     Management (IAM) roles.

6. **Reporting and Documentation:**

   - Put together the results into a comprehensive report that covers the
     breadth of the incident, how long it lasted, and what effect it had.

   - Provide stakeholders with insights and update incident response
     playbooks as needed.

Challenges and Best Practices

Understanding common hurdles and proven strategies helps you build a stronger, more
effective forensic and incident response approach in AWS.

Challenges

Handling security evidence comes with tough hurdles – from keeping data trustworthy
to managing huge volumes and meeting complex legal rules.

- Ensuring that evidence remains untampered and legally admissible
  throughout the collection and analysis stages

- Efficiently handling and processing massive volumes of log and event
  data across multiple systems

- Navigating the complex landscape of legal and regulatory
  requirements that vary across jurisdictions and may affect how
  evidence is collected, stored, and shared

Best Practices

Follow proven steps to ensure thorough logging, consistent forensic readiness, and
effective use of tools for stronger security.

- **Enable Comprehensive Logging:**

  - Use **AWS Organizations** to enforce that logging is enabled across
    all member accounts.

  - For streamlined access and analysis, logs should be in a secure
    Amazon S3 bucket.

- **Standardize Forensic Procedures:**

  - Create standard operating procedures (SOPs) for forensic
    investigations.

  - Instruct AWS forensic tools and workflows to security teams.

- **Leverage AWS Marketplace Solutions:**

  - Investigate external forensic tools available in AWS Marketplace
    to augment functions.

- **Test and Refine Processes:**

  - Carry out frequent exercises to confirm forensic processes and
    guarantee operability.

Within the AWS ecosystem, effective incident response and forensics require robust
planning, automation, and skilled execution. AWS services and best practices can help
an organization reduce the potential impact of security incidents, ensure compliance,
and continuously improve the security posture of an organization. By following outlined
steps, your organization can navigate AWS Cloud securely, no matter your industry
or field.

What You Have Learned

In this chapter, you have learned how to build a solid security position on AWS with
three legs: continuous monitoring, compliance, and incident response in a Zero-Trust
framework.

You began learning how continuous monitoring and anomaly detection give real-time visibility into system activity so you can catch threats early before they spiral out of control. You learned the most critical AWS services such as CloudWatch, GuardDuty, and Lookout for Metrics and how you can design an effective monitoring pipeline using automation.

You discovered next how you could make practices for compliance within policies and those in the industry align. You delved into how security features like AWS Config and Security Hub provide monitoring for configuration drift, automate compliance checking, and reduce audit fatigue with real-time insight and remediation.

Then you focused on incident response in a Zero-Trust architecture. You learned how to build an incident response plan (IRP), enforce strict access controls, and react with velocity using Lambda, EventBridge, Systems Manager, and Amazon Detective. In a hands-on walkthrough, you observed how the services collaborate as a reaction to a breached EC2 instance.

Finally, you explored AWS security incident response playbooks, automation techniques, and cloud forensics. You saw firsthand how evidence is collected, stored, and analyzed natively within the cloud and how to automate processes to reduce time to containment, maintain compliance, and maintain evidence in the event of future analysis or legal review.

Summary

This chapter provided a comprehensive review of how cloud security can be improved by leveraging continuous monitoring, compliance, and incident response methodologies on AWS.

You discovered how to leverage services like CloudTrail, GuardDuty, and Security Hub to allow real-time detection and automated response to threats. We explored how Zero-Trust principles reduce attack surfaces and enforce tight access across your AWS environment. You also discovered forensic analysis and how to collect and maintain evidence following an incident.

Through the chapter, you gained hands-on experience to

- Detect and respond to threats with AWS-native tools.

- Streamline compliance across multi-account environments.

- Create and automate Zero-Trust–consistent response workflows.

- Perform post-incident forensics that drive legal, operational, and security outcomes.

By using these practices, your organization is more resilient and better capable of anticipating, detecting, and responding to today's cloud threats.

CHAPTER 8

Advanced Threat Protection and UEBA: Strategic Network Security on AWS

Organizations in the digital world today face a myriad of cyber threats that are anything but simple. As these cyber adversaries become more sophisticated and many are supported by nation-states, our basic security controls increasingly fall short. **Advanced Threat Protection** (**ATP**) fills this gap. When we talk about ATP, we're not just covering the how-to of Zero Trust (though that's certainly part of it; we have delved into Zero Trust in earlier chapters in detail). **Advanced Threat Protection** is more about the what and why of modern threat detection and prevention. How do organizations keep pace with the seemingly endless evolution of cyber threats? What advanced technologies and strategies do they use? And what allows them to achieve a state where they're not just reacting to what has already happened (and might even be happening right now) but are also operating securely in a future where anything could happen?

A key component of the ATP is the deployment of advanced network security controls, which give organizations much better visibility and control over their network traffic. Unlike traditional firewalls and intrusion detection systems, which can only look at the traffic to and from the network edge, these advanced controls allow you to look deep into the traffic itself. This means that if a threat actor tries to sneak into the network using malware that disguises itself as "legitimate" traffic or tries to communicate outbound using encrypted communications, the network security controls will catch it and stop it. The only way a threat actor has to "win" is if they can manage to get past the

© Syed Rehan 2025
S. Rehan, *Cybersecurity with AWS*, https://doi.org/10.1007/979-8-8688-1554-6_8

network, and the way the network is designed to work, to the host itself, or to "run the gauntlet" of all the ways into a host. There are also ways these network security devices can segment a network to "enclose" parts of it securely.

In this chapter, we will also explore **User and Entity Behavior Analytics (UEBA)**, a powerful tool for detecting malicious insiders and other unusual activities. While **Zero Trust** focuses on strong identity governance – ensuring that only verified, authorized users can access systems – **UEBA** adds an additional intelligence layer by monitoring behavior patterns in real time. It uses machine learning and artificial intelligence to establish a baseline of "normal" behavior for users and systems and then flags deviations that could indicate threats. This enables organizations to spot and act on threats quickly, even when they originate internally.

Where Does UEBA Fit?

UEBA is often part of a broader **Advanced Threat Protection (ATP)** strategy but can also operate independently. Think of ATP as the overall umbrella of proactive security techniques to detect, prevent, and respond to advanced attacks. UEBA, in this case, is one of the critical engines inside ATP, helping spot anomalies that traditional signature-based defenses might miss.

Even with strong governance controls and a well-architected Zero-Trust system, threats can emerge unexpectedly. UEBA ensures that if something unusual happens, the system notices and reacts before serious damage can occur.

In a world where everything is connected, the new security paradigms that require that we must shell out the same old workhorses like firewalls, intrusion detection systems (IDSs), and other network controls simply aren't enough. Calls for employing "Zero Trust" are now louder than ever, and with good reason. Privileged accounts and access are the cybercriminals' best friends, and they are compromised more often than we like to think. And when we do think about it, it's often these accounts that we recognize as the "way in." Once in, the intruder can go in any direction they please. Go further, and it's not just account-level security or app-layer security that gets you to where you need to go with Zero Trust. It's these elements in combination, working together, that must get us to a place where we can have some confidence that we're secure and resilient.

Advanced Threat Protection: Focus on Network Security Controls

Advanced Threat Protection (ATP) is a critical component of modern cybersecurity strategies, designed to safeguard your organization's data, applications, and infrastructure from sophisticated cyber-attacks.

Although the previous chapters covered the Zero-Trust (ZT) framework, with its emphasis on strict access controls and verification of every user and device, we now need to extend our protection by focusing on Advanced Threat Protection (ATP). While Zero Trust minimizes risk by reducing the attack surface and assuming breach by default, ATP complements it by providing the detection, prevention, and response capabilities needed to deal with sophisticated threats that manage to bypass even strong Zero-Trust defenses. In essence, ATP builds an active security layer on top of ZT, continuously monitoring, identifying, and mitigating advanced, persistent threats that might otherwise remain undetected. This layered approach ensures that organizations are not only hard to breach but also quick to detect and respond when breaches occur, strengthening the overall resilience of the system.

In cloud environments such as AWS, ATP leans heavily on security controls to monitor, analyze, and block nefarious activity across the network.

This chapter will look at a sequential, straightforward guide to putting ATP into action within AWS, aimed at groups that are still learning about data strategy and cloud security.

Key AWS Network Security Controls for ATP

A set of native tools and services helps enforce sophisticated network security. Here are the main components to prioritize:

- **Amazon Virtual Private Cloud (VPC)**
- **Security groups and network access control lists (NACLs)**
- **AWS Network Firewall**
- **AWS GuardDuty**
- **AWS WAF (Web Application Firewall)**
- **VPC Flow Logs**

Amazon Virtual Private Cloud

- **Function**: Segregates your AWS resources into a logically defined network.

- **ATP Implementation**:

  - **Subnet Segmentation**: Split your VPC into public and private subnets. Place essential resources (like databases) in private subnets.

- **Route Tables**: Control traffic flow between subnets to limit lateral movement.

- **Example**: Use web servers in a public subnet and databases in a private subnet, with them all strictly routed between the aforementioned subnet types.

Security Groups and Network Access Control Lists (NACLs)

When it comes to controlling who can talk to your AWS resources, security groups and NACLs form the first line of defense in your network perimeter.

- **Security Groups**: Are virtual firewalls per EC2 instance that manage incoming and outgoing traffic. They are essential since they let you highly manage which ports and protocols to expose, reducing the attack surface. Everything is defaulted to being denied, and you only permit traffic explicitly that's required for application functionality. This prevents there from being open ports or interfaces that are unnecessary for the particular application flow. Additionally, you can define not only what traffic is permitted (e.g., TCP on port 443), but also who can communicate (e.g., only traffic from particular IP addresses or other security groups). Security groups are stateful, hence implicitly permitting return traffic when an inbound rule is allowed and hence simpler to manage flows without sacrificing security.

- **Best Practice**: Apply the principle of least privilege when setting up security groups, i.e., make web servers permit incoming HTTPS connections (TCP port 443) from specific, trusted hosts instead of opening all ports to the internet.

- **Network Access Control Lists (NACLs)**: Offer another layer of network-level protection at the subnet level. NACLs are stateless – unlike security groups – so inbound and outbound rules need to be specified separately, enabling more detailed control of all traffic entering and exiting a subnet. NACLs are helpful when you need to place wider restrictions on large numbers of resources, e.g., blocking whole IP ranges before the traffic even reaches the individual servers.

- **ATP Use Case**: NACLs are extremely useful in the Advanced Threat Protection (ATP) context to block known bad IP addresses or networks at the subnet perimeter. This keeps malicious traffic from even reaching your critical workloads, minimizing the threat of lateral movement in your environment.

AWS Network Firewall

- **Function**: It is a managed firewall service for VPCs, providing intrusion detection/prevention.

- **ATP Features**:

  - **Rules Defined by the User**: Prevent known threats (like those associated with ransomware) from being able to do harm.

- **Suricata Rules**: Anomaly detection uses open source Suricata rules.

- **What Is a Suricate Rule**: Rules for Suricata are taken from the open source community and are used by AWS Network Firewall to spot and stop odd network traffic (malicious). They aren't what you'd normally think of as firewall rules. Instead, they're more like guidelines. Suricata examines real-time data to find incriminating patterns. You can imagine it sort of like a three-dimensional model of the network traffic that the firewall is responsible for watching over. When Suricata sees something in that model that's suspicious, it can mark it as such and then issue a warning, which you can use to carry out proactive action.

- **What Is a Three-Dimensional Model**: The "three-dimensional model" refers to how Suricata analyzes network traffic from three key perspectives at the same time:

  - **Source and Destination**: Who is sending the traffic and who is receiving it (IP addresses, ports, protocols)

  - **Content and Payload**: What the packet contains (application data, file types, embedded commands)

  - **Behavior Over Time**: How the traffic behaves across sessions (e.g., repeated login attempts, data exfiltration patterns, or abnormal communication sequences)

- By simultaneously considering these three dimensions – identity, content, and behavior – Suricata can detect sophisticated and stealthy attacks that traditional firewalls may overlook, enabling more effective threat prevention.

- **Example**: Prevent traffic from the geographical areas where your organization has no business.

AWS GuardDuty

- **Function**: An AI-driven threat detection service that examines VPC Flow Logs and DNS logs, analyzes Amazon S3 data events, and monitors Amazon Aurora login events and runtime activity for Amazon EKS, Amazon EC2, and Amazon ECS, including serverless container workloads on AWS Fargate and CloudTrail events.

- **ATP Implementation**:

  - Activate GuardDuty to find atypical conduct (e.g., mining for cryptocurrency, making unauthorized API calls).

  - Consolidate discoveries with AWS Security Hub for centralized alerts.

AWS WAF (Web Application Firewall)

- **What It Accomplishes**: Shields web applications from widespread attacks (e.g., SQL injection and cross-site scripting)

- **Use Case for ATP**:

  - Make rules to stop malicious payloads from getting through in HTTP/HTTPS traffic

VPC Flow Logs

- **Method of Operation**: Captures metadata concerning network traffic (source/destination IP, ports, protocols).

- **ATP Implementation**:

  - Examine flow logs using either Amazon Athena or third-party SIEM (Security Information and Event Management) tools (e.g., Splunk), to find the following types of traffic patterns that could indicate a **security problem**:

    - Large amounts of data being sent to an unusual number of destinations

    - Unusual amounts of requests being sent to an unusual number of destinations

    - Repeated communication attempts over a short period of time

Step-by-Step Implementation Plan

Let's walk through a practical roadmap to build and secure your AWS network from the ground up.

Phase 1: Assess Current Network Architecture

1. Identify current AWS resources (EC2, S3, RDS, etc.) and their network configurations.

2. Identify assets that are at high risk (for instance, customer data kept in S3 or databases or essential APIs).

Phase 2: Design a Secure Network Architecture

1. One or more VPCs should be created depending on organizational needs – single VPCs are often sufficient for smaller environments, while multiple VPCs (organized by business unit, environment, or security requirements) provide better isolation and scalability.

2. Use security groups and NACLs to restrict traffic and enforce the principle of least privilege.

3. Implement AWS Network Firewall with tailored rules to "**counteract**" known threats, helping to prevent unauthorized access and malicious activities within the network.

Phase 3: Enable Monitoring and Threat Detection

1. Activate VPC Flow Logs and direct them to Amazon S3 for centralized storage and deeper analysis.

2. Enable AWS GuardDuty and configure notifications to be sent through AWS Security Hub for streamlined incident visibility.

3. If you have web applications, establish AWS WAF rules to protect against common web exploits. For non-web applications, consider additional protections like AWS Shield for DDoS mitigation or implementing tighter network-level controls through security groups and NACLs.

Phase 4: Automate Response

1. Leverage AWS Lambda to set up automated responses to findings from GuardDuty (e.g., isolate compromised instances).

2. Work with AWS Systems Manager to patch vulnerabilities seamlessly and automatically.

Best Practices for Sustaining ATP in an AWS Environment

Keep your AWS environment resilient and secure by following these practical, layered strategies tailored for long-term protection.

*   **Secure Network Communications**: Use AWS Certificate Manager (ACM) for SSL/TLS encryption.

- **Auditing on a Monthly Basis**: Perform routine reviews every month of security groups and NACLs.

  - While "monthly" is a general best practice for many organizations, **more critical systems** may require **weekly** or even **continuous auditing** depending on the risk profile.

- **Least-Privilege Access**: Use AWS IAM to limit roles and permissions for IAM users.

- **Layered Security**: Mix network defenses with application-layer security (e.g., AWS Shield for DDoS protection).

Compliance, Cost, Resources, and Audits

Keeping cloud environments secure also means staying compliant, managing costs smartly, and using the right tools to audit and optimize your security posture.

- **Compliance**: Use AWS Artifact and AWS Config to align with standards such as GDPR, HIPAA, or PCI DSS.

- **Cost Optimization**:

  - Utilize AWS Cost Explorer to keep an eye on the expenses associated with Network Firewall, GuardDuty, and WAF.

  - Remove unnecessary resources (like orphaned security groups).

- **Resources**:

  - **AWS Trusted Advisor**: Leverage this tool for real-time security recommendations.

- **Regular Audit Template (Example)**:

  Use the following example template to ensure consistent reviews of your AWS network security controls. Customize based on your organization's needs (Table 8-1).

Table 8-1. *Regular AWS Network Security Audit Checklist*

Check	Status (Pass/Fail/ Review)	Findings	Action Items
VPC Configuration			
- Subnets are segmented (public/private).			
- Route tables restrict unnecessary traffic between subnets.			
Example: Private subnets for databases have no direct internet access.			
Security Groups			
- No security groups allow inbound traffic from 0.0.0.0/0 unless explicitly required.			
- Outbound traffic is restricted to necessary ports/ protocols.			
Example: Web servers only allow HTTP/HTTPS inbound.			
NACLs			
- NACLs block known malicious IP addresses.			
- Rules are ordered correctly (e.g., deny rules precede allow rules).			
AWS Network Firewall			
- Custom Suricata rules are updated with latest threat signatures.			
- Firewall logs are enabled and analyzed.			
GuardDuty and WAF			
- GuardDuty findings are reviewed regularly.			
- AWS WAF rules block SQL injection and cross-site scripting attempts.			

(continued)

Table 8-1. (*continued*)

Check	Status (Pass/Fail/ Review)	Findings	Action Items
IAM and Access			
- IAM policies follow least-privilege principles.			
- Unused IAM roles/keys are deactivated.			
VPC Flow Logs			
- Flow logs are enabled for all critical subnets.			
- Logs are analyzed for unusual traffic patterns (e.g., spikes in rejected connections).			

Audit Frequency:

Regular audits help ensure your cloud security posture stays strong and aligned with both internal standards and regulatory requirements.

- **Monthly:** Perform baseline testing of security groups, network ACLs (NACLs), and IAM configurations to detect and correct any deviations.

- **Quarterly:** Analyze firewall rules in depth, GuardDuty trends, and network configurations for compliance with organizational and regulatory requirements.

- **Accountability:** The cloud security team and IT operations are responsible for carrying out audits. Store audit results in a shared version-controlled repository such as an AWS S3 bucket or third-party product, so that it is transparent, traceable, and readily available to stakeholders.

To implement ATP in AWS, you must start with a strategic focus and collaborate closely with business leaders. The challenge of network segmentation becomes paramount: without effective and enforced access controls, the internal attack surface remains highly exposed. This risk is further heightened if the AWS deployment lacks real-time monitoring. To ensure that ATP implementation is actionable and not just theoretical, a set of recommendations we provided will serve as a solid starting point.

The key is to work alongside business leaders and secure approval for your ATP plan from your organization's AWS cloud stakeholders, those responsible for upholding the shared responsibility model.

ATP Plan Approval Authorizer (Typical):

These are the key stakeholders typically involved in reviewing and approving the ATP security plan before implementation.

- Security Team Leader

- Architect of Cloud

- Director of Information Technology

- Head of Cybersecurity for Cloud

- CISO (Chief Information Security Officer)

- IT Director

- VP of Security (or business leader)

UEBA and Insider Threats

User and Entity Behavior Analytics (UEBA) is a security practice that uses artificial intelligence (AI), specifically its subset machine learning (ML), to monitor and analyze the behavior of entities (e.g., servers, applications) and users (e.g., employees) within your environment. UEBA detects unusual or suspicious activities that could indicate insider threats, such as

- **Malicious Insiders:** Malicious insiders deliberately taking information

- **Compromised Accounts:** Hackers taking over compromised credentials

- **Accidental Misuse:** Inadvertent disclosures of sensitive information

Why UEBA in AWS?

Organizations moving to cloud need to move beyond service-based perimeter-only security. UEBA detects threats in your environment in AWS through behavior patterns, not through rules.

Key AWS Services for UEBA

AWS offers native services for implementing UEBA. The key services are

AWS GuardDuty

- **Function**: A threat detection service that employs machine learning to perform an analysis of AWS logs (such as CloudTrail, VPC Flow Logs, and DNS logs).

- **Use Case for UEBA**: Observes unusual API call behavior, unauthorized access attempts, or active user behavior that is unusual (e.g., logging in from unexpected locations and/or logging in to non-validated and not regular user login destination in tandem).

AWS CloudTrail

- **Function**: Captures every API interaction within your AWS account (e.g., the individuals behind the creation and deletion of resources).

- **Use Case for UEBA**: Monitor deviations in normal user behavior, i.e., actions taken by users that are unexpected or uncharacteristic like when a developer accesses finance-related data.

Amazon Detective

- **Function**: To analyze automatically CloudTrail, GuardDuty, and VPC Flow Logs and visualize them to show user/entity behavior.

- **Use Case for UEBA**: Incidents can be investigated by constructing user activity timelines (e.g., mapping a compromised account's actions).

Amazon Macie

- **Function**: Employs machine learning to identify and classify private information (e.g., PII, credit card numbers) located within Amazon S3.

- **Use Case for UEBA**: Notifications when anything but the ordinary occurs with the access to or sharing of sensitive data.

AWS IAM (Identity and Access Management)

- **Function**: Controls who can use AWS resources and how they can use them.

- **Use Case for UEBA**: Insiders are less likely to abuse their privilege when that privilege is limited. Hence, UEBA can enforce least-privilege access as an insider risk control.

Step-by-Step Implementation Plan

Break down the UEBA (User and Entity Behavior Analytics) setup into clear, actionable phases for better threat detection and response.

Phase 1: Enable Logging and Visibility

1. Turn on AWS CloudTrail.

    - Enable logging for all AWS regions.

    - Store logs in an S3 bucket with encryption enabled.

2. Enable VPC Flow Logs.

    - Monitor network traffic for anomalies (e.g., unexpected data transfers).

3. Activate AWS GuardDuty.

    - Automatically analyze logs for threats.

Phase 2: Configure UEBA Tools

1. Set up GuardDuty findings.

    - Create alerts in Amazon CloudWatch or AWS Security Hub for critical findings (e.g., *UnauthorizedAccess:IAMUser*).

2. Use Amazon Detective.

    - Link GuardDuty findings to Detective to visualize user behavior (e.g., map a user's API calls over time).

3. Deploy Amazon Macie.

   - Scan S3 buckets for sensitive data and set alerts for unusual access patterns.

Phase 3: Define Baseline Behavior

1. Analyze historical data.

   - Use GuardDuty and Detective to establish "normal" behavior for users/roles (e.g., typical login times, accessed resources).

2. Create custom GuardDuty rules.

   - Flag deviations (e.g., a user accessing AWS regions they've never used).

Phase 4: Automate Responses

1. Use AWS Lambda for remediation.

   - Automatically revoke access or quarantine resources if GuardDuty detects high-risk activity (e.g., disable an IAM user with suspicious logins).

2. Integrate with AWS Systems Manager.

   - Patch vulnerabilities triggered by UEBA findings (e.g., update instances with exposed ports).

Phase 5: Train Teams and Monitor (Recurring Task)

1. Educate employees.

   - Train staff on recognizing phishing attempts and secure data handling.

2. Regularly review findings (depending on organization size, weekly/monthly).

   - Hold meetings to analyze GuardDuty/Detective reports and refine baselines.

Best Practices for UEBA in AWS

Follow these practical steps to strengthen your User and Entity Behavior Analytics (UEBA) setup and reduce security risks in your AWS environment.

- **Least-Privilege Access**: Limit IAM permissions with policies (e.g., "Effect": "Deny" for sensitive actions).

- **MFA Deployment**: Require MFA for all IAM users.

- **Periodic Audits**: Employ the following template to examine UEBA configuration settings.

- **Ensure Encryption of Sensitive Data**: AWS KMS (Key Management Service) can safeguard your data at rest.

- **Ensure Encrypted Data Transfer**: When using your custom service end points, use AWS KMS to encrypt data transfer.

- **Unused Accounts**: A critical security risk—60% of the security incidents I've investigated with customers had a recurring vulnerability: stale user accounts and roles and unmanaged credentials. These accounts created but never used present a major security problem. Because the accounts are under-managed, they're vulnerable to exploitation.

To counter this, companies must implement a stringent policy for identifying and handling user accounts that are no longer needed. Inactive accounts should be disabled or deleted after a defined period of dormancy, which should be established by the security lead based on user activity patterns.

For production accounts, a good practice is to keep them deactivated by default and only enable them when a user attempts to log in. At that moment, an additional verification step such as multi-factor authentication (MFA), identity confirmation via an admin approval workflow, or an automated identity validation system should be required before granting access. This approach can be implemented using AWS IAM access policies, AWS Single Sign-On with conditional access controls, or integration with identity providers (IdPs) that support just-in-time (JIT) provisioning and reactivation mechanisms. By enforcing this flow, organizations reduce the number of dormant accounts that could otherwise be exploited by threat actors, ensuring accounts are only usable when actively validated and needed.

UEBA Audit Template

Use the following example template to ensure consistent reviews of your UEBA within the environment. Customize based on your organization's needs (Table 8-2).

Table 8-2. *Example UEBA Audit Template*

Check	Status (Pass/Fail)	Action Items
GuardDuty enabled		
CloudTrail logging active		
IAM policies follow least privilege		
Macie scans sensitive S3 buckets		
Detective investigations conducted monthly		
MFA enforced for all users		
Unused accounts count		
Disabled stale accounts (audit tracking)		

Example Use Case: Detecting a Compromised Account

Scenario:
An attacker steals an employee's AWS credentials.

UEBA Detection:
Track and respond to suspicious user behavior in real time using AWS security tools working together.

- GuardDuty flags *UnauthorizedAccess:IAMUser* from an unusual IP address.

- Amazon Detective maps the attacker's activity (e.g., launching EC2 instances for crypto-mining).

- Lambda triggers an automated proactive response: revoke the user's access immediately, terminate all resources, and notify the security team.

Compliance and UEBA

UEBA supports regulatory compliance by continuously monitoring user access patterns and helping generate audit-ready reports.

Adherence:
UEBA is aligned with GDPR, HIPAA, and PCI DSS, as it is monitoring the access to data. For compliance reports, use AWS Artifact.

What You Have Learned

In this chapter, we explored the critical role of Advanced Threat Protection (ATP) and how network security controls strengthen overall cybersecurity within AWS environments. We examined the core AWS services that underpin ATP, outlined a structured step-by-step plan for its implementation, and provided best practices to sustain these controls over time. A sample audit template was also introduced to help standardize security assessments.

Recognizing that robust perimeter defenses alone are insufficient, we shifted focus to User and Entity Behavior Analytics (UEBA) to address the growing risk of *insider threats*. We explored how UEBA, supported by AWS services like GuardDuty, CloudTrail, and Detective, enables proactive threat detection based on behavioral patterns rather than static rules. Finally, we detailed a comprehensive UEBA implementation strategy, shared best practices, and provided an audit template to ensure continuous monitoring and improvement.

Summary

User and Entity Behavior Analytics (UEBA) in AWS transforms how organizations defend against insider threats by shifting security from rigid, rule-based detection to dynamic, behavior-driven insights.

Traditional security tools often rely on predefined signatures or static rules (such as blocking certain IP addresses), but these approaches struggle to catch sophisticated, evolving threats like account compromise or insider misuse. UEBA fills this gap by leveraging machine learning (ML) to learn what *"normal"* behavior looks like for each user and entity in your environment. For example, if a marketing employee suddenly accesses financial databases at 2:00 AM from an unusual location, UEBA flags this activity as suspicious even if no specific rule was technically broken.

By integrating AWS services like GuardDuty, CloudTrail, and Detective, organizations can build an intelligent, layered defense against insider risks. GuardDuty acts as the real-time alarm system, continuously analyzing logs (CloudTrail, VPC Flow Logs, DNS) for unauthorized patterns or anomalies. CloudTrail provides the critical audit trail of every API action, forming the foundation for behavior baselining. Detective serves as the investigator, helping security teams reconstruct timelines and uncover *"this shouldn't be happening"* scenarios when things go wrong.

Crucially, UEBA is **not** a "**set and forget**" solution; it thrives on continuous improvement. This proactive, iterative approach ensures that your organization not only detects emerging threats but also builds a resilient culture of security awareness and operational agility. As your environment evolves, regularly revisit and refine your baselines, automate where possible, and maintain a behavior-first detection mindset. By doing so, you use AWS tools in a way that not only scales with your needs but also stays resilient against the growing reality of ***insider-driven*** threats.

CHAPTER 9

Advanced Security Operations in AWS

When organizations move their most important workloads to the cloud, but still need strong security, having solid security operations in AWS makes even more sense.

Security operations within AWS (AWS SecOps) become advanced by necessity, and there's a better-than-average chance they'll also become more automated, more integrated, and more responsive than most security operations you'll encounter outside AWS.

Why? Because AWS's native security tools offer advanced automation and integration if you're going to leverage their full potential.

You might call this chapter an instruction manual. It's not exhaustive; it's broad and high-level with many paths and steps to take, and it could easily double as a tour through the AWS security service portfolio.

First, let's look at how to effectively write detection logic and SIEM (Security Information and Event Management) rules using AWS services like CloudTrail, Config, GuardDuty, and Security Hub. When used together, these services enable clear, real-time identification and analysis of suspicious or near-suspicious activities that might pass through an organization's AWS perimeter such as login attempts by humans or bots. With a solid understanding of how each service works individually and how they complement each other, you can craft detection logic and SIEM rules that accurately spot suspicious actions, whether they are isolated incidents or part of a larger pattern.

Next, we explore how to bring Endpoint Detection and Response (EDR) solutions into the fold and look at how AWS Systems Manager and Amazon Inspector help safeguard workloads from endpoint vulnerabilities and configuration challenges.

Critical components of advanced security operations are the capabilities of incident response. We, therefore, cover standard processes of incident response and examine AWS's dedicated services that streamline and enhance your response strategies.

© Syed Rehan 2025
S. Rehan, *Cybersecurity with AWS*, https://doi.org/10.1007/979-8-8688-1554-6_9

Next, we tackle the significant task of sustaining knowledge over AWS services and matching technologies. These include not just the technology of the services themselves, but also the public cloud infrastructure as a whole; the authentication systems that work with it; "vulnerability management" solutions (i.e., those technologies that are not designed to be used in production, but are essential for finding flaws in the systems that are safely deployed); and the network infrastructure (including how to secure virtual private clouds (VPCs) and connected systems) that makes everything work. The security teams benefit from the context that having such a broad base of expertise brings.

Moreover, we elaborate on how to design and automate the detection and alerting pipelines that form the basis for scalable security operations. When using such pipelines, we want to achieve two primary goals:

- Increasing operational efficiency
- Minimizing response times

Let's look at each of those in turn.

This chapter ultimately provides a detailed investigation into the dissection of attacker methodologies and techniques by building on what we learned in our earlier chapters. It is vitally important for anyone interested in building on AWS to understand the tools and tactics that common attackers use. This knowledge allows you to tailor your defensive strategies in ways that are meaningful and effective.

These advanced operational practices, when mastered, will enable security professionals to

1. Anticipate threats.

2. Rapidly mitigate incidents.

3. Safeguard AWS deployments.

Writing Detections and SIEM Rules

This section focuses on creating effective detections and SIEM (Security Information and Event Management) rules using key AWS services that are specifically suited for detection logic and security monitoring.

For writing detections and SIEM rules, the core AWS services are

- **AWS CloudTrail**: Records API activity for auditing and security investigations

- **AWS Config**: Tracks configuration changes and evaluates compliance against defined rules

- **Amazon GuardDuty**: Provides continuous threat detection using machine learning and threat intelligence

- **AWS Security Hub**: Aggregates security findings from AWS services and third-party solutions, providing a centralized view

Each of these services plays a specific role in capturing activity, identifying misconfigurations, detecting threats, and aggregating findings, helping to enable faster and more accurate detection of security incidents.

AWS SIEM Capabilities: Broader View

While the above services are directly used for writing detections, AWS also provides a broader suite of services that together deliver **full SIEM functionality** (data collection, normalization, analysis, and alerting). These include

- **Amazon Security Lake**: Centralizes and normalizes security data from AWS and third-party sources for analytics

- **Amazon GuardDuty**: Threat detection based on ML models and anomaly detection

- **AWS CloudTrail**: API activity tracking for audit and investigation purposes

- **AWS CloudWatch Logs**: Real-time log ingestion, monitoring, and alert generation

- **AWS Security Hub**: Consolidates and prioritizes security alerts from various AWS services and partner tools

- **AWS Config**: Resource configuration tracking and compliance evaluation

AWS native services can also integrate with third-party SIEMs (like Splunk, Sumo Logic, etc.) via AWS Marketplace offerings, allowing organizations to customize and extend their detection and incident response workflows as needed.

Table 9-1 highlights the AWS services essential for writing detections and SIEM rules and, separately, those that contribute to delivering broader SIEM functionality within AWS environments. It helps clarify which services are directly used for creating detection logic and which ones collectively support centralized security monitoring, threat detection, and compliance management.

Table 9-1. *AWS Native and Extended Services for Security Detection and SIEM Integration*

AWS Core Services for Detection	AWS Broader SIEM Ecosystem
AWS CloudTrail	Amazon Security Lake
AWS Config	Amazon GuardDuty
Amazon GuardDuty	AWS CloudTrail
AWS Security Hub	AWS CloudWatch Logs
	AWS Security Hub
	AWS Config

AWS CloudTrail

As we learned in an earlier chapter, AWS CloudTrail is a service that allows you to govern, comply, and audit the operation and risk of your AWS account. CloudTrail records events in your account, including all API calls and related activities made by you and certain AWS services. CloudTrail offers you a choice of three different levels of event logging: logging for read-only events, logging for write-only events, and logging for all events.

Writing Detections:
To create AWS CloudTrail detections, you need to set up specific patterns or conditions within CloudTrail logs that tell you when a security incident has happened or is in progress.

For example, you might set up detections for unauthorized access attempts or for anomalous behavior that could indicate an attack.

Steps:

Follow these straightforward steps to set up effective monitoring and detection in your AWS environment.

1. **Enable Logging for CloudTrail**: Ensure that CloudTrail is both activated and logging and storing those logs in an S3 bucket.

2. **Specify Detection Standards**: Decide which actions or API calls you deem suspicious or in need of surveillance.

   a. For instance, monitoring actions like *"DeleteBucket"* in S3 or *"CreateUser"* in IAM

3. **Configure EventBridge Rules**: Employ Amazon EventBridge to create patterns that correspond to certain API calls or events. **Pattern Example**:

```
{
  "source": ["aws.iam"],
  "detail-type": ["AWS API Call via CloudTrail"],
  "detail": {
    "eventName": ["CreateUser", "DeleteUser", "AttachUserPolicy"]
  }
}
```

4. **Integrate with SIEM Solutions**: Centralize log storage and processing with a full-featured SIEM. Correlate the rich set of logs and events generated by the program with the rest of the organization's suspicious activities.

Best Practices for CloudTrail Monitoring:

Keep your cloud activity transparent and secure by following these essential CloudTrail monitoring tips.

- Make certain that CloudTrail is active in every single region.

- Keep a watchful eye on the activities of the root account.

- Send notifications when there are alterations to policies (for instance, when there are changes to IAM roles).

- Pay attention to any changes made to the configurations for logging and monitoring.

AWS Config

AWS Config gives a fine-grained and precise view of the configuration of AWS resources in your account. It continuously watches over and notes the configurations of resources that you set up.

Writing Detections:

You can use AWS Config to find out whether configuration drift has occurred (i.e., whether it has configured anything in the environment that it doesn't know about), whether any security devices have been misconfigured (e.g., if a security group in front of an EC2 instance has been set up to allow any and all traffic through), or whether the organization as a whole is complying with the policies it has set.

Steps:

Here's a clear, step-by-step process to set up and monitor your AWS Config rules for continuous compliance.

1. **Activate AWS Config**: Make sure AWS Config is active and registering adjustments in the setups of relevant resources.

2. **Define Custom Rules**: Create custom Config rules that utilize AWS Lambda functions or AWS Config rules.

   a.   **Example Rule**: Identify unencrypted S3 buckets.

3. **Assess Adherence**: Consistently assess assets against specified regulations.

4. **Configure Notifications**: Use EventBridge or SNS to inform when resources no longer conform to requirements.

Best Practices:

Follow these practical steps to maintain strong, up-to-date security and automate routine tasks effortlessly.

- Turn on AWS Config in every region.

- Continuously reassess rules and tune them to keep up with changing security conditions.

- Use Systems Manager Automation or Lambda functions to automate remediation.

Amazon GuardDuty

In earlier chapters we discussed Amazon GuardDuty, which is a service that continuously monitors your AWS environment for malicious or unauthorized behavior, helping to protect accounts, workloads, and data. It serves as a strong first line of defense by analyzing three primary data sources: VPC Flow Logs to detect suspicious network traffic, AWS CloudTrail events to identify unauthorized API activity, and DNS logs to uncover attempts to connect to known malicious domains.

Writing Detections:
GuardDuty offers out-of-the-box managed threat detection rules. However, a strong security posture requires that you customize alerts and integrate them with SIEM systems.

Steps:
Follow these practical steps to set up and optimize GuardDuty for effective threat detection and response across your AWS environment.

1. Activate GuardDuty across every AWS account and in all regions.

2. **Set Up Trusted IP Lists and Threat Intelligence Lists**: Establish lists to permit or prohibit recognized IP addresses.

3. **Findings of the Review**: Track GuardDuty findings in the console or with CloudWatch Events.

4. **Custom Rule Creation (via SIEM)**: Ingest GuardDuty findings into a SIEM solution to apply additional rules and correlations.

   a. **Example**: If GuardDuty reports *"Recon:EC2/ PortProbeUnprotectedPort"*, this is indicating a port scanning attempt. Then you should raise a high-priority alert in your SIEM and optionally trigger automatic isolation of the targeted EC2 instance.

Best Practices:
Keep your security strong by regularly reviewing findings, automating fixes for serious issues, and continuously updating your threat intelligence.

- Investigate and review findings regularly and fine-tune rules based on your environment and account usage.

- High-severity findings should have automated remediation that takes place right away.

215

- Keep updating your threat intelligence lists continuously. Security is a continuous iterative cycle.

AWS Security Hub

AWS Security Hub is a thorough source from which to get a look at the security alerts and overall security posture of your AWS accounts. If you have multiple AWS accounts, they can all be pulled into Security Hub, and then you can get this one pane of glass from which to see your security posture and alerts across all those accounts.

Writing Detections:

Aggregated findings from a number of AWS services plus some third-party tools are collected by Security Hub. The AWS services currently supplying findings to Security Hub include Amazon GuardDuty, Amazon Inspector, Amazon Macie, AWS Firewall Manager, AWS IAM Access analyzer, Amazon Route 53 Resolver DNS Firewall, AWS Systems Manager Patch Manager, AWS Config, and AWS IoT Device Defender. The straightforward way to get started with Security Hub is to enable it in your AWS account and have it aggregate findings from the services mentioned above. If you want to go beyond what those exciting services are doing and get a really fine-grained look at your overall security posture, you can then write custom rules for Security Hub. Writing a custom rule really amounts to creating a standard or control to use in evaluating the services' findings against your overall, desired security baseline.

Steps:

Here's a clear, step-by-step guide to set up and automate your security monitoring and response with AWS services.

1. **Enable Security Hub**: Enable Security Hub for every account and region.

2. **Define Custom Insights**: Construct insights to **filter and prioritize** findings based on specific parameters.

   a. **Example**: From GuardDuty, filter out the findings that are of "High" severity.

3. **Integrate with AWS Config (and Other Services)**: While AWS Config is often used to send compliance data to Security Hub, you can also integrate findings from multiple services like GuardDuty, Inspector, Macie, and others for a more complete security posture.

4. **Automate Remediation**: Use AWS Lambda or Step Functions to automatically fix certain findings.

Best Practices:

Here are simple habits to stay ahead of security issues and keep your environment running smoothly.

- Keep an eye on discoveries and review them constantly.

- Make insights fit your organization.

- Automate responses to findings that are critical. Always do this where possible.

Integrating Endpoint Detection and Response (EDR)

AWS offers a set of native services that fulfil traditional Endpoint Detection and Response (EDR) functions, enabling organizations to monitor, detect, and respond to threats across AWS workloads such as EC2, containers, and serverless functions.

Key AWS Services Supporting EDR Functions:

These AWS tools work together to help detect, investigate, and respond to security threats effectively.

- **Amazon GuardDuty**: Threat detection based on VPC Flow Logs, CloudTrail, and DNS logs

- **AWS Systems Manager**: Secure endpoint access, patch management, compliance monitoring, and automated remediation

- **Amazon Inspector**: Vulnerability management and continuous scanning

- **AWS Security Hub**: Centralized aggregation of findings and security posture insights

These services together form a native EDR-like ecosystem within AWS, providing real-time endpoint monitoring, behavioral anomaly detection, and automated incident response workflows without relying on third-party EDR solutions.

Real-Time Monitoring:

AWS services like GuardDuty and Inspector offer visibility into endpoint activities (e.g., network connections, process execution) with continuous monitoring for malicious behavior.

Behavioral Analysis:

GuardDuty leverages machine learning to detect unusual API activities, compromised instances, and lateral movement attempts.

Automated Response:

Automated workflows using AWS Lambda and Systems Manager Runbooks can isolate compromised endpoints, revoke IAM permissions, or quarantine suspicious containers.

AWS Services for Endpoint Security (EDR)

AWS provides specialized services that focus on protecting specific compute resources like EC2, containers (ECS, EKS, Fargate) and serverless functions (Lambda). These services deliver endpoint security capabilities needed for modern EDR strategies.

AWS Systems Manager

A powerful tool that helps you manage, secure, and respond to your endpoints all from one place.

Role in EDR: Systems Manager acts as the **control plane** for endpoint management:

- **Visibility**: Inventory management and operational metadata collection.

- **Patching**: Automates vulnerability remediation for EC2 and on-prem resources.

- **Secure Access**: Session Manager eliminates the need for SSH keys, using IAM for auditable instance access.

- **Incident Response**: Automation documents enable predefined workflows for threat response.

Best Practices:

Here are simple steps to keep your systems secure, up to date, and well-monitored.

- Keep patches up to date with Patch Manager.

- Restrict access using Session Manager with least-privilege IAM roles.

- Monitor compliance status regularly using Systems Manager Compliance.

Amazon Inspector

Automate vulnerability scanning to keep your workloads secure and up to date.

Role in EDR:

Inspector provides automated vulnerability scanning:

- **Scan Targets**: EC2 instances, container images in Amazon ECR, and Lambda functions

- **Continuous Assessment**: Rescans workloads upon updates or CVE disclosures

- **Prioritize Findings**: Ranks vulnerabilities based on exploitability and network exposure

Best Practices:

Maximize security by integrating tools and automating responses to critical findings.

- Integrate Inspector with Security Hub for centralized visibility.

- Automatically trigger patching workflows for high-severity vulnerabilities.

Use Case Example:

See how automated scans and remediation protect your deployments in real time.

- Scan ECR container images before deployment and block unapproved deployments automatically.

- Detect vulnerable EC2 instances exposed via misconfigured security groups and remediate them with Systems Manager Automation.

Combining AWS Services for EDR Capabilities

Bring together AWS tools to build a strong Endpoint Detection and Response system.

Preventive Measures:

Here are steps to stop threats before they cause harm.

- Use Inspector to identify vulnerabilities early.

- Apply Patch Manager to automatically remediate severe CVEs.

Detective Controls:

Here are ways to spot suspicious activity quickly and clearly.

- Forward Systems Manager logs to CloudWatch for baseline monitoring.

- Integrate third-party findings into Security Hub if desired.

Automated Response:

Automatically react to security incidents to minimize damage.

- Quarantine compromised resources with Lambda workflows or Systems Manager Automation.

- Roll back unauthorized changes using AWS Config remediation rules.

Use Case: Cryptojacking

See how AWS tools work together to detect, analyze, and respond to cryptojacking threats effectively.

- **Detection**: You can use GuardDuty to identify abnormal CPU usage on an EC2 instance.

- **Analysis**: Use Inspector to confirm outdated, exploitable software.

- **Response**: Use Systems Manager and Lambda to isolate the instance automatically and revoke IAM credentials to prevent escalation (damage control).

EDR and XDR in AWS

Discover how endpoint and extended detection solutions combine to provide comprehensive security across your AWS environment.

Why Both Matter:

Learn why having both EDR and XDR is essential for protecting everything from individual resources to your entire cloud ecosystem.

- **EDR** secures individual endpoints like EC2 instances, containers, and Lambda functions.

- **XDR** expands visibility across cloud workloads, identities, network traffic, and APIs, necessary for defending complex cloud-native architectures.

To fully understand the complementary roles of EDR and XDR in AWS security, it helps to compare their features side by side. Table 9-2 highlights how each approach addresses different layers of protection and integrates within the AWS ecosystem.

Table 9-2. *Comparing AWS EDR and XDR: Capabilities and Integration for Comprehensive Security Detection*

Feature	Endpoint Detection and Response (EDR)	Extended Detection and Response (XDR)
Scope	Endpoint-focused (EC2, containers, serverless)	Extends detection to multiple layers, including endpoints, networks, cloud workloads, and more
Data sources	Data collection from endpoint devices, such as system logs, file activity, and process events	Aggregates data from endpoints, network traffic, cloud applications, SaaS platforms, email systems, and identity management
Threat detection	Detection of endpoint-specific threats like malware, ransomware, or endpoint compromise	Identifies advanced threats across multiple vectors, including insider threats and sophisticated attacks
Response	Provides incident response for endpoint-based threats	Offers coordinated responses across diverse attack surfaces
Integration	Endpoint security tools	Centralizes multiple security tools like IAM, SIEM systems, firewalls, etc.
Visibility	Limited to endpoints	Provides unified visibility across the AWS ecosystem (single pane of glass)
Threat hunting	Typically lacks proactive threat-hunting capabilities (Basic)	Includes advanced and proactive threat hunting across all integrated layers
Complexity	Easy to manage due to scope being aligned to only endpoints	Requires more resources and expertise to configure and manage leading to being comprehensive

By tightly integrating **AWS-native services** such as GuardDuty, Inspector, Systems Manager, Security Hub, and Detective, organizations can **achieve strong EDR capabilities** and **extend them into an XDR framework**, building a multi-layered security defense entirely inside the AWS environment, without immediate reliance on third-party endpoint products.

Extending to XDR: AWS-Native and Hybrid Solutions

Extended Detection and Response (XDR) enables a unified approach to detect, investigate, and respond to threats across endpoints, cloud, network, and identity systems.

AWS services provide a strong foundation for XDR, leveraging its native services to deliver full visibility and response capabilities across cloud-native and hybrid environments.

Unlike earlier sections focused on configuring detection for individual services, this section highlights **how AWS services interoperate** to uncover and respond to **complex multi-stage attacks**. Let's quickly see in Table 9-3 how these services correlate to detect different types of attack vector.

Table 9-3. *AWS Services and Their Roles in Detecting Multi-stage Attack Vectors*

AWS Service	Role in XDR	Example Attack Detected
Amazon GuardDuty	Threat detection	Account compromise
AWS Security Hub	Cross-service correlation	Privilege escalation
Amazon Detective	Root cause analysis	Insider threat

AWS Services Enabling XDR

Discover the key AWS tools that work together to provide Extended Detection and Response across your cloud environment.

Amazon GuardDuty: Real-Time Threat Detection Engine

Discover how GuardDuty continuously monitors your AWS environment to spot threats as they happen.

Role in XDR:

GuardDuty provides ongoing threat detection by analyzing multiple AWS telemetry sources and highlighting suspicious or unauthorized behaviors across accounts.

Threat Detection Sources:

To effectively detect threats, it's important to understand the key sources of security data that reveal suspicious activity early.

- **CloudTrail Logs**: Capture API misuse and credential attacks.

- **DNS Logs**: Detect suspicious domain lookups (C2 channels, tunneling).

- **VPC Flow Logs**: Identify lateral movement, port scans, or data exfiltration.

Use Case:

Account compromise and lateral movement

Scenario:

In the account compromise scenario, GuardDuty can detect multiple failed login attempts across AWS accounts, followed by a successful login from an unfamiliar IP. Shortly after, it notices unusual multi-region traffic flow between EC2 instances.

Implementation Steps:

Follow these practical steps to set up and automate threat detection and response across your AWS environment.

- Enable GuardDuty across all AWS accounts and regions.

- Integrate GuardDuty findings into AWS Security Hub for correlation.

- Set up AWS Lambda to automatically disable the suspicious IAM user and quarantine compromised instances.

AWS Security Hub: Centralized Aggregation and Correlation

Bring together security findings from multiple sources to give you a clear, unified view of potential threats.

Role in XDR:

Security Hub can aggregate findings across AWS services and external security tools to correlate related events and prioritize security incidents holistically.

Why It's Needed in XDR:

It connects isolated detections into cross-service, multi-layered attack stories, exactly what XDR aims to do.

Aggregation Sources:

Collect and unify security findings from various services to gain comprehensive visibility across your environment.

- Amazon GuardDuty

- Amazon Inspector

- AWS Config

- Third-party security solutions

Use Case:

Privilege escalation and configuration drift

- **Scenario:**

  - GuardDuty would report anomalous API behavior from an IAM user.

  - AWS Config can identify the same user disabling MFA immediately after gaining access.

- **Implementation:**

  - Enable Security Hub to aggregate and correlate findings.

  - Develop custom Security Hub insights that flag suspicious IAM behavior.

  - Trigger AWS EventBridge to launch an automated rollback of IAM permissions and enforce reapplication of MFA the moment detection has occurred.

Amazon Detective: Root Cause Investigation and Analysis

Quickly uncover the full context of security incidents with visuals and automated insights that connect the dots across your environment.

Role in XDR:

Detective simplifies complex investigations by automatically linking entities and events, providing visual graphs and timelines that map the relationships between users, IPs, and resources.

Why It's Needed in XDR:

It provides **rapid root cause analysis** and visual evidence chains across multiple services, accounts, and regions.

Use Case:

Insider threat and data exfiltration

- **Scenario:**

   Amazon Detective can trace an IAM user's suspicious behavior when

   - Elevation of privileges occurs.

   - A user updates a policy to open S3 bucket permissions.

   - A threat actor is trying to bulk download sensitive data from S3.

- **Implementation:**

   - Enable Amazon Detective across accounts using AWS Organizations.

   - Investigate GuardDuty and CloudTrail findings through Detective.

   - Identify and visualize unauthorized activities tied to the insider threat, enabling rapid containment actions.

Third Party (Open Source): Wazuh XDR Solutions for AWS Hybrid Setup

Wazuh is an open source security platform with good capabilities for providing threat detection, ensuring compliance, and generating responses in the sorts of mixed-platform environments – cloud, hybrid, and on-premises – that some organizations are still using. It works quite well with AWS environments, adding considerable cover to the sorts of security-native capabilities AWS itself provides but for on-premises setup.

Key Capabilities of Wazuh:

Discover how Wazuh helps you stay ahead with real-time threat detection, comprehensive workload security, and automated response across your AWS environment.

- **Threat Detection in Real Time:** Works with AWS CloudTrail, CloudWatch, and VPC Flow Logs to keep an ever-watchful eye on things and instantly lets you know when something just isn't right

- **Endpoint and Cloud Workload Security**: Provides active oversight of AWS EC2 instances, containers (EKS/ECS), and serverless deployments (Lambda functions)

- **Automated Response and Remediation**: Works with AWS Systems Manager (SSM) to help automate incident response tasks and provides an automatic isolation capability that incident response teams can use when needed

- Automates the checking of compliance against CIS benchmarks and other regulatory standards

Implementation Guidance for AWS Integration:

Wazuh Manager can be set up inside AWS as an EC2 instance.

1) Set up AWS integrations with IAM roles and policies to allow Wazuh to access AWS logs and metadata in a read-only fashion. Allow IAM roles set in Wazuh to access certain AWS services (like CloudTrail) and AWS resources with an IAM policy that grants read-only access.

2) Create specific, personalized rules and alerts that fit the unique requirements of your AWS environment. When necessary, use multiple AWS log sources to rule out false positives in the identification of complex and sophisticated threats (e.g., combining GuardDuty alerts with Wazuh's abnormal activity reports on area/operation security in an AWS cloud).

Recommended Actions:

To use XDR effectively in AWS environments, the following are recommended:

- Utilize services that are native to AWS (GuardDuty, Security Hub, Detective) for the integrated detection, correlation, and response to threats.

- Create your own insights and correlation rules in Security Hub to improve visibility across different services.

- If you have hybrid setup (AWS plus your own data center), an open source solution like Wazuh can be augmented with AWS native services to broaden your threat detection and response capabilities to endpoints and hybrid environments. This could give you comprehensive XDR coverage.

Building an XDR Architecture on AWS (Hands-On Guide)

When creating an effective XDR (Extended Detection and Response) architecture in AWS, it's necessary to integrate and normalize critical security data sources. With those at hand, you can then do the step of correlating XDR for advanced threat detection and finally automating your security responses.

Data Collection and Normalization

To build a strong security foundation, it's important to gather and organize key data from various AWS services, giving you clear visibility and control.

CloudTrail (API Activity)

AWS CloudTrail captures detailed API activity logs across your accounts.

Hands-On Setup:

Let's walk through the practical steps to set up CloudTrail and get your logging and monitoring ready.

a.   Access the AWS Console and navigate to CloudTrail.

b.   Select Create trail.

c.   Identify the trail to be named, designate an S3 bucket in which to store the associated log files, and activate logging for all kinds of management events that control access to the trail and the data events that indicate usage of the S3 bucket after the trail has been enabled.

d.   Enable CloudWatch Logs to be integrated if it is necessary to monitor and alert in real time.

VPC Flow Logs (Network Traffic)

Records traffic passing through your VPCs, essential for spotting anomalies.

Hands-On Setup:
Let's walk through the simple steps to set up your VPC Flow Logs quickly and securely.

a.   Go to the VPC Console. Navigate to your VPC. Select Flow Logs.

b.   Select the destination for the flow log (CloudWatch or S3). Then, click Create Flow Log.

c.   Set IAM role permissions for all traffic, and then save.

Amazon GuardDuty Findings (Threat Intel)

Provides continuous monitoring of your AWS environment to detect and alert on known bad activity.

Hands-On Setup:
Let's walk through the simple steps to get the GuardDuty service set up quickly.

a.   Navigate to the AWS Console and select GuardDuty.

b.   Enable GuardDuty to start detecting threats right away.

c.   Centralize and delegate administration of GuardDuty to a single account (using AWS Organizations).

Amazon Security Lake (OCSF Schema)

Security Lake gathers and structures security information from AWS and many external sources. And it does so by using a standard schema, i.e., an "OCSF schema" (OCSF is shorthand for "Open Cybersecurity Schema Framework").

Hands-On Setup:

Follow these steps to initiate and configure Amazon Security Lake for collecting and normalizing your security data.

1. Go to the AWS Console and select Amazon Security Lake.

2. Select Enable Security Lake.

3. Choose data origin points (CloudTrail, VPC Flow Logs, GuardDuty).

4. Identify regions, establish IAM authorizations, and validate to commence with the ingestion and normalization of logs.

Correlation and Analytics

Collecting data is sophisticated enough; when you add the correlating and analyzing part into the mix, it becomes even more complex. But doing this work means we can find and understand the most dangerous threats that cut across not just our AWS services but also third-party platforms. And when we find these sophisticated threats, we neutralize them.

Workflow Example:

A workflow can contain several types of tasks. Each of these tasks can be executed in the way depicted in the example below. They can also be executed in parallel or in series. In a series execution, a task continues executing until it reaches its own end or a stop condition. When it reaches that condition, the next task in the series gets executed. In a parallel execution, tasks can be executed in any order (including the order depicted in the example), as long as execution within a task does not interfere with execution in another task.

GuardDuty Detects Anomalous EC2 Behavior:

GuardDuty produces a conclusion (for instance, an EC2 instance is participating in cryptojacking).

Security Hub Correlates It with Inspector Vulnerability Data:

AWS Security Hub combines the results from GuardDuty and Inspector, and it does so in a way that not only identifies the security issues in an AWS account but also gives the security personnel a path to remediating those issues. Security Hub integrates with several other AWS services, including GuardDuty and Inspector, both of which are used for threat detection and security assessments.

Hands-On Setup:

Let's walk through a simple step-by-step setup to enable Security Hub and integrate key tools for customized security insights.

1. **Turn On Security Hub**: Navigate to the AWS Console and then Security Hub, and click Enable.

2. Integrate GuardDuty and Inspector.

   a. Under Integrations, enable outcomes from Amazon GuardDuty and Inspector.

3. Insights can be formed to customize and meet your individual needs.

   a. You can do this in the following ways:

      i. Select Insights, and then select Create Insight.

      ii. Define rules to correlate EC2 vulnerabilities (Inspector) and threat alerts (GuardDuty), e.g., "Vulnerable EC2 instances with high-severity threats."

Automated Response

Using AWS Lambda, EventBridge, and AWS Systems Manager, you can automate security incident response.

Example:

Automate EC2 instance isolation.

Hands-On Setup:

Follow these clear steps to set up the AWS Lambda function for automating security incident response.

Step 1: Create an AWS Lambda Function

- Lambda Console ➤ Create function.

- Choose runtime (e.g., Python 3.x).

- Add permissions for Systems Manager (SSM) to isolate EC2 instances:

```
{
  "Version": "2012-10-17",
  "Statement": [{
    "Effect": "Allow",
    "Action": "ssm:SendCommand",
    "Resource": "*"
  }]
}
```

- Here's an example Python Lambda snippet to isolate instances:

```
import boto3
ssm = boto3.client('ssm')
def lambda_handler(event, context):
    instance_id = event['detail']['resource']['instanceDetails']
    ['instanceId']
    response = ssm.send_command(
        InstanceIds=[instance_id],
        DocumentName='AWS-RunShellScript',
        Parameters={'commands': ['sudo iptables -A INPUT -j
        DROP']}
    )
    return response
```

Step 2: Configure Amazon EventBridge

Next, set up EventBridge to catch critical GuardDuty alerts and trigger your Lambda automatically.

- EventBridge Console ➤ Rules ➤ Create Rule.

- Set a trigger for event patterns that match critical GuardDuty findings.

- Target your Lambda function for automatic execution.

Mapping Practical AWS (Cloud) Scenarios to EDR and XDR Approaches

In an earlier section we learned what EDR and XDR are. We know they aren't like other security tools that do mostly one job, for instance, stop a piece of malware from running. EDR and XDR are not point solutions; they are part of an overall security strategy and should be pretty integrated to fulfil their roles effectively in a wider cybersecurity strategy for your organization.

EDR-Specific Scenario:
Let's explore a real-world example of how Endpoint Detection and Response tackles insider threats effectively.

Scenario:
Insider threat – data exfiltration from EC2 via unauthorized tools

- **Problem**: When a rogue employee installs a custom file transfer tool on an EC2 instance to slowly exfiltrate sensitive business data without triggering alarms.

- **Detection Flow**: Amazon Inspector can flag unauthorized software or binaries not approved by the organization's baseline.

- **Systems Manager Inventory**: Can detect unexpected software installations or changes on the instance.

- **GuardDuty**: Will Identify unusual outbound traffic patterns (e.g., slow but steady data transfer to external IPs).

EDR Role:
Is to catch the unauthorized software installation early, isolate the affected instance, and prevent further data leakage, all before significant damage is done.

XDR-Specific Scenario:
Let's walk through a real-world example to see how XDR helps detect and respond to threats across AWS services.

Scenario:
Cross-service ransomware attack in AWS

- **Problem**: Let's say an external attacker exploits a misconfigured public S3 bucket, gains a foothold, and then encrypts sensitive EBS volumes attached to EC2 instances, threatening ransom if decryption keys aren't paid for.

- **Detection Flow**: AWS Config will identify misconfigured (public) S3 buckets.

- **GuardDuty**: Will detect unusual API activity on S3 and suspicious EC2 instance behavior (e.g., sudden spike in EBS snapshot creation and encryption).

- **Security Hub**: Should be used for correlating S3 misconfiguration and EC2 ransomware behavior into a single high-severity finding.

- **Amazon Detective**: Will map the attacker's lateral movement from S3 to EC2, showing full blast radius.

XDR Role:

In this scenario is to connect storage, compute, and identity anomalies into a full ransomware chain, allowing automated response like quarantining resources and triggering backup restores immediately.

Key Takeaways:

Let's wrap up the key points to help you understand how EDR and XDR work together for a stronger, more complete cloud security strategy.

- EDR is crucial for catching targeted threats directly at the compute layer (like insider misuse on EC2), but it operates mainly at the endpoint level.

- XDR extends protection by connecting dots across multiple AWS services (storage, compute, IAM) to uncover complex, multi-stage attacks like cloud ransomware campaigns.

- In modern cloud environments, both EDR and XDR are essential. EDR stops fast-moving endpoint threats early, while XDR builds a complete attack story and enables rapid, coordinated defense across layers.

- Organizations that combine endpoint-focused visibility (via Amazon Inspector, Systems Manager) with cross-service correlation and investigation (via GuardDuty, Security Hub, Detective) build a resilient security posture that can withstand even sophisticated adversaries.

Challenges and Best Practices

Understanding common hurdles and practical ways to overcome them ensures your AWS security stays strong and efficient.

- **AWS-Specific Challenges:**

  Here are key AWS challenges and how to address them effectively.

  - **Ephemeral Workloads (Lambda, ECS):** Limited EDR agent runtime.

    - **Reduction in Risk:**

      - Shift security left, embedding security checks during continuous integration/continuous deployment (CI/CD) pipelines.

      - Use agentless vulnerability scanning (Inspector).

      - Set up runtime threat detection using Amazon Web Services (AWS) native services (CloudWatch, GuardDuty).

  - **High Log Volume Costs (CloudTrail, VPC Flow Logs):** Managing log data effectively helps control costs while keeping the important security insights you need.

    - **Mitigation:**

      - Some of the key controls we can put in place are as follows:

        - **Use Log Filtering and Lifecycle Policies:** For S3, that means ensuring filters are applied to as full a range of logs as possible, which isn't straightforward, and then using S3 Intelligent-Tiering and Glacier for long-term storage and retrieval.

        - **Prioritize Critical Logs:** For AWS CloudTrail and similar services, that means ensuring as complete a delivery of logs as possible and then using the controls AWS provides to manage those logs (i.e., control access, encrypt, etc.).

- **Use Sampling and Intelligent Filtering on VPC Flow Logs:**
  This means using a range of different methods to apply sampling and filtering that ensures that VPC Flow Logs are as manageable (and as useful) as possible.

- **Best Practices:**

  Let's wrap up with practical tips to keep your AWS security efficient, automated, and cost-effective.

  - Ensure security management is handled centrally in AWS Organizations.

  - Make sure that Security Lake (OCSF) is used for assimilation of data.

  - Automate all responses and remediations using Lambda and EventBridge.

  - Review the AWS bill regularly and make sure that logging is cost-optimized.

Best Practices for XDR on AWS

Putting best practices in place makes certain that your XDR architecture is watertight, connected, and economical. We will look at straightforward, direct-to-the-point actions and clear, full-bodied explanations of how to make the best, most efficient use of AWS-native services and integrations.

Prioritize OCSF-Compatible and Native Tools:
When building your XDR architecture, prioritize tools that either **support** or **natively adopt** the Open Cybersecurity Schema Framework (OCSF). Tools that are *compatible with OCSF* can export or ingest data formatted to the OCSF standard, easing integration across systems. However, tools that *natively work with the OCSF data model* go a step further: they structure, store, and analyze security events internally according to the OCSF schema, providing deeper normalization, more accurate correlation, and faster threat detection. Visualize this like a pyramid: at the base are OCSF-compatible tools, and at the top are tools truly built on the OCSF foundation, offering the strongest XDR capabilities.

Amazon OpenSearch Service:

Amazon OpenSearch Service (renamed from Amazon Elasticsearch Service) makes it easy to deploy, secure, and operate OpenSearch clusters at scale in the cloud. Using the service, you can run searches across large amounts of data in near real time. It provides a multitenant search engine with a secure user experience and a set of tools for analyzing and visualizing data. Because OpenSearch is open source software, you can build on top of it, contribute back to it, and use what other users create.

AWS Verified Access:

AWS Verified Access allows you to replace a VPN with a more secure, seamless, and easy-to-manage access solution. VPNs work by

a. Securely connecting users to company resources

b. Enforcing security policies that are specific to the resources being accessed

In contrast, AWS Verified Access

- Provides direct access to applications hosted in AWS

- Works with any identity provider

- Does not require user tunnelling or virtual desktops

- Enforces fine-grained security policies based on application context

Hands-On Setup:

Let's walk through the practical steps to get these AWS security tools up and running seamlessly.

Amazon Security Lake:

Start by enabling Security Lake and connecting your key data sources for centralized security data collection.

- Access the AWS Console and navigate to the Amazon Security Lake Console.

- Select Enable Security Lake (unless already enabled).

- Select origins (CloudTrail, VPC Flow Logs, GuardDuty, and external integrations) to obtain your data.

- Identify an S3 bucket for consolidated storage.

- Set up IAM roles to give secure cross-service access.

Amazon OpenSearch Service (Security Analytics):

Next, set up OpenSearch to analyze your security data and build dashboards for real-time threat insights. OpenSearch Service works with Security Lake for threat detection and advanced security analytics.

- Access the AWS Console and navigate to the OpenSearch Console.

- Select the option to create a new domain:

    - Choose the most recent version of OpenSearch.

    - Set up protections (identity and access management policies, SAML authentication, fine-grained access control for data and resources).

- Retrieve OCSF logs from Security Lake:

    - Set up AWS Glue or AWS Lambda to send logs from Security Lake (S3) to OpenSearch.

- Set up dashboards and alerts for fast threat evaluation.

AWS Verified Access:

Now, configure Verified Access to secure remote logins and gain detailed user-level visibility across your environment.

- Open the AWS Console and navigate to AWS Verified Access.

- Select Create Verified Access Instance.

- Establish guidelines that are centered on identity providers (such as AWS IAM Identity Center or Okta).

- Send logs to Amazon Security Lake or OpenSearch using EventBridge for centralized analytics.

AWS AppFabric:

AWS AppFabric collects and organizes the logs from security applications (e.g. Office3665, Salesforce, Okta) used together with AWS services. Finally, connect your security apps with AppFabric to streamline log collection and enhance cross-service threat detection.

- Access the AWS Control Center and then navigate to AWS AppFabric.

- Select Connect application.

- Select a Software as a Service (SaaS) application such as Okta, Slack, Zoom, and Office 365.

- Set up potential logging destinations. You can use either Security Lake or OpenSearch, and you can send logs to them via Kinesis Data Firehose.

- Logs will automatically be ingested in OCSF format. Automatic ingestion of cross-service threat detection is being enhanced with this format.

Use AWS Organizations for Multi-account Visibility:

AWS accounts management is made simple with AWS Organizations. It allows one to control security and governance on a number of AWS accounts. These features make AWS Organizations particularly suited to the needs of large company divisions or projects. AWS Organizations offers these enhanced control features in two key ways.

Advantages:

- Brings together management of GuardDuty, Security Hub, Inspector, and Detective

- Simplifying incident response and security policy enforcement

Hands-On Setup:

Discover how unified management of key security tools makes incident response and enforcement simpler.

Stage 1:

Start by creating or organizing your AWS accounts in AWS Organizations to centralize management. To activate AWS Organizations

- Navigate to the AWS Console ➤ AWS Organizations.

- To create an organization, click the button labeled Create Organization, and then proceed to invite any pre-existing AWS accounts that you would like to join your organization.

Stage 2:

Activate and delegate your security services GuardDuty, Security Hub, Inspector, and Detective in one central account.

- Navigate to GuardDuty ➤ Settings ➤ Delegated Administrator ➤ Establish a central security account.

- Security Hub ➤ Settings ➤ Delegate management ➤ Add the security account.

- Assign administration of Inspector and Detective to the central security account in the same way as GuardDuty and Security Hub.

Stage 3: Central Logging

Enable logging in one place. Make sure that Amazon Security Lake or your S3 buckets can be reached from many different accounts.

- Securely set IAM cross-account permissions.

Operational Recommended Practices:

Keeping your security strong means regularly testing, tuning, and automating responses to stay ahead of threats.

- Regularly validate the flow of logs and the mechanism of alerts.

- Validate the overall setup regularly by checking all tools, integrations, and alerts. Better safe than sorry.

- Eliminate false positives. Involve as many scenarios as possible.

- Conduct simulated attacks (AWS CloudShell, Kali Linux EC2 instance) to assess XDR configuration.

- AWS Lambda provides an excellent way to automate incident response and take action when AWS services detect potential security problems.

  - Using AWS Lambda, you can run code in response to events.

  - You can use it as part of your incident response plans, e.g., to run a series of commands to remediate issues either in a serverless fashion or to spin up EC2 instances when needed.

- Set up scripts for auto-remediation (e.g., isolating EC2 instances or blocking IAM principals), which can be preconfigured and invoked automatically in response to security threats.

Incident Response in AWS

Cybersecurity incidents demand rapid response if they are to be contained and mitigated satisfactorily. The AWS platform and its associated toolset offer a rich set of possibilities for implementing effective incident response processes, and these have been aligned well with industry-standard frameworks like those from NIST.

Standard Incident Response Processes

The normal steps of the IR process typically are

- **Preparation**: Establish policies, tooling, logging, and training to lay the groundwork.

- **Detection and Analysis**: Quickly recognize and evaluate occurrences.

- **Containment, Eradication, and Recovery**: Isolate and remediate affected systems.

- **After an Incident**: Review what happened, improve processes, and bolster the foundation of your security.

Cloud IR Framework

Aligning incident response phases exactly with AWS services allows a way of working that is not just rapid and effective but also beautifully structured.

AWS-Specific NIST Alignment:
Modern incident response in the cloud demands structure without sacrificing speed. By mapping AWS-native services (Table 9-4) directly to each phase of the NIST IR framework, organizations can build a faster, clearer, and more resilient incident response process. The table below outlines how AWS tools support preparation, detection, containment, eradication, recovery, and post-incident review, ensuring cloud-native operations stay aligned with recognized security standards.

Table 9-4. *Mapping AWS Services to the NIST Incident Response Framework*

NIST Phase	AWS Services and Tools
Preparation	AWS CloudFormation, IAM, CloudTrail, Security Hub, GuardDuty
Detection and analysis	GuardDuty, Security Hub, CloudWatch, Amazon Detective
Containment	AWS Systems Manager Automation, AWS Lambda, EC2 security groups
Eradication	Inspector, Systems Manager Patch Manager
Recovery	AWS Backup, Systems Manager Automation, CloudFormation
Post-incident activity	Amazon CloudWatch Logs Insights, AWS Audit Manager

Hands-On Setup:

Here's how to use AWS Systems Manager for containment.

Isolate an EC2 instance that has been compromised:

- Access the AWS Console and navigate to Systems Manager.

- Go to Documents ➤ Look up AWS-IsolateInstance.

- Choose the ID of the EC2 instance that has been compromised.

- Run the command to automatically quarantine the instance.

  - This command performs the following actions, which are also described in more detail in the next section:

    - Makes the instance inaccessible to the outside (removing security groups and disabling network interfaces)

    - Isolates the instance from other instances

Immutable Evidence Preservation:

Making sure the evidence is unchangeable guarantees reliable forensic examination after the event.

AWS Backup (Forensic Snapshots):

AWS Backup helps you create forensically sound snapshots to preserve critical AWS data, making it possible to recover quickly and securely if a breach occurs. This ensures data integrity during investigations and supports compliance with regulatory requirements.

Hands-On Setup:

Let's walk through the practical steps to create backups in AWS.

1. **Access the AWS Backup Console**

   - Go to the AWS Management Console and open the AWS Backup service.

2. **Create a Backup Plan**

   - Select "Create backup plan."

   - Choose target resources: EC2 instances, EBS volumes, RDS databases.

   - Define backup frequency (hourly, daily) and retention rules.

   - Enable Vault Lock to protect backups from deletion or tampering.

3. **Implement Access Controls**

   - Configure IAM roles and permissions to tightly restrict who can access backups.

   - Apply encryption using AWS KMS for data at rest.

4. **Perform Ad Hoc Backups**

   - Trigger manual backups if unusual activity or an incident is detected.

   - Store these incident-related backups in separate, secure backup vaults.

Recovery Process After Breach:

Here's how to safely restore your systems after a security incident.

1. **Identify the Recovery Point**

   - In AWS Backup, locate the relevant backup based on the timestamp before the incident.

2. **Initiate Restore**

   - Choose "Restore" on the selected recovery point.

   - Restore into an isolated, controlled environment (new VPC or quarantine subnet).

3. **Validate the Restore**

- Verify system integrity and confirm no indicators of compromise are present on the restored resources.

4. **Return to Production (Caution)**

- Once thoroughly validated, move the clean resource into production or rehydrate data into original workloads.

Key Reminders:

Keep these important tips in mind to maintain a strong backup and recovery strategy.

- Always restore to a safe environment first to avoid reintroducing compromised systems.

- Use IAM policies and Vault Lock to enforce backup immutability.

- Regularly test backup and recovery workflows to ensure readiness.

Amazon S3 Object Lock (Immutable Logs) – Securing Forensic Evidence:

While immutable logs are not an active incident response action, they are a crucial part of preparing for and investigating security incidents. Amazon S3 Object Lock ensures that critical logs cannot be altered or deleted after they are written, preserving the integrity of forensic evidence.

Hands-On Setup:

Let's walk through the practical steps to securely set up your S3 bucket with Object Lock for protecting your critical logs.

- Navigate to the AWS Console ➤ Amazon S3.

- Create or select a bucket. Go to Properties ➤ Object Lock ➤ Enable.

- While uploading logs, turn on Object Lock and select either Governance or Compliance mode for retention.

- Configure key security logs, such as AWS CloudTrail and VPC Flow Logs, to be stored in this locked S3 bucket.

By enabling immutable logs, you ensure that in the event of a security incident, trusted and tamper-proof records are available for accurate detection, analysis, and compliance reporting.

Chaos Engineering for Resilience

Test your incident response mechanisms and resilience in a proactive way by simulating security incidents with AWS Fault Injection Simulator (FIS). By using this tool you can perform fault injection experiments that simulate network outages, infrastructure failures, and service disruptions, among other scenarios.

Simulate Attacks Using AWS Fault Injection Simulator:
Controlled fault insertion through AWS FIS enables real-world security incident simulation for testing incident response (IR) processes.

Example:
Triggering GuardDuty findings

Hands-On Setup:
Let's walk through setting up a practical fault injection experiment to test and validate your GuardDuty alerts and automated response workflows.

    Step 1: AWS Fault Injection Simulator setup.

- Access the AWS Console and open Fault Injection Simulator.

- Select Create Experiment Template.

- Name the experiment, e.g., "Simulate GuardDuty Crypto-mining Alert."

Step 2: Specify actions (imitate CPU stress).

- **Actions:**

    - Choose the action type: **AWS-FIS-CPUStress**.

    - Establish duration (for instance, 5–10 minutes).

Step 3: Determine your targets (simulated compromise of an EC2 instance).

- Choose EC2 instances or auto-scaling groups to inject.

Step 4: Define stopping conditions.

- Automatically stop if certain thresholds are breached by critical metrics.

Step 5: Run the experiment and confirm reply.

- Select "Start Experiment."

- Confirm that GuardDuty identifies crypto-mining irregularities.

- Verify that automated incident response workflows are set up to use either Lambda or Systems Manager to perform isolation and remediation tasks. These workflows should trigger automatic actions to contain any security incidents affecting your environment.

Developing Detection and Alerting Pipelines

Creating automated identification and alerting pipelines is vital for quickly spotting and ranking security threats and remediating them. The following is a step-by-step, copiously detailed guide to implementing such a system using AWS services.

Automating Alerts:
Automation allows security teams to reduce their response times because it can provide them with an enriched context almost immediately.

AWS-Native Automation:
AWS native tools work together seamlessly to enhance and automate your security alert handling.

- **EventBridge plus Lambda**: You can enrich alerts with additional context from DynamoDB (e.g., tagging compromised resources). AWS EventBridge captures security alerts from various AWS services such as GuardDuty and Security Hub and routes them to AWS Lambda functions. These Lambda functions can enrich the alerts by adding important metadata, e.g., querying DynamoDB tables that store resource tags, owner information, or criticality levels. This enriched context improves incident triage, prioritization, and automated response workflows without altering the original alert payload.

Hands-On Setup:
Let's walk through the practical steps to get everything set up from storing context data to automating alerts and tagging resources.

    Step 1: Set up DynamoDB (for contextual data storage).

- Open the AWS Console and then the DynamoDB Console.

- Select Create Table:

  - **Table Name**: *ResourceContext*

  - **Partition Key**: ResourceId (String)

- Insert an example item into the DynamoDB table:

```
{
   "ResourceId": "i-1234567890abcdef0",
   "Owner": "security-team@example.com",
   "Criticality": "High"
}
```

Step 2: Create an AWS Lambda function (alert enrichment).

- AWS Management Console ➤ Lambda ➤ Create function:

  - **Environment**: Select latest Python, i.e., Python 3.x.

  - **Read and Tag AWS Resources**: Attach a policy to read DynamoDB and tag AWS resources.

Here's an example Lambda function (Python):

```python
import boto3

dynamodb = boto3.resource('dynamodb')
table = dynamodb.Table('ResourceContext')
ec2 = boto3.client('ec2')

def lambda_handler(event, context):
    resource_id = event['detail']['resource']['instanceDetails']['instanceId']

    response = table.get_item(Key={'ResourceId': resource_id})
    context_data = response.get('Item', {})

    # Tag EC2 instance with contextual data
    tags = [{'Key': k, 'Value': v} for k, v in context_data.items() if k !=
    'ResourceId']

    if tags:
        ec2.create_tags(Resources=[resource_id], Tags=tags)

    return {'status': 'Resource tagged successfully', 'tags': tags}
```

Step 3: EventBridge rule (trigger Lambda on GuardDuty alert).

- AWS Console ➤ EventBridge ➤ Rules ➤ Create rule:

  - **Name**: GuardDutyEnrichment.

  - **Event Source**: AWS events.

  - **Event Pattern**:

    ```
    {
      "source": ["aws.guardduty"],
      "detail-type": ["GuardDuty Finding"]
    }
    ```

- **Target**: Choose your Lambda function created above.

GenAI for Triage with Amazon Q:

Amazon Q Developer now enables you to rapidly generate, test, and deploy Python scripts that parse and prioritize CloudWatch alerts. With Amazon Q, you can automate the triage process, ensuring security alerts are swiftly analyzed and routed according to severity.

Hands-On Setup:

Let's get practical. Here's how to set up your environment and start generating code with Amazon Q step by step.

Step 1: Prepare your environment.

- Ensure you have the latest AWS Toolkit and Amazon Q Developer extension installed in your IDE (e.g., VS Code).

- Authenticate with your AWS credentials.

- Activate Amazon Q Developer in your IDE if not already enabled.

Step 2: Generate Python code with Amazon Q.

- Commence crafting Python comments that are descriptive enough to act as prompts for Amazon Q, for example:

```
# Function to parse CloudWatch alarm events and prioritize alerts
based on severity
# Input: JSON event from CloudWatch
# Output: Prioritized alerts list (Critical, High, Medium, Low)
```

- Amazon Q Developer will automatically generate the appropriate Python code for you.

Example Output:

```
import json

def prioritize_alerts(event):
    alerts = event.get('alerts', [])
    priority_map = {"Critical": [], "High": [], "Medium": [],
    "Low": []}

    for alert in alerts:
        severity = alert.get('severity', 'Low')
        priority_map[severity].append(alert)

    prioritized_alerts = priority_map["Critical"] + priority_
    map["High"] + priority_map["Medium"] + priority_map["Low"]
    return prioritized_alerts
```

- You can further refine the generated code by conversing with Amazon Q Developer, asking for enhancements, error handling, or integration with other AWS services.

Step 3: Integrate with AWS Lambda and notification services.

- Use the generated code in an AWS Lambda function to automate CloudWatch alert triage.

- Route prioritized alerts to incident management platforms such as SNS, Slack, or Jira by extending your Lambda function with the relevant AWS SDK integrations.

Proactive Threat Hunting:

Amazon OpenSearch: Machine learning–based anomaly detection on VPC Flow Logs using Random Cut Forest (RCF) proactively detects anomalous network activities by leveraging the built-in machine learning capabilities of Amazon OpenSearch.

Hands-On Setup:

Let's walk through the practical steps to get your Amazon OpenSearch environment ready for analyzing VPC Flow Logs and detecting anomalies.

Step 1: Configure your Amazon OpenSearch domain.

- Navigate to Amazon OpenSearch from the AWS Console:

  - **Version:** The most recent supported version of OpenSearch.

  - **Security:** Allow for highly detailed access controls to be enforced (IAM roles).

Step 2: Take in VPC Flow Logs and put them into OpenSearch.

- Configure CloudWatch Logs to accept Amazon VPC Flow Logs:

  - Create a log group in CloudWatch Logs:

    - AWS Console ➤ VPC ➤ Flow Logs ➤ Set up with CloudWatch

- Stream CloudWatch Logs to OpenSearch:

  - Set up a subscription for CloudWatch Logs that sends the log data into Amazon Kinesis Data Firehose. Firehose will then serve as the data delivery mechanism to OpenSearch.

Step 3: Set up anomaly detection to use Random Cut Forest (RCF).

- Navigate to the AWS Console and then OpenSearch. Select your domain. Then choose OpenSearch Dashboards.

- Navigate to Anomaly Detection and select Create detector:

  - **Name:** *VPCFlowAnomalyDetector*.

  - **Pattern for Index:** (vpc-flow-logs-*).

  - **Feature:** Aggregate by network metrics (e.g., bytes transferred, number of connections).

  - Choose the Random Cut Forest (RCF) algorithm.

- Arrange for the alerts to be sent out automatically:

  - Utilize the OpenSearch alerts plugin to set up notifications through email, SNS, or Lambda when anomalies occur.

Example of an Alert Being Triggered:

The alert condition has been met, and for this example its action is to notify an interested party, typically a human.

Send alerts about anomalies to SNS ➤ Lambda for automatic reaction.

Dissecting Attacker Methodologies and Techniques in AWS

This section shifts its focus to the evolving trends in how threat actors are exploiting cloud environments. Adversaries no longer attack at just one level; they operate across multiple layers, using a mix of techniques (how they achieve their goals) and tactics (what their goals are).

Here, we break down prominent attack methods, forensic footprints (what is left behind for analysts to find), and emerging defensive strategies that are increasingly shaping the future of cloud security.

Keep in Mind: The cybersecurity landscape evolves rapidly. Regardless of when you are reading this material, always refer to the latest AWS, Azure, and GCP documentations and trusted cybersecurity sources to stay aligned with current and future developments.

Analyzing Attacker Tactics:
Understanding and analyzing attacker tactics helps you better defend your cloud environment by recognizing common threats and how AWS protects against them.

MITRE ATT&CK for Cloud: AWS-specific techniques

- **Credential Access:** Exploiting Instance Metadata Service version 1 (IMDSv1) to steal temporary AWS credentials.

- **How It Works:** An SSRF (Server-Side Request Forgery) vulnerability in a web application allows an attacker to induce the application to make arbitrary HTTP requests. When the web application is running on EC2 and has an SSRF vulnerability, the attacker can use it to unsafely access the local AWS environment, in this case the IMDS.

- **AWS Mitigation:** IMDSv2 should be enforced. AWS Systems Manager can be used to enforce IMDSv2 automatically by using Launch Templates or EC2 Instance Metadata Defaults.

- **Hardening IAM Roles:** Attach IAM roles with the least-privilege permissions (e.g., deny *sts:AssumeRole*).

- **AWS Config Rule:** Non-compliant EC2 instances should be flagged by enabling imdsv2-check.

Impact – Ransomware Targeting Elastic File System (EFS):

Let's explore how ransomware can exploit Amazon EFS through compromised EC2 instances and what steps AWS offers to help protect against this risk.

Flow of Attack: Attackers break into Amazon EC2 instances. These compromised instances use Amazon Elastic File System (Amazon EFS – *elasticfilesystem:ClientWrite*) and contain the ransomware. After the attack, when the system is compromised, the security risk levels of not having the right access control in place are demonstrated. The compromise of these types of instances could allow attackers to increase their foothold in the environment.

AWS Mitigation:

AWS offers powerful tools to protect your file systems and monitor suspicious activity effortlessly.

- **AWS Backup:** Turn on automatic backups for EFS and make them immutable for as long as you want.

- **EFS File Policy:** Use IAM conditions (e.g., *aws:SourceVpc*) to restrict access.

- **Amazon GuardDuty:** Detect abnormal file activity through EFS audit logs (e.g., *elasticfilesystem:ClientRootAccess*).

Forensic Deep Dives with AWS Services:

Let's explore how AWS tools help you dig deep into security incidents and trace complex attack paths.

CloudTrail Lake:

Reconstructing IAM role chaining

Use Case: An attacker takes on a role in Account A and then moves to a role in Account B to steal S3 data.

AWS Tooling:

CloudTrail Lake allows us to perform analysis across accounts and on data types that were not previously accessible. You can run basic or advanced SQL queries on the event data stored in CloudTrail Lake. Here's an example SQL query for CloudTrail Lake:

```
SELECT eventSource, eventName, userIdentity.arn, sourceIPAddress
FROM cloudtrail_logs
WHERE eventName = 'AssumeRole'
```

```
AND userIdentity.type = 'AssumedRole'
AND eventTime > '2024-01-01T00:00:00Z'
```

Integrate:

Send results to Amazon Detective for attack path visualization.

GuardDuty EKS Audit Log Monitoring:

Purpose:

To escalate privileges in an EKS cluster by detecting a malicious *kubeclt* exec command.

AWS Tooling:

EKS GuardDuty Protection: Monitors for findings such as *Kubernetes/ ContainerPrivilegeEscalation* by scrutinizing the audit logs from Kubernetes.

Mitigation Response: Utilize AWS Systems Manager Incident Manager to isolate the pod and eliminate the associated IAM roles.

Defensive Strategies (AWS-Native):

Let's explore built-in AWS tools and best practices to proactively protect your environment and enforce strong access controls.

Proactive IAM Policy Guardrails:

- **AWS Control Tower SCPs:**

  - **Example Policy:** For all accounts in an AWS organization, denying high-risk actions:

    ```
    {
      "Version": "2012-10-17",
      "Statement": [
        {
          "Sid": "BlockDestructiveActions",
          "Effect": "Deny",
          "Action": [
            "s3:DeleteBucket",
            "cloudtrail:DeleteTrail",
            "rds:DeleteDBInstance"
          ],
    ```

```
      "Resource": "*"
    }
  ]
}
```

- Control Tower's Service Control Policies (SCPs) deploy enforcement.

Permission Boundaries:
Use boundaries to restrict IAM roles and prevent privilege escalation (e.g., limit roles to specific regions or services).

AI-Driven Threat Hunting with Amazon SageMaker:
Harness AI to proactively detect threats by analyzing your cloud activity with smart machine learning models.

Workflow:
Follow a clear step-by-step process to gather data, train your model, detect anomalies, and respond automatically.

Step 1: Data Gathering

- Retrieve CloudTrail logs from Amazon S3 and use AWS Glue for preprocessing.

Step 2: Train the Model

- Leverage Amazon SageMaker to train a bespoke machine learning model using the established, well-defined cloud security APIs.

Step 3: Inference and Alerts

- Use the model to identify unusual events (e.g., *AssumeRole* and *s3:PutObject* coming from a new geography) and notify AWS Security Hub.

Mitigate:

- Trigger a Lambda function and suspend the IAM role until investigation has been completed and the role is not compromised.

What You Have Learned

This chapter covered the advanced aspects of security operations in AWS and provided an in-depth discussion on the strategies involved in threat detection, incident response, and threat mitigation in cloud environments. The key takeaways included

Detection Engineering with AWS-Native Tools:

Amazon Web Services CloudTrail and GuardDuty form the backbone of threat detection, enabling near-real-time API activity monitoring and malicious behavior detection. You learned to use Amazon EventBridge to craft custom SIEM rules and integrate findings into AWS Security Hub for truly centralized visibility.

AWS Config offers always-on compliance, unearthing incorrect setups like S3 buckets that are not encrypted or security groups that are too permissive. With custom rules and continuous compliance monitoring, AWS Config ensures that the security baselines you want to enforce across your AWS account are followed.

Endpoint Security (EDR) and Extended Detection (XDR):

Amazon Inspector and AWS Systems Manager are two vital services for endpoint hardening. Systems Manager's Patch Manager is the primary service that automates the remediation of vulnerabilities. It does so by patching instances. Amazon Inspector is another of the key services that identify network exposures and vulnerabilities in your applications.

AWS uses cross-service telemetry (CloudTrail, VPC Flow Logs, GuardDuty) in its XDR to correlate threats across endpoints, identities, and networks. Amazon Detective maps attack chains, and third-party solutions (e.g., Palo Alto Cortex XDR) do hybrid log analysis and enrich AWS threat intelligence.

Proactive Defense Strategies:

AWS Control Tower implements IAM policies as guardrails. These guardrails enforce least-privilege access. They block high-risk actions like *s3:DeleteBucket* or *cloudtrail:DeleteTrail*. They allow all other actions at the specified permission level.

Using Amazon SageMaker for AI-driven threat hunting in CloudTrail logs allows us to detect anomalous behavior, like strange AssumeRole chains or API calls that are outside the normal geographic boundaries of where we expect our users to be.

Incident Response and Forensic Analysis:

AWS Systems Manager Automation and Lambda are used to contain (e.g., isolate compromised EC2 instances). For keeping evidence, we use AWS Backup and S3 Object Lock to make sure it is immutable.

The forensic investigation powers of CloudTrail Lake and GuardDuty EKS Audit Log Monitoring are unparalleled. They allow for the precise reconstruction of IAM role chaining and the detection of malicious Kubernetes activity. That's not to say they are perfect. For them to perfectly accomplish these tasks would require IAM roles that are securely configured and more than just a tacit adherence to security best practices across the board.

Emerging Attacker Tactics:

You examined techniques from the AWS-specific version of the MITRE ATT&CK framework, such as credential theft through exploitation of the Instance Metadata Service version 1 (IMDSv1) and ransomware targeting Amazon's Elastic File System (EFS). Your countermeasures consist of enforcing use of the second version of the IMDS (IMDSv2), making EFS immutable, and monitoring the file system with AWS's GuardDuty service.

Summary

In this chapter, we provided a comprehensive exploration of advanced security operations in AWS, emphasizing the integration of native services to build a resilient, automated security posture. We began with detection engineering, leveraging CloudTrail, GuardDuty, and Security Hub to craft SIEM rules that identify suspicious activities, from unauthorized API calls to cryptojacking. The discussion expanded to endpoint security, with Systems Manager and Inspector automating and managing vulnerability conditions, while XDR solutions like Amazon Detective and third-party tools break down silos to correlate cross-domain threats.

Proactive defense strategies were put in the spotlight, showcasing IAM guardrails and anomaly detection with AI. The chapter also dissected the modern attacker, going through our playbook of sorts and the better forensic techniques it takes these days to find out when and how an attacker moved through a system, "role chaining" especially, or to figure out if they used Kubernetes to pull off some kind of privilege escalation stunt.

In the final analysis, the chapter showed just how critical automation and integration are in AWS security.

When Security Hub, Lambda, and SageMaker work together, they serve up an astonishing common operational picture that's not just insightful but actionable in real time, at cloud speed, and against evolving attack patterns. All of this is aimed at the bad guys not making a successful entry.

You have mastered these concepts and are now prepared to architect and enforce security operations that are not just reactive but predictive, turning AWS environments into fortified, intelligent ecosystems.

CHAPTER 10

Generative AI and Cybersecurity in AWS

How organizations innovate is being transformed by generative AI (GenAI). It automates tasks such as code generation, threat analysis, and the creation of synthetic data. But the integration of generative AI into cloud environments brings new cybersecurity challenges. This chapter examines the potential of generative AI for AWS users while also addressing many of the risks associated with it, such as adversarial attacks where attackers use generative AI against you for data leaks, model exploitation, and other cybersecurity exploitations. We will also explore how to use generative AI to help secure your AWS environment.

Generative AI As a Cybersecurity Tool

While generative AI introduces new threats, it also provides organizations with powerful opportunities to strengthen their defenses. When properly applied, generative AI can act as a force multiplier in cybersecurity programs, enhancing threat detection, accelerating incident response, and improving compliance efforts. In this section, we will explore how generative AI can be leveraged as a proactive tool to bolster cloud security across detection, simulation, automation, and defense strategies.

Threat Detection and Response

Organizations can leverage generative AI in two ways to enhance threat detection. First, they can train custom models using Amazon SageMaker on AWS CloudTrail logs, GuardDuty findings, and VPC Flow Logs. This approach helps build tailored models that learn the environment's specific behaviors and can pinpoint suspicious patterns, such as

257

© Syed Rehan 2025
S. Rehan, *Cybersecurity with AWS*, https://doi.org/10.1007/979-8-8688-1554-6_10

API calls made by unauthenticated users. Alternatively, pre-trained GenAI models can be applied directly to security logs to detect anomalies without extensive retraining. In both cases, GenAI can also assist by auto-generating remediation playbooks to maintain compliance and accelerate incident response.

Example:
A model trained on S3 access logs detects abnormal data transfers between AWS accounts and triggers an automated Lambda workflow to contain the threat.

Phishing Simulation and Defense

As part of a proactive, Blue Team-focused training strategy (where the Blue Team defends, the Red Team simulates attacks, and Pink Teams collaborate between attackers and defenders), organizations can use Amazon Nova (LLM) to safely generate simulated phishing emails, helping employees recognize common attack patterns without exposing them to real threats.

These controlled exercises are essential for strengthening user vigilance and promoting a culture of cybersecurity awareness. Additionally, Amazon Comprehend can assist by scanning communications for social engineering tactics, enabling security teams to fine-tune detection rules and automate responses. Together, these tools form part of a broader educational and defensive approach to prepare the workforce against evolving phishing campaigns.

Automated Compliance

Instead of building models (LLM) from scratch, organizations can now *leverage* powerful foundation models (such as those available through Amazon Bedrock, i.e., Amazon Nova, or third-party ones like Claude) to streamline compliance efforts. These models can be *prompted* without additional training to map AWS Config rules against industry standards like GDPR and HIPAA and to generate audit-ready reports. This approach provides a level of compliance assurance comparable to what traditional external auditors offer while remaining adaptable to future models as technology evolves.

Securing Generative AI Workloads on AWS

As organizations increasingly adopt generative AI, the AI systems themselves become attractive targets. Key risks to address include

- **Data Poisoning**: Malicious or corrupted data used to manipulate model behavior.

- **Prompt Injection**: Unsanitized user inputs leading models to leak sensitive information or behave unexpectedly.

- **Model Inversion**: Attackers reconstruct training data from model outputs.

AWS Best Practices to Mitigate These Risks:
Each security best practice below maps directly to mitigating one or more of the risks outlined above.

- **Data Privacy (Mitigates Data Poisoning and Model Inversion)**

  - Encrypt all training and inference data using AWS Key Management Service (KMS).

  - Classify and protect sensitive data in S3 buckets with Amazon Macie before any model training or fine-tuning.

  - Deploy GenAI environments in dedicated VPCs and use AWS PrivateLink to keep Bedrock and SageMaker API traffic private and isolated.

- **Input and Output Validation (Mitigates Prompt Injection and Model Inversion)**

  - Use Bedrock Guardrails to inspect and filter unsafe prompts and responses (both inputs and outputs).

  - Amazon API Gateway can help with basic validation layers (e.g., input schema checking), but for advanced GenAI-specific filtering, Bedrock Guardrails are recommended.

- **Model Monitoring and Anomaly Detection (Supports Defense Against All Three Risks)**

  - Use Amazon CloudWatch to track inference performance, including anomalies such as high inference latency (potential DDoS) or unexpected output entropy (potential hallucination or poisoning attempts).

- **Access Control (Reduces the Risk of Unauthorized Access and Prompt Injection)**

  - Enforce least-privilege IAM roles for developers and applications interacting with GenAI workloads.

  - Use Amazon Q Developer to check codebases for hardcoded credentials or insecure API usage.

By tying these defensive measures directly to the risks they address, organizations can build a security-first approach to deploying and maintaining generative AI systems on AWS.

Case Study: Securing a GenAI-Powered Chatbot

A company in the healthcare sector uses AWS to run an Amazon Bedrock–powered chatbot that responds to patient inquiries. Here's how to ensure its security:

Data Isolation
Encrypted patient information is stored in an Aurora database, separate from the model's knowledge base.

Input Sanitization
Modern input sanitization for LLM prompts requires moving beyond basic regex validation to address sophisticated injection attacks and contextual threats. While API Gateway regex rules can enforce basic syntax checks (e.g., blocking blatant SQL-like operators such as *SELECT* or *UNION*), they lack the semantic understanding to detect disguised adversarial intent, such as prompts like "Generate user details formatted as a *CSV* or *JSON* list" that bypass pattern-matching. For robust protection, integrate Amazon Bedrock Guardrails, which uses natural language processing (NLP) to analyze prompt intent and context. Guardrails automatically blocks harmful requests, including data

extraction attempts, PII leaks, or indirect prompt injections, by enforcing customizable content policies (e.g., denying topics like "user enumeration" or "structured data output"). It also redacts sensitive information and validates both inputs and LLM outputs, ensuring compliance with regulations like GDPR. Pair this with API Gateway's regex as a first-layer filter, and add AWS WAF for threat-specific rules (e.g., rate limiting), creating a multi-layered defense that adapts to evolving LLM security risks.

Output Filte9ring

Bedrock Guardrails protects against the risk of disclosing protected health information (PHI) and ensures our responses are compliant with HIPAA.

Monitoring

If the response rate of the bot exceeds thresholds (potential brute-force abuse), then CloudWatch alarms trigger and mitigation action taken.

Challenges and Mitigations

Let's explore the common challenges you might face and how to tackle them effectively.

Securing Generative AI Workloads: Practical AWS Strategies

Here are practical ways to safeguard your AI models using AWS tools you can rely on.

Adversarial Threat Detection and Mitigation

Here's how to detect and stop tricky attacks designed to fool your AI in real time:

- For applications using Amazon SageMaker with custom or fine-tuned models:

  - Use SageMaker Debugger to monitor training and inference metrics (e.g., gradient shifts, confidence anomalies) and detect signs of adversarial manipulation during both model training and real-time inference.

- If retraining is feasible (large enterprises), enrich data sets with synthetic adversarial examples using frameworks like Adversarial Robustness Toolbox (ART) and trigger automated retraining pipelines with SageMaker Training Jobs.

- For organizations deploying models via Amazon Bedrock (where models are managed by AWS and not retrained by the customer):

  - Focus on securing user inputs at runtime. Use Bedrock Guardrails to filter and block malicious or adversarial prompts before they ever reach the model (e.g., prompt injection attacks).

  - Guardrails enforces intent-based policies without needing to modify or retrain the underlying model.

AI Supply Chain Integrity

Keep your AI safe by making sure every piece you use is secure and trustworthy.

- Scan any third-party libraries (e.g., PyTorch, Hugging Face transformers) used in SageMaker custom builds with Amazon Inspector for vulnerabilities.

- Validate container images with Amazon ECR Image Scanning, and enforce Software Bill of Materials (SBOM) checks to ensure no hidden malicious dependencies enter critical cloud environments.

Compliance and Governance for GenAI Workloads

Easily meet regulations and protect sensitive data while running your AI workloads.

- **Regulatory Alignment**: Automate audit evidence using AWS Audit Manager mapped to AI-specific frameworks like NIST AI RMF, ISO/IEC 42001, and the EU AI Act.

- Enforce data residency, sovereignty, and privacy via AWS Control Tower Guardrails and Amazon S3 Object Lambda for runtime masking of sensitive data.

Zero-Trust Enforcement Across AI Environments

Lock down access and keep a close eye on everything happening in your AI systems.

- Apply fine-grained IAM permissions with session tagging to tightly control user access to Bedrock and SageMaker APIs.

- Enable CloudTrail Lake to maintain immutable audit trails across both training/fine-tuning activities (SageMaker) and inference (Bedrock).

Secure Innovation Framework for Generative AI

AWS generative AI services offer revolutionary cybersecurity opportunities from **threat detection** (e.g., GuardDuty anomaly models) to **automated incident response**, but they require a multi-layered security approach:

- **Data Security:**

  Protect your AI training and fine-tuning data at every stage whether at rest or in transit using AWS tools that secure your data and validate inputs in real time.

  - Protect training/fine-tuning data at rest and in transit with AWS KMS.

  - Validate user/system inputs at runtime using Bedrock Guardrails and API Gateways.

- **Proactive Threat Simulation:**

  Stay ahead of potential attacks by simulating threats against your AI pipelines to uncover and address vulnerabilities before they can be exploited.

  - Use AWS Threat Composer to simulate attacks against AI pipelines and expose hidden weaknesses.

- **Continuous Security Assurance:**

  Keep security ongoing and integrated by embedding intelligent monitoring and automated responses throughout your AI development and operations.

  - Embed Amazon Q Developer for secure AI-driven development and use AWS Security Hub to monitor security events across services.

Generative AI security demands **defense in depth**: combining native AWS protections (KMS, IAM, Guardrails), adversary-resilient application design, and continuous stress-testing via a well-documented framework like ***AWS Well-Architected Generative AI Lens***. What we must keep in mind always is security must evolve alongside models and data-driven toolkits and be operationalized, which is not a one-time project but an iterative process.

Leveraging Amazon Generative AI to Secure Your AWS Environment

Generative AI models on Amazon Bedrock (e.g., Amazon Nova, Claude 3) can transform AWS security by enhancing threat detection, identity management, compliance, and code security. Below are five practical areas to integrate AI into your cloud defense, with real AWS services.

Automate Threat Detection and Response

Leverage intelligent automation to quickly identify and respond to security threats with minimal manual effort.

Tools:
Amazon Bedrock (Nova or latest Claude model), GuardDuty, CloudTrail, Security Hub, Lambda

Implementation:
At the time of writing, there are few options on implementation, but notable ones are using Amazon Bedrock or using Strands Agents using SDK.

- **Detection**: Feed CloudTrail logs and GuardDuty findings into an LLM via Bedrock for real-time anomaly analysis, or you can use open source AI agents by utilizing Strands Agents.

- **Response**: Lambda triggers auto-remediation (e.g., disabling compromised IAM credentials).

Example:

GuardDuty flags unusual S3 API activity. An EventBridge rule triggers Lambda to gather related logs and send them to a Bedrock model (or Strands Agents by using SDK), which analyzes the activity, concludes credential misuse, and automatically revokes access through Lambda.

Secure Access and Identity

Start by understanding the tools that help protect your user access and identities in AWS.

Tools:

Bedrock (Nova or latest Claude model), Amazon Q Developer, IAM, Security Hub

Implementation: Next, see how these tools work together to actively monitor and improve your security policies.

- **IAM Review**: Use AI to detect overly permissive policies and suggest least-privilege alternatives.

- **Access Audit**: Ask Bedrock-based assistants questions like "Which IAM users haven't used admin privileges in 90 days?"

Example:

Finally, explore a real-world scenario showing how AI can simplify and strengthen access controls. A developer asks an AI assistant to generate a policy allowing EC2 to access only a specific S3 bucket. The model drafts correct JSON with least privilege enforced.

Protect Data and Ensure Compliance

Use powerful AWS tools to find, protect, and report on sensitive data with ease.

Tools:

Bedrock (Nova or latest Claude model), Macie, AWS Config, Audit Manager

Implementation:

Step-by-step actions that turn data insights into effective protection and reporting.

- **Data Discovery**: Summarize Macie findings to prioritize sensitive data risks.

- **Compliance Reporting**: Auto-generate GDPR and HIPAA compliance reports by mapping Config rules.

Example:

A real-world scenario showing how AWS helps spot risks and guide you to secure your data.

Macie identifies unencrypted PII in S3. An LLM summarizes high-priority risks and recommends remediation, including enabling encryption and blocking public access.

Secure Code and Infrastructure

Let's explore the tools and steps that help you build and maintain secure code and infrastructure from development through deployment.

Tools: Amazon Q Developer, Bedrock (Nova or latest Claude model), CodePipeline, Inspector, CloudFormation

Implementation:

Easily integrate security into your development and infrastructure with smart tools guiding you every step.

- **Secure Development**: Q Developer suggests secure coding practices during development (e.g., avoid hardcoded secrets).

- **IaC (Infrastructure as Code) Review**: Bedrock models analyze CloudFormation templates for misconfigurations.

Example:

Here's a practical scenario that shows how this works in real life. An LLM flags a CloudFormation security group open to the world and suggests restricting it or using Systems Manager Session Manager for secure access.

Guard Against Generative AI-Specific Risks

Key tools and strategies to protect your systems from risks unique to generative AI.
Tools: Bedrock Guardrails, PrivateLink, KMS, CloudWatch

Implementation:
Here's how to put these protections in place seamlessly and securely.

- **Input/Output Filtering**: Use Bedrock Guardrails to detect harmful prompts, PII leaks, and hallucinations.

- **Private Access**: Invoke Bedrock via PrivateLink and encrypt data with KMS.

Example:
A practical illustration to help you understand the concept in action. A security chatbot is protected using Guardrails to block prompt injections and PII leaks. All interactions are logged and monitored via CloudWatch. Sensitive information never leaves the AWS environment.

What You Have Learned

In this chapter, you have understood how generative AI (GenAI) has the power to transform the area of cybersecurity in AWS environments. You learned that GenAI is a two-bladed sword: both a strongly effective defender increasing threat detection, compliance, and automation and an upcoming new attack surface.

You might see how AWS services such as Amazon Bedrock, SageMaker, and Amazon Q Developer can strategically be used in combination with GuardDuty, CloudTrail, Macie, and Security Hub to add more security features. We covered hands-on examples, including applying Bedrock models for real-time anomaly detection, IAM policy auditing at scale, compliance report generation on AWS Config rules, and code and infrastructure hardening based on AI recommendations.

But the chapter also emphasized the key need to protect GenAI itself. You learned how to secure training and inference data with AWS KMS, segregate GenAI workloads with PrivateLink and dedicated VPCs, authenticate inputs and outputs with Bedrock Guardrails, monitor behavior with CloudWatch, and enforce hard IAM policies. Threats such as data poisoning, prompt injection, and model inversion were one to one mapped to defensive controls you can implement today.

Finally, you recognized that securing a GenAI-powered environment means constant watchfulness and implementing Zero-Trust architecture and adversary-resilient designs, thinking about security as a continuous setup rather than a static setup – a dynamic, adaptive approach incorporated into your AWS operating model.

Summary

Generative AI is not only another addition to the cybersecurity toolset; it is a paradigm changer for security managed in cloud deployments.

For AWS customers, GenAI provides three important advantages:

1. **Improved Threat Analysis**: GenAI enhances existing systems by breaking down sophisticated security signals, uncovering patterns, and enhancing situational awareness more quickly than possible with human processing alone.

2. **Forecasting and Prioritization of Threat Risk**: GenAI models can predict future threats by identifying anomalies in logs, configurations, and user activity, enabling earlier and more intelligent defensive response.

3. **Accelerating Decision-Making and Response**: When a threat or anomaly is detected, GenAI systems can suggest or automate response (e.g., Lambda functions, IAM role revocation), with much shorter time to containment.

While GenAI excels at analyzing, forecasting, and suggesting actions, the actual automation of defense tasks is typically handled by agents, workflows, or traditional automation tools, not GenAI itself. This is why human intervention remains critical, providing a multi-modal, human perspective essential for effective cybersecurity decision-making.

By combining Amazon's core security services (i.e., IAM, GuardDuty, KMS, Config, etc.) with GenAI services (Bedrock, SageMaker, Q Developer), you can create an AWS environment that learns to adapt, resist, and evolve against new threats.

Remember:

Generative AI is a force multiplier, not a replacement for cybersecurity professionals. Its real power lies in **enhancing human judgment**, not bypassing it. AI can accelerate detection, recommend faster responses, and strengthen defenses, but **human oversight, critical thinking, and decision-making remain essential** to interpreting AI outputs, validating actions, and adapting defenses in a constantly evolving threat landscape.

CHAPTER 11

AWS Security Best Practices and Future Outlook: Compliance, Post-Quantum Readiness, and Strategic Advantage

As cloud adoption speeds up, guaranteeing the security and compliance of identities and workloads in AWS becomes all the more vital. The protection of sensitive data and the maintenance of trust demand a serious, proactive approach in the rapidly evolving world of cloud computing. In this book, we've covered a huge amount of ground across many substantial security topics in AWS.

Now, in this final chapter, we're going to bring it home and cover a few key strategies and some essential tools to provide robust, resilient security in AWS.

This chapter offers detailed, actionable best practices for securing AWS environments. It stresses complete identity management, workload protection, and advanced threat detection as essential elements of a secure AWS environment.

Moreover, it walks you through some of AWS's robust compliance and governance capabilities (such as AWS Artifact and AWS Control Tower) that help you to effectively rule your environments in accordance with necessary regulatory standards while also keeping them securely auditable. And because it's impossible to cover AWS security without addressing the completely dynamic nature of security threats, we also give some thought to AWS's post-quantum cryptography (PQC) readiness.

© Syed Rehan 2025
S. Rehan, *Cybersecurity with AWS*, https://doi.org/10.1007/979-8-8688-1554-6_11

Organizations can bolster their resilience by taking advantage of AWS's security ecosystem and ensuring that they are always compliant. To this end, I would encourage current and prospective customers to take the following step: adopt a security governance framework that can be mapped to the AWS shared responsibility model.

Strategies for Securing Cloud Workloads and Identities in AWS

Securing workloads and identities in AWS requires a multi-layered approach that combines strong identity and access controls, robust workload protection mechanisms, and proactive threat detection capabilities.

Identity and Access Management (IAM):
The frontline defense for securing AWS resources is IAM.

Best Practices:
Follow these essential tips to strengthen your AWS identity and access security.

- **Least-Privilege Principle**: Provide the least amount of access necessary for users and roles.

- **MFA (Multi-factor Authentication)**: Ensure that all users with access to the console and API are subjected to MFA.

- **Access Based on Roles**: Use roles instead of users to improve security and to make things more flexible.

Steps to Secure IAM: A Hands-On Guide

Use this practical checklist to harden IAM configurations and reduce security risks in your AWS environment:

- Enforce strong password policies.

- Use IAM roles for EC2 instances and Lambda functions.

- Apply the principle of least privilege (PoLP).

- Regularly review IAM users, groups, and permissions.

- Enable multi-factor authentication:

- MFA adds an extra layer of security to your AWS account by requiring additional verification beyond just a password. Even if credentials are compromised, unauthorized access is blocked without the second factor.

    - **To enable MFA via the AWS Console**, navigate to **IAM Console ➤ Users ➤ [Your Username] ➤ Security credentials ➤ Manage MFA.**

        This is where you can assign a virtual or hardware MFA device for the selected IAM user.

Create IAM Roles:

Go to the Identity and Access Management Console (IAM). Choose Roles ➤ Create role. Define trusted entities (e.g., AWS services, federated identities).

IAM Access Analyzer:

IAM Access Analyzer helps you identify the permissions you need to grant to your identities so they can access your resources. Access Analyzer has three main components:

1. **Analyzers**: You create an analyzer to monitor the permissions granted to your identities across your AWS accounts and organize them by region. Analyzers also find and generate access maps for resources shared with your identities.

2. **Findings**: Findings tell you when a resource is accessible by any identity (not just the ones you expect). And findings are not just a flag that tells you when something is wrong. They also help you understand the resources shared with your identities that you might not expect.

3. **Access Maps**: Access maps give you a visual representation of the findings, showing you how the resources are shared across IAM identities.

    a. Go to IAM Console ➤ Access Analyzer. Schedule regular reviews of external access findings and remediate any excessively permissive policies.

Workload Protection – Securing AWS Compute, Storage, and Networking Services:

Protect your applications and data across compute, storage, and network layers with layered AWS security controls.

Compute (EC2, Lambda, Containers):

Keep your compute environments secure and compliant with automated scanning and patching tools.

- For continuous vulnerability scanning, employ Amazon Inspector.

- Use AWS Systems Manager Patch Manager to routinely and properly patch your EC2 instances, ensuring they remain secure and compliant.

Storage (S3, EBS, EFS):

Encrypt and control access to your data at rest to prevent unauthorized access and ensure privacy.

- **Encrypt Data at Rest with AWS KMS**: Turn on server-side encryption (SSE-KMS for S3 objects, "Encryption by default" for EBS volumes, and "Enable encryption" for new EFS file systems). The data key is protected by a KMS customer-managed key, so anything written to disk is unreadable without the right KMS permissions.

- **Harden S3 Bucket Access**: Replaces broad ACLs with least-privilege bucket policies that name only *authorized principals* (specific IAM roles, service principals, or partner accounts). Add a VPC gateway/interface endpoint or AWS PrivateLink to keep traffic on the AWS backbone, and then enable **Block Public Access** as a safety net. **Result**: The bucket is reachable only from your VPC and only by the identities you specify.

Networking:

Use robust network protections and secure development practices to minimize exposure and mitigate threats early.

- Leverage AWS Network Firewall and AWS WAF to safeguard against network dangers.

- Enforce a DevSecOps culture that focuses on security. Embed security practices in all development and operational processes.

- Conducting threat modelling and then using the models to guide architectural decisions help ensure that the right design patterns and security controls are selected.

- Eliminate vulnerabilities early in the **Secure Software Development
  Life Cycle (SSDLC)**, the practice of weaving security into every SDLC
  phase (planning, design, implementation, testing, deployment, and
  maintenance). By applying threat modeling during design, enforcing
  secure coding standards in development, automating static and
  dynamic vulnerability scans in CI/CD pipelines, and conducting
  regular security reviews, you catch and fix flaws long before they
  reach production. These secure design decisions not only reduce
  the number of issues and breaches but also make your systems and
  applications intrinsically more resilient against future attacks.

Checklist:

Use this quick-reference checklist as an example to validate your cloud security
controls. Customize it to fit your specific cloud (AWS) environment, and incorporate
the best practices and hands-on guides shared throughout this book. Regularly using
a tailored checklist like this will help you maintain a sound audit process and ensure
comprehensive security management.

Below is an example consolidated checklist (Table 11-1) based on detailed guidance
from earlier chapters to help you verify and enforce your cloud security controls
end to end.

Table 11-1. *Checklist Example*

Check	Tasks
IAM permissions and access	• Enforce least privilege on all IAM users, groups, and roles. • Schedule and review IAM Access Analyzer findings monthly.
MFA enforcement	• Require MFA for "**all**" console and API users. • Verify virtual/hardware MFA device assignment (*IAM Console › Users › Security credentials › Manage MFA*).
Password and credential hygiene	• Apply strong password policy (length, complexity, rotation). • Disable or remove unused IAM users and access keys.
IAM role usage	• Use IAM roles for EC2, Lambda, and cross-account access. • Review role trust relationships and session duration.

(continued)

Table 11-1. (*continued*)

Check	Tasks
Vulnerability management	• Enable Amazon Inspector for EC2, ECR, and Lambda assessments. • Confirm Systems Manager Patch Manager is automating OS/package patching for all managed instances.
Data encryption at rest	• Enforce SSE-KMS for S3, "Encryption by default" for EBS, and encryption for new EFS file systems. • Rotate and audit customer-managed KMS keys regularly.
S3 bucket hardening	• Apply least-privilege bucket policies listing only authorized principals. • Enable Block Public Access and require VPC gateways/interface endpoints or PrivateLink.
Network protections	• Deploy AWS Network Firewall in each VPC. • Configure AWS WAF rules on ALBs/API Gateway. • Enable VPC Flow Logs and integrate with GuardDuty.
Secure SDLC integration	• Automate static/dynamic scans in CI/CD pipelines. • Conduct threat modeling during design and validate with periodic code reviews.
DevSecOps practices	• Embed security checks (Inspector, Config rules) into deployment pipelines. • Train development teams on secure coding and SSDLC best practices.
Continuous monitoring and auditing	• Enable GuardDuty, Security Hub, and CloudWatch alarms for key findings. • Ensure CloudTrail is logging in all regions to an immutable S3 bucket.
Incident response automation	• Have EventBridge + Lambda workflows for common detections (e.g., GuardDuty findings). • Maintain and test Systems Manager Automation runbooks for containment and recovery steps.

Cloud Security Compliance and Governance Overview

AWS offers a complete set of services to make compliance and governance simple. They help organizations stay aligned with regulatory standards and internal policies.

Here are some key services and tools provided by AWS (most if not all we have covered in detail but given here for completeness):

- AWS Artifact

- AWS Config

- Amazon CloudWatch

- AWS CloudTrail

- AWS Security Hub

- AWS Identity and Access Management (IAM)

- AWS Key Management Service (KMS)

- Amazon GuardDuty

- Amazon Inspector

- AWS Audit Manager

Ultimately, achieving and maintaining compliance is your responsibility; no one knows your business better than you. AWS offers a range of reports and services to help you meet and demonstrate your compliance objectives.

AWS Compliance Program

AWS maintains a wide range of "compliance-ready" services, each independently audited against major global frameworks:

- **GDPR** (European data protection)

- **HIPAA** (US health information privacy)

- **PCI DSS** (payment card security)

- **SOC 2** (service organization controls)

- **FedRAMP** (US federal cloud security)

Being "*compliance ready*" means AWS services include the technical building blocks, encryption at rest and in transit, granular IAM controls, comprehensive logging, and more; these features give you the controls and reporting capabilities required to satisfy your specific regulatory obligations.

That said, compliance is a shared effort:

1. **Choose Thoughtfully**: Pick the right AWS services and regions for your data sovereignty needs (e.g., storing EU customer data in EU regions).

2. **Configure Carefully**: Enable and manage features like encryption keys, VPC isolation, access logging, and retention policies in line with your obligations.

3. **Operate Consistently**: Maintain your data lifecycle, retention, archival, and deletion, according to your internal policies and external regulations.

4. **Demonstrate Transparently**: Use AWS Config, CloudTrail, and AWS Audit Manager to record settings and generate the evidence you'll provide to auditors.

By combining AWS's audited infrastructure with your own secure configurations and processes, you create a robust, well-documented foundation for meeting compliance requirements, without unnecessary complexity or anxiety.

The independent, regular audits that AWS has in place give the necessary assurance to you as a customer to have confidence in the compliance of AWS with their own relevant programs. In fact, the assurance goes further than that; it covers not just the AWS platform as a whole, which is what most of our customers are directly concerned with, but also the individual services that make up the platform, but let me reiterate this – your environment and your overall cloud applications and your tech stack need your own efforts to meet the compliance required by your own business or industry verticals you operate in.

AWS Artifact

A central repository within AWS, AWS Artifact provides simple access to all compliance reports and agreements concerning AWS.

A practical use of the tool involves running multiple analyses on a data set at once. This can save considerable time when working with large amounts of data. In this section, we will go through the process of using the tool to work with some real data. For most of analyses performed in the previous chapters, we used some simulated data sets. Now, it is time to switch gears and work with some real data.

Hands-On Setup:

Let's walk through how to get started with AWS Artifact and access key compliance documents in just a few clicks.

- Go to AWS Artifact through the AWS Management Console.

- Download fundamental compliance paperwork (e.g., SOC, PCI DSS, ISO) and acquiesce to compliance agreements electronically for GDPR and data processing addendums.

AWS Control Tower

AWS Control Tower is a service that simplifies governance and compliance management across multiple AWS accounts. It provides a reliable and repeatable way to set up and govern a secure, compliant, multi-account AWS environment.

Main Features:

Here's what makes AWS Control Tower a powerful and easy way to manage your AWS environment at scale.

- Preventive guardrails (deny high-risk actions) and detective guardrails (alert on policy violations) are automatically deployed.

- The dashboard is centralized: visibility and governance oversight is provided across AWS accounts.

- Accounts management is simplified. You can now efficiently provision accounts through the Account Factory. This makes it easier than ever to ensure everything is compliant. And because it's "by design," there's no extra work needed to make it so.

AWS Control Tower simplifies governance and compliance management across multiple AWS accounts.

Key Features:

AWS Control Tower streamlines multi-account setup and governance by combining automation, guardrails, and centralized monitoring into one cohesive experience.

- **Landing Zone Setup**: AWS Control Tower creates a well-architected multi-account environment using AWS Organizations and Organizational Units (OUs).

- **Guardrails**: Preventive and detective guardrails are applied to enforce security and compliance best practices.

- **Account Vending Machine (AVM)**: Automates account creation with predefined policies.

- **Centralized Monitoring**: Through AWS Organizations, aggregates logs and configuration data from all member (nested/child) accounts into Amazon CloudWatch, AWS Config, and AWS CloudTrail for unified logging, auditing, and alerting.

Hands-On Setup:

The system is made up of several key components. Here's a schematic overview:

- Navigate to the AWS Console ➤ Control Tower. Initiate the landing zone setup.

- Set up accounts for auditing and archiving logs.

- Enforce personalized pre-emptive guardrails such as prohibiting the deletion of essential resources:

```
{
  "Sid": "PreventResourceDeletion",
  "Effect": "Deny",
  "Action": ["s3:DeleteBucket", "ec2:TerminateInstances"],
  "Resource": "*"
}
```

- This policy can be applied at the OU level to enforce restrictions across all accounts in the OU.

Detective Guardrails:

- Setup compliance "*guardrails*" as AWS Config rules that continuously
  evaluate resource configurations against your governance
  policies. When a rule is violated, such as an open security group or
  unencrypted volume, AWS Config raises an alert, enabling rapid
  remediation through AWS Systems Manager Automation or a custom
  remediation Lambda.

Compliance Frameworks:

- AWS Control Tower supports compliance frameworks like CIS, NIST,
  PCI DSS, GDPR, etc., by enabling relevant controls.

Ongoing Governance:

- The dashboard provides a single pane of glass to monitor compliance
  status, guardrail violations, and account activity across all managed
  accounts.

Upcoming and Future Outlook

As the cloud evolves further, so do security capabilities for customers. Customers should
learn and educate themselves with the new challenges of a changing world such as
threats arising from quantum computing and strict new regulatory mandates.

Post-quantum Readiness in Cloud

Traditional cryptography could be threatened by upcoming quantum computing.
Progressing post-quantum cryptography (PQC) adoption is a way that cloud providers
will ensure the protection of their customer communications and data.

1. **For Data in Transit**: Use hybrid PQ TLS to future-proof TLS
   connections to AWS services like KMS or Secrets Manager for API
   endpoints.

2. **For Data at Rest**: Continue using AES-256-GCM (already
   quantum-resistant) and monitor AWS announcements for future
   enhancement of PQ key management features.

Regulatory Mandates (GDPR and CCPA) for PQC Preparedness

Emerging data protection laws like the EU's GDPR and California's CCPA increasingly emphasize strong cryptographic safeguards. While neither currently requires post-quantum cryptography (PQC), many experts anticipate that future updates could mandate demonstrable PQC preparedness to ensure long-term data confidentiality against quantum threats. Designing today's systems with PQC in mind will position your organization to meet and exceed tomorrow's compliance expectations.

Implications for Organizations:

Understanding how quantum threats could shape future compliance helps you stay ahead of evolving regulatory expectations.

- **GDPR and CCPA Compliance**: Organizations might have to document their plans to be ready for quantum-safe cryptography as part of their data protection strategies.

- **Taking the Initiative**: Using the current PQC capabilities will far better enable us to meet the many compliance obligations we "may" see in the future.

Recommendations:

Here are practical steps you can take today to prepare your systems and data for a quantum-resilient future.

- Assess sensitive data that necessitates enduring safeguarding.

- Explore and enable post-quantum–capable options in AWS services, such as AWS KMS (for hybrid PQC key exchange in TLS), and experiment with custom PQC libraries in Nitro Enclaves, where appropriate for your most sensitive workloads. Regularly check AWS documentation for updates on PQC support in ACM Private CA and other services.

- Document your quantum-readiness efforts by recording cryptographic configuration choices in AWS Artifact, Audit Manager, or your compliance records. This will help you demonstrate proactive risk management and quantum-safe preparedness to auditors, regulators, and customers.

- **Stay current with official AWS cryptography announcements**:

- Follow the AWS Security Blog, AWS News Blog, and service-specific release notes so you can adopt new encryption features and guidance as soon as they are published.

Competitive Advantage Through Early PQC Adoption

By taking the initiative to adopt post-quantum cryptographic security measures, organizations stand to ensure a substantial competitive advantage. They position themselves to mitigate future risks associated with emerging quantum computing technologies in a proactive manner. What is more, they can avoid delaying until it becomes absolutely necessary to re-architect their systems. And when it is necessary, they can avoid doing so in a highly reactive, disorganized, and, therefore, expensive manner. In many ways, securing against the "Q threat (*quantum threat*)" offers a low-cost, high-return opportunity.

Strategic Recommendations:
Here's how to future-proof your systems against quantum-era threats with AWS.

Immediate Actions:
Start with quick wins to boost your post-quantum readiness today.

- **Enable Hybrid PQ TLS:** Secure API endpoints (KMS, Secrets Manager) with AWS's built-in PQ TLS.

Collaborate and Educate:
Work with industry leaders and empower your teams to stay ahead of the curve.

- **Engage with Consortia:** Join initiatives like the Post-Quantum Cryptography Alliance (PQCA) and leverage AWS's partnerships for interoperable solutions.

- **Train Teams:** Build internal expertise on NIST-approved algorithms (e.g., CRYSTALS-Kyber) and AWS's evolving PQ features.

Document and Communicate:

Build trust by planning clearly and sharing your post-quantum journey transparently.

- **Create a Roadmap**: Align PQC adoption with NIST's timeline (e.g., CNSA 2.0 by 2030) and AWS's updates.

- **Leverage Trust Frameworks**: Highlight PQ readiness in compliance reports (e.g., GDPR, CCPA) to build stakeholder confidence.

What You Have Learned

In this chapter, you explored the core strategies and essential tools for securing workloads and identities in AWS. You learned how applying the principle of least privilege within Identity and Access Management (IAM), combined with regular reviews using IAM Access Analyzer, creates a strong baseline for safeguarding cloud resources. You also discovered the importance of encrypting data at rest using AWS KMS, scanning for vulnerabilities using Amazon Inspector, and monitoring network traffic with AWS Network Firewall to achieve defense in depth. Beyond workload and identity security, the chapter explained how AWS services, such as AWS Control Tower and AWS Artifact, streamline compliance efforts by providing guardrails and documentation for regulatory obligations (GDPR, CCPA, etc.).

Lastly, you delved into post-quantum cryptography (PQC) readiness, understanding that early adoption of quantum-safe cryptographic measures can provide both future-proof security and a competitive edge.

Summary

This final chapter served as a culmination of the security topics covered throughout the book, emphasizing AWS's robust ecosystem of services and best practices for maintaining a secure and compliant environment. First, it underscored IAM as a frontline defense mechanism, stressing tight access controls, MFA enforcement, and the need for regular policy audits. Next, it highlighted workload protection, from routine patching and vulnerability scans to data encryption and secure network design using AWS Network Firewall, ensuring multiple layers of defense.

The chapter then turned its focus to governance and compliance, showcasing how
AWS Control Tower can centrally manage guardrails and how AWS Artifact facilitates
access to compliance documentation for audits. This ensures organizations remain fully
aligned with both internal governance frameworks and external regulatory mandates.
Finally, looking to the future, the chapter introduced AWS's post-quantum readiness. As
quantum computing evolves, early adoption of PQC, especially around TLS connections
and key management, will be vital to maintain confidentiality over the long term. By
proactively integrating these PQC strategies, organizations can differentiate themselves
in the marketplace and be well-prepared for emerging compliance requirements tied to
quantum-safe cryptography.

Index

A

GPSR Compliance
The European Union's (EU) General Product Safety Regulation (GPSR) is a set
of rules that requires consumer products to be safe and our obligations to
ensure this.

If you have any concerns about our products, you can contact us on

ProductSafety@springernature.com

In case Publisher is established outside the EU, the EU authorized
representative is:

Springer Nature Customer Service Center GmbH
Europaplatz 3
69115 Heidelberg, Germany